DEVIANCE

DEVIANCE

ANTHROPOLOGICAL PERSPECTIVES

EDITED BY MORRIS FREILICH,
DOUGLAS RAYBECK,
AND JOEL SAVISHINSKY

BERGIN & GARVEY

New York • Westport, Connecticut • London

Library of Congress Cataloging-in-Publication Data

Deviance : anthropological perspectives / edited by Morris Freilich,
   Douglas Raybeck, Joel Savishinsky.
      p.   cm.
   Includes bibliographical references and index.
   ISBN 0–89789–205–4 (alk. paper). — ISBN 0–89789–204–6 (pbk. :
alk. paper)
   1. Deviant behavior—Cross-cultural studies. 2. Interpersonal
relations—Cross-cultural studies.   I. Freilich, Morris.
II. Raybeck, Douglas.   III. Savishinsky, Joel.
GN493.5.D48   1991
302.5'42—dc20   91–2037

British Library Cataloguing in Publication Data is available.

Library of Congress Catalog Card Number: 91–2037
ISBN: 0–89789–205–4
ISBN: 0–89789–204–6 (pbk.)

First published in 1991

Bergin & Garvey, One Madison Avenue, New York, NY   10010
An imprint of Greenwood Publishing Group, Inc.

Printed in the United States of America

The paper used in this book complies with the
Permanent Paper Standard issued by the National
Information Standards Organization (Z39.48–1984).

10   9   8   7   6   5   4   3   2

CONTENTS

TABLES AND FIGURES

TABLES

FIGURES

PREFACE

The impetus for this book began several years ago when Hamilton College sponsored a talk by Morris Freilich on the subject of deviance. This was followed by a series of congenial arguments between Freilich and Douglas Raybeck, who was also interested in deviance and who had arranged for the talk. During this period, both came to realize that their differing approaches to the subject matter were more complimentary than contradictory and that the field of deviance in anthropology was woefully understudied, if not unrepresented.

Freilich and Raybeck began to redress this situation by organizing a series of symposia at meetings of the American Anthropological Association. At the first of these, they were joined by Joel Savishinsky who had an interest in and an approach to deviance which differed from and enhanced the approaches Freilich and Raybeck were developing. These three were gratified to encounter various anthropologists who found the theme of significant interest and who discovered they had appropriate material in their field notes which, due to the relative invisibility of the topic, they had previously neither organized nor published.

This book is the result of considerable intellectual exchange and growth during which we editors have revised our essays and made them available to the six other contributors to this book. Happily, these contributors have not chosen to ignore our theoretical models, but have either adopted portions of them, or used them as a point of reference for their ethnographic treatments of deviance.

As in any complex endeavor, especially in creative ones, there need be numerous acknowledgements for assistance and support. We want first to thank our respective families for putting up with us throughout this effort and for enduring the often formidable demands on our time and schedules that this book occasioned. We must acknowledge the generous assistance of Hamilton College which underwrote the costs of typing the entire manuscript, and also provided other forms of support, such as Raybeck's transportation to meetings, and summer funding for his research efforts. In particular, we want to thank Jan Pieroni who typed what must have seemed like endless variations of the manuscript, yet managed to avoid either rampant confusion or a loss of composure. We quickly learned that when she politely raised a question about some aspect of our manuscript, her query generally presaged the discovery of a shortcoming or omission that we had yet to note.

Additionally, we wish to acknowledge the assistance of both Ithaca College, which furnished Joel Savishinsky with released time and summer support to facilitate his work on this book, and Northeastern University, which provided Morris Freilich with stimulating colleagues and sufficient financial support to attend conferences and to help organize panels on the anthropology of deviance.

We also want to thank the people at Greenwood Publishing Group, whose efforts have markedly improved the quality of this book. Sophie Craze, senior editor for anthropology at Bergin & Garvey, helped considerably with initial organizational matters and was a constant source of support throughout the rather protracted birth of this work. David Baker, whose contributions as copy editor are so significant that we three would rather others remain ignorant of the degree of assistance he provided. Finally, we want to thank Meg Fergusson, the production editor who oversaw the process of publishing this work.

We have striven to create a work that will be attractive to a wide range of potential readers. At one level, we would like students and interested lay people to find the ideas and observations in this book an intriguing and stimulating introduction to one of the oldest concerns of social science: the relationship of the individual to the group, especially the necessary tension that exists between the freedom of the former and the order of latter. However, we also hope that this book will be read by anthropological colleagues who will find increased interest in the topic of deviance, and that some of these may even dust off their field notes in search of hitherto neglected observations of the unusual, the unaccepted, the deviant.

INTRODUCTION: THE ANTHROPOLOGY OF DEVIANCE

Anthropologists are latecomers to the study of deviance. Our tardy arrival is largely due to the nature of our traditional subject matter. Since the nineteenth century anthropological research has tended to focus on small-scale systems, societies that westerners generally view as primitive, exotic, and mysterious. To counter such myths, anthropologists have tried to discover sense where others have imputed nonsense, to perceive structure and meaning where others have found only noise. As anthropologists have struggled to discern (and sometimes impose) patterns and structures, irregularities were played down. If they were mentioned at all, it was to highlight the actual pattern which had been discovered (Benedict 1934). Put otherwise, anthropologists have tended to view deviance as a mole, a disruptive animal that messes up the neatness and symmetry of our carefully manicured cultural lawns.

While lagging far behind sociologists in the systematic study of deviance, anthropologists have displayed a long, though intermittent, interest in this phenomenon (e.g., Malinowski 1964). Indeed, there even exists a deviance text reviewing theoretical distinctions that have been made or employed by anthropologists (Edgerton 1976). Generally, however, the concerns of those researchers have been quite different from the ones reflected in this volume.

We wish to introduce deviance as a specialized field, a subdiscipline of anthropology with close links to sociology. In prior studies, deviance has been treated in piecemeal fashion, cut up and packaged under a variety of labels, including suicide, alcoholism, legal systems, and physical abuse.[1] Since currently there is no field called "The Anthropology of Deviance," investigators are neither sharing data on deviance nor developing common theoretical approaches to the study of deviance. We propose a comparative study of deviance in which societal and ethnographic data, and theoretical formulations, inform one another. Such research, we suggest, can improve not only our understanding of deviance, but also our understanding of the general sociocultural order.

Anthropology provides a wealth of fieldwork data that offer novel, comparative understandings of deviance. Anthropology's concerns with social phenomena at varying levels of complexity can increase our appreciation of the manner in which micro-level and macro-level phenomena are interrelated. Put otherwise, our involvements with complex and simple, nonwestern societies leads to a better recognition of the way in which deviance is affected by sociocultural scale. Additionally, concerns with fieldwork and with differing levels of sociocultural integration combine to promote a better appreciation of the processes that generate deviance. Finally, an anthropology of deviance is likely to create new models, models that permit the individual to reappear as a viable actor who creates and recreates sociocultural systems.

FIELDWORK AND THE IMPORTANCE OF QUALITATIVE DATA

Curiously, anthropologists are often accused by "soft" social scientists of using "soft" methodologies. In truth, we have been chary of employing quantitative, statistical approaches in studying our subject matter. However, we believe we have good reason for this. Our concern has been to attempt an understanding of other cultures in terms that are meaningful to the participants of those cultures. We pursue and try to capture emic meaningfulness, the understandings of insiders. Our search for data that are meaningful to the people being studied produces results which are necessarily imperfect. But the data are as sensitive to the contexts of other cultures as our talents and skills permit.

Qualitative information, we argue, must precede attempts at meaningful, cross-cultural comparison, especially those that utilize statistics. Quantification necessarily involves a simplification of cultural reality. Social scientists who employ quantitative approaches in their research reduce complex phenomena to a series of types. These types are assigned to a limited number of pigeonholes and then treated statistically. Given the major concerns with cultural context, and the subtle and not-so-subtle differences that exist among cultures, anthropologists are generally reluctant to simplify their data through quantification. Siding with Locke, we believe that a lack of precision does not necessarily mean a lack of scientific rigor.

Our qualitative concerns lead us to give primacy to what people actually do, rather than what they say they do. Traditionally we engage in fieldwork, a prolonged period during which the anthropologists live within the societies they seek to describe. As a result we experience a personal and rich introduction to another system of rules, behaviors, sentiments, and beliefs. We record not only what people do, but how they react to the behaviors and utterances of others. We study not only the rules, what people ought to do, but how they feel about their current situations and their future prospects. We also note what sorts of beliefs, prejudices, and attitudes people espouse and, when possible, what failings, errors, faults, and blemishes they see themselves as manifesting. Researchers who employ such an approach gain an appreciation of both the consistencies and the inconsistencies that give texture to social life. Anthropologists find that contextual concerns define both deviance and the reactions of society's members to it. Further, manifestations of deviance can alter the nature of the cultural context and, in some instances, lead to the emergence of new cultural patterns.

Despite our belief that the methodologies and subject matter of anthropology are likely to yield new insights into the nature and functioning of deviance, we are cognizant of some limitations of anthropology's traditional approach. If our qualitative observations are arguably more inclusive and more sensitive to the sociocultural context than those of most social scientists, these same observations often prove difficult to replicate. Our conclusions frequently rest upon insights that resist being tested. All methodologies have trade-offs. The ones that anthropologists usually subscribe to favor comprehensiveness and sensitivity over replicability and testability. Still, like Alice examining the Queen's croquet game, we believe there are interesting and important questions to be asked and we can't wait for the perfect opportunity.

MICRO-LEVELS, MACRO-LEVELS, AND THE SIGNIFICANCE OF SOCIAL SCALE

Anthropologists live among those being studied. The intimate experiences that characterize such an enterprise have impressed us with the importance and distinctiveness of face-to-face encounters. Such encounters are rich in interpersonal meaning and in the nuances that accompany social exchanges, be they material or nonmaterial. We are conscious of the complexity that exists even within a seemingly simple, small band.

Further, we propose that the scale of a social unit has profound implications for the content, structure, and processes that one encounters in most social situations.

Small-scale social units are either independent and self-reliant (such as a hunting and gathering band) or are part of a large-scale social unit (such as a tribe or state). They are distinguished in part by a limited population, and by the personalistic, three-dimensional ties that interconnect members of the system. In a small-scale social unit, most people know each other well. Their interdependence and shared circumstance promote an interest in each other's background, personality, past history, and current behavior. Access to such a rich social context affects the way in which the members of small-scale social units view and treat acts that depart from the proper. Moreover, it allows them to rely principally on informal sanctions to control deviance.

Large-scale social units are fundamentally different from small-scale social units in both qualitative and quantitative ways. Like a Ma and Pa grocery that balloons into a chain of supermarkets, large scale social units lose the personalistic, three-dimensional relationships that are common in small-scale entities. While small units are independent, self-sufficient, and possessed of relatively few specialized institutions, large scale ones possess numerous specialized institutions that exhibit a great deal of interdependence rather than independence. In small units, relations between individuals are personalized and particularistic; often *who* one is related to is a major defining element of one's social identity. In contrast, the sheer size and scope of large scale entities means that most members will be unfamiliar with the other individuals who make up the population of their social world. Consequently, many relationships in large-scale social units such as that of buyer-seller, or even employer-employee, are formalized, structured and commonly devoid of personal content.

The impersonal nature of relationships in large-scale social units means that most members will have low visibility. Further, they will enjoy a degree of freedom from interpersonal social pressures that does not and cannot exist at a smaller scale of social life. This very freedom, however, requires a greater reliance on the formal mechanisms of state control. These characteristics, as well as those mentioned above, have significant implications for the manifestation of deviance and for the reactions of others to deviant acts and actors.

Discussion of large- and small-scale social units has emphasized contrasts between the two. It should be remembered, however, that these are not mutually exclusive categories. Indeed, large units are comprised of small ones, and it is in these latter that people live. Thus, even in a large and complex nation-state such as the United States, people live in towns, in neighborhoods, on blocks, or, in the most impersonal of contexts, within apartment buildings. Generally, individuals recognize their membership in several small units even though these are enwrapped within a large one that makes its own demands upon them.

Membership in units of differing social scale has considerable significance for the study of deviance. Anthropologists and other social scientists have long recognized an important and basic distinction concerning the nature of social life. At an ideal level of analysis one may focus upon formal systems and codes. Such formal statements concerning the "rules of the game" are more characteristic of complex societies. The latter possess a plethora of specialized institutions, some of which are charged with the responsibility for developing and/or implementing conceptions of appropriate behavior. At the micro-level, the one at which we all live, people are concerned with conceptions of appropriate behavior and beliefs that are not institutionalized, but that nonetheless are shared informally among society's members (cf. Goffman 1959, 1963b). Informal conventions or "smart-rules" may be found both in small-scale societies and in small social units within complex societies (cf. Freilich, Chapter 1).

A concern with deviance and sociocultural order will necessarily involve the manner in which these two interact. This in turn has ramifications for our understanding of the relations between the micro- and macro-levels. Defining deviance is a sociocultural act but one that involves individual perceptions. The latter tend to vary from audience to audience (see Savishinsky, Chapter 3). Given the existence of varying definitions of deviance, several interesting questions arise. How are deviants identified? What does their deviant behavior do to their relationship to the wider sociocultural order? What steps are taken formally and informally to regulate deviance? What differences characterize the sanctions at these two levels?

SOCIAL PROCESS AND THE GENERATION OF NEW MODELS

Deviance involves a dialectic between the individual and the group, the exceptional and the normative. As we argued earlier, a concern with deviance and sociocultural order necessarily involves examining the manner in which these two interact. This, in turn, has ramifications for our understanding of the relations between the micro- and macrolevels.

We agree with labeling theorists who hold that deviance is not a given, but rather that it is subject to negotiation and change. We also believe that diachronic studies of deviance, with attention to its emergence and alteration over time, can yield significant insights into general social processes.

We argue that a dialectical approach to the study of deviance encourages investigators to view emerging cultural patterns as a synthesis between established or "proper" cultural patterns and the range of often discrepant or "smart" behaviors manifested by individuals and groups. This dialectic between the "proper" and the "smart" enables us to understand social and cultural change in a new way. We can locate the impetus for change in the deviant behaviors of individuals and groups. More specifically, a simple hypothesis now makes much sense: Some deviant behavior becomes, first, "smart" and then "proper" (cf. Freilich, Chapter 1).

In a very real sense, the study of deviance is the study of social and cultural reality, rather than the study of idealized social and cultural abstractions. In examining the reality captured by a focus on deviance, we encounter ourselves, as we are and as we'd like to be. Arguably, deviance not only promotes sociocultural change, its existence is a necessary condition for the maintenance of culture and society. It seems past time to examine this phenomenon more closely. The dialectic approach here promoted triggers in the creation of models that are more faithful to "reality" at both the macro- and the micro-level. The value of being pushed to create better models is difficult to overstate. After all, deviance lies in the eyes of beholders. And beholders, Plato long ago taught, get truth second-hand. We see the forms of truth only after they have been filtered through objects housed in a cave. Put otherwise, we see shadows and call them reality. Plato's image of realizable reality has been superseded by an image shared by all who work in modern science.

Human experience is no longer analyzed in Platonic terms. We now consider experience as monitored by models. And once we plan and record experiences systematically and scientifically, once we collect data, we again talk of models. Now we say, data are dumb—they need models to speak for them. The model appears to be a necessary servant of science. But with so much power can the model remain a mere servant? By grabbing a given model do we not have a tiger by the tail? Actually, as we will shortly demonstrate, work with models is even trickier than thus far discussed. This is so because the tiger, models, often moves around in disguise. Like Blake's beast of the same name, models—as tigers—present us with a kind of "fearful symmetry." What this tiger is, and what this tiger does, often is misrepresented by myths. Clearly, before we can present our own three models of deviance we must clarify the meaning of this term "models."

MODELS, SCIENCE, AND MYTH

Models are strange servants of science. As servants, models should be subservient, yet they dominate much scientific activity. Models solve some scientific problems, but they create special problems for all model users. Moreover, the functions of models are difficult to clearly identify and fully understand. This is because the relationship between Science and Model is muddled by the interference of a third party, namely, Myth. In short, to provide an accurate and adequate exposition on models it is necessary to discuss the set: Model-Science-Myth. Let us begin this tricky exposition by focusing on a key issue: the functions of models are tied to the purpose of science, and the purpose of science is not obvious. Indeed the purpose of science is not what it is generally believed to be; it is not to discover truth. When the purpose of science is misrepresented, then functions of models, likewise, are misrepresented. So before we can discuss models sensibly, we must examine the major misrepresenter of science, namely, the myth of what science is. After science is stripped of its mythical mask, we can move to the core questions about models: (1) What is a model? (2) How does a servant called models dominate its master, science? (3) Why do scientists use such a bossy servant? (4) What problems arise from the use of models? First, then, we must clear away mythical misunderstandings of science.

Science and myth seem like natural enemies. Science is serious, myth is playful. Science pursues truth, myth revels in fantasy. Science deals with reality, myth juggles fictions. How can there be a serious relationship between science and myth? The answer, actually, is quite simple: scientists are human, and all humans have a serious relationship with myth. Myth makes life more meaningful and less stressful for everyone by providing instant solutions to basic problems (Freilich 1975). What basic problems does myth solve for scientists?

Science, as daily activity, has little of the glamor and glory that many attribute to it. The work generally is hard, long, and intense, with little positive feedback on a regular basis. And this is so even when the work is later acknowledged to be pathbreaking. Indeed, the history of science provides many examples of brilliant work that initially was ridiculed or (perhaps worse for the scientist) ignored. Somehow the work continues; somehow, and generally, researchers remain dedicated to far distant goals. How can this dedication be explained? Science, with the aid of myth, gets transformed from a job to a calling: a mission that can be assumed only by the sensitive and the gifted. Like missionaries, scientists develop, first, a passion and then an obsession for the calling. The scientific obsession is truth. Myth takes a passionate obsession with truth and gives it meaning, legitimacy, and nobility. Myth loudly proclaims: "Science Discovers Truth." Most of us listen and nod agreement. Since the task of science is to find truth, then scientists need an obsession with truth. Such an obsession almost becomes a professional requirement. In a materialistic world an obsession with truth is an instant halo-bringer. How wonderful it must be to dedicate one's life to the discovery of truth! Put otherwise, the myth "Science Discovers Truth" creates an intellectual climate within which scientists tend to define their labors as extremely special. Hard work, often misunderstood and unappreciated, can be seen as worship: the worship of truth. While hard work is difficult to maintain without regular, positive feedback, such is not the case with worship. Worship brings its own special reward—achieving grace. In sum, in the relationship between science and myth there is real reciprocity. Myth gives science a pseudo-religious image. In return, science stays silent as myth enriches itself with two extra myths. First, that science is the pursuit and discovery of truth. Second, that science and myth are natural enemies.

The myth "Science Discovers Truth" tells us that truth is the goal of scientific work. Actually, the goal of scientific research is far more modest than finding truth. Each scientific project has its own rather specific goal; yet it is useful to speak of the overall goal of science, a goal to which each specific project makes a contribution. The real, general goal of science is *not* to discover truth or unchanging reality: since what some call truth today, may be proven false tomorrow. Actually, science tries to bring us ever closer to truth by chopping away the false. The real goal of science, then, is *to discover the false*. As Albert Einstein once noted, "scientific laws do not assert that something exists or is the case: they deny it. They insist on the nonexistence of certain things" (Popper 1968:69).

From a scientific perspective a false idea is one that does not meet given empirical tests. And empirical testing of ideas lies at the heart of the scientific enterprise. Each science has its own special ways of testing ideas empirically. In anthropology, the most popular manner of empirically testing ideas is to do fieldwork. In the field—the place into which the anthropologist moves and lives, and where among other things anthropologists do participant-observation research—a mountain of data sits ready to be collected and tested. The potential mass of data is too large to handle. It must be cut down to a manageable size. To do such chopping and maintain some peace of mind, it is necessary to make two assumptions: first, that all the data collectible are not equally important; second, that a set of data exists that is of critical importance. The problem for all scientists is: How does one know ahead of time what this set of critical data looks like? The answer comes by jumping out of the empirical world and into conceptual reality. In the world of ideas sits a strange, bossy servant called a model. A model tells us what data are critical. Further, a model provides categories into which data can be lodged, and presents concepts that allow us to weave categories of data together to create a system. In sum, and using technical terms, a model identifies paths of success and points to paths of failure.[2]

A model appears to be a perfect companion for a researcher. Sadly, nothing—from idiots to models—is perfect. Let us briefly discuss the model's imperfections. A model makes research manageable by providing pragmatic tools: including blinders, which limit vision; lenses, which direct vision; a network of categories, which distinguish and house data; and potent postulates, a set of underlying ideas that assure us that only a certain path—the path identified by the model—leads to success. However, each model comes with its own pragmatic tools. By appointing one model as our bossy assistant, we reject other models. How do we know which model to embrace and which models to reject? The answer here is disappointing, particularly so for those who think science is simple. We do not know whether our choice of model is the best choice. Indeed, at the time of choosing it is impossible to know this very important bit of information.

We have just identified the model's Achilles heel: It is possible to work with a model for months, even years, and then discover that some other model is far superior for the purposes of the research. Each model says to us (so to speak), "Act as if I am a perfect companion. If our association disappoints you, you can get another model." Clearly, while models provide much aid they also provide much insecurity. Given the insecurity linked to the use of models, why do we use them?

Models, as already discussed, take a mountain of possible data and reduce it into a pool of manageable information. What merits much repetition is that this reduction cannot be achieved in a rational manner without a model. True, models generate insecurities; but the comfort of certainty is not part of the scientific enterprise. Science and its bossy companion, models, are aspects of human life in general. Like the rest of human life, science and models have two faces: a happy face, which mirrors the joys of pursuing ever-elusive reality, and a sad face, which reflects the pains of living with uncertainty.

Let us take stock of our discussion so far. It includes three propositions: (1) Scientists use models to make research manageable; (2) models have a serious flaw; and (3) models, while flawed scientific tools, are necessary scientific tools. For those who find this picture of science strange, we add a fourth proposition: (4) Whether we want to or not, we use models anyway. Proposition 4 when fully explained makes it easier to understand the other three propositions. Our explanation begins with an analysis of the inner workings of an imaginary organization.

Imagine a club called PEWs (short for Pure Empirical Workers). PEWs has a constitution which begins with the following directive: "Every PEW must promise to work without models!" Now, irrespective of promises made, and irrespective of what any PEW thinks she is doing, all PEWs (along with the rest of us) regularly use models. We seem to have thrown you the reader a curve ball and hit you with paradox. The supposed paradox disappears, however, when we realize that (1) PEWs, like all of us, do much of their thinking with metaphors; and (2) metaphors are one of the disguises that our "tiger," the model, takes on. Let us explicate this by looking at some metaphorical models from everyday life.

Everyday experience includes concepts that are so complex that the experts, philosophers, are baffled. Curiously, the general public juggle these ideas without any perceivable problem. How is this curiosity to be explained? The ditty "Ignorance is bliss, 'tis folly to be wise" comes to mind. But this simplistic formulation confuses the picture. Let us go to a specific example and see where it leads. *Argument* is a complex concept that provides most of us with no problem of meaning. How do we know what is meant by "argument"?

Following George Lakoff and Mark Johnson (1980:4) when the term *argument* comes to mind, we remember key words used in actual arguments; words such as those presented below in italics:

Your claims are *indefensible*.

He *attacked every weak point* in my argument.

His criticisms were right *on target*.

I *demolished* his argument.

I've never *won* an argument with him.

You disagree? Okay, *shoot*!

If you use that *strategy*, he'll *wipe you out*.

He *shot down* all of my arguments.

From such key words and their supporting sentences, we conclude, correctly: In modern North American culture, WAR is the metaphor for Argument. Once it is known that Argument equals WAR, the concept *argument* is easy to use. During an argument, just as when fighting a war, the goal is to demolish opponents. The strategy is to keep attacking weaknesses until the enemy surrenders. Still following Lakoff and Johnson, a given culture includes many metaphors each of which explain things, events, and processes, which could create confusions in daily interactions. Since metaphors or sense-making agents are always available, the general public go about their lives (largely) free of intellectual puzzles. To better understand the function of metaphors, consider some other metaphors from Lakoff and Johnson's insightful work *Metaphors We Live By* (1980:15-32):

happy = up ("You're in high spirits . . . I'm feeling up . . .").

sad = down ("I'm feeling down . . . depressed . . .").

mind = machine ("He broke down" . . . "She has a screw loose").

Some events = containers: "He's *in* love. We're *out of* trouble now. He's coming *out of* a coma, I'm slowly getting *into* shape. He *entered* a state of euphoria. He fell *into* a depression."

Why is the metaphor a popular, sense-making system? A lengthy treatment of this question is beyond the confines of this work. However, the answer provided by Lakoff and Johnson (1980:6) appears very persuasive: "human thought processes are largely metaphorical." Put otherwise, humans use metaphors for thinking because they must; that is the way the human mind works.[3] Since *metaphor* is one of several words for model—map, representation, frame, structure, image, metaphor—then what appeared a moment ago to be a paradox is no paradox at all. PEWs (the Pure Empirical Workers) use models, but these take the form of metaphors. PEWs do it this way because, like the rest of us, they must. The question "Shall I use a model?" is not a meaningful question. The real question about models is rather "Should I use a model for unconscious reasons—a model that probably comes from one or more metaphors which exist in my culture?" or "Should I rationally and thoughtfully select a model that appears to serve the purposes of my research?" Once the real options are presented, only one sensible answer appears to exist: Rationally select a model! Actually an even better answer exists: Rationally select several models that can be used jointly. This "better answer" builds on a bit of wisdom grabbed from the marketplace: "There is no such thing as a free lunch." Let us explain.

A model takes a mountain of collectible data and shrinks it into a pool of manageable information. However, there is no such thing as shrinkage without a cost! Whether we are talking about science or weight loss, "reducing" things is a service we usually have to pay for. Shrinkage too has its price—much uncertainty. This is so because, as Paul Meadows has put it (1957:4), each model stipulates only "some correspondence with reality." Social science, it is well known, is soft-science, still in a primitive state of development. If the models used in the hard-sciences—physics, chemistry, and biology, for example—have only "*some* correspondence with reality," then the models used in soft, social science must have a very limited correspondence with reality. A weak, social science model, therefore, is like a beam of light used on a dark night and directed to a limited area. The spot hit by the beam is nicely illuminated. However, surrounding areas are left darker than they were before the light was used. If several models are cleverly used together—when several beams of light are strategically utilized—then a much larger area can be illuminated.

Our volume offers students of deviance three new models for deviance research. These models, we suggest, can be used in a variety of combinations, with models currently in vogue. Our models have emerged while struggling with data collected in systems that the deviance experts, sociologists, may consider "unusual." In attempting to frame our cross-cultural data within existing models of deviance, we discovered a lack of fit. We felt encouraged to develop our own models by learning that the experts too were not totally satisfied with existing models. For example, Lawrence Cohen and Richard Machalek recently proposed that "Social scientists have yet to explain why 'normal' individuals operating in unexceptional environments deviate and commit crimes" (1988:465). Our models, we hasten to add, provide additional perspectives, rather than total solutions to the problem discussed by Cohen and Machalek. Moreover, while our models are constructed in response to data, perhaps unusual from a sociological perspective, their core ideas are not completely novel. Put otherwise, the "new" in our new models must be understood within a context created by linking two metaphors. The first states: "Those who grovel and almost sink in rich marshlands, learn to see deeper" (Freilich 1990). The second, attributed to Sir Isaac Newton, states: "If I have seen further, it is because I have stood on the shoulders of giants." Woven together, these two metaphors present the following proposition: Those who grovel in confusions developed by superior minds tend to gain two talents: special vision to see creative labor, and the courage to climb on the shoulders of creative laborers. We have groveled and done some climbing. Whether we have chosen the right shoulders to climb upon and whether we actually "see further" is a judgment best left to those whose expertise is the study of deviance.

Our models, along with much supporting data, are fully presented below. First, in order to give our work a quick historical perspective, each model will be given a brief introduction.[4]

MODELS FOR CROSS CULTURAL RESEARCH

Smart and Proper Strategies: SAPS

SAPS seek to solve two problems: First, what image best captures the essential nature of humans? Second, how is the "best" image most elegantly presented? Twenty-four centuries ago Sophocles submitted a splendid solution to the first problem:

> Wonders are many, but none,
> None is more wonderous than man. . .
> Cunning, cunning is man,
> Wise though his plans are,
> Artful beyond all dreaming,
> They carry him to good and evil.

Strangely, Sophocles' image of the human condition is rarely referred to. Rather we hear, over and over again, an image grabbed from one of Shakespeare's minor plays, *As You Like It* (2:7):

> All the world's a stage
> And all men and women merely players:
> They have their exits and their entrances;
> And one man in his time plays many parts.

Humans-As-Actors (HAA) present us as "merely players," mere performers. Used creatively, beyond the Bard's limitations, the HAA image yields valuable insights (cf. Chapter 3). However, when HAA is simplistically used—all too often in the social science literature[5]—we get a curious presentation of an animal with the prestigious label *Homo sapiens*. Wise men and women appear to live mechanistic lives: mouthing lines already written, moving in ways already choreographed. As text, "All the world's a stage" sounds innocent enough. As subtext, the message—at least the message heard by some—is false and dangerous. The message "Humans are Puppets" comes with various visions, each of which describes how we, puppets, are manipulated, and who is "in charge." Some say the puppeteer is "culture"; for others the hidden power is "social structure," or "social institutions." The label of the puppeteer, surely, is a trivial issue. As Shakespeare almost said, a puppeteer by any other name still smells the same: still pulls the strings, still calls the shots.

Climbing on the shoulders of Sophocles, SAPS tries to help us see further, beginning with the notion that humans are wonderous beings: cunning, wise, artful, good and evil. Our amazing creativity takes these and other talents and utilizes them to create distinctly different conceptual worlds. In these worlds or cultures, everything knowable and imaginable gets a definition which, essentially, is arbitrary. For example, each conceptual reality or "culture" defines, in its own distinct manner, what it means to be good. A certain form of goodness becomes "legitimized" as the opposite of evil. "Legitimized" is a concept that comes from law. Often there is no legal or lawful process involved in "legitimizing" a certain form of goodness. Perhaps we should say: A certain form of goodness becomes "institutionalized." "Institutionalized," however, is a vague concept, one that even the experts, sociologists, have trouble explaining. Yet something does occur, some process makes a given set of decisions good in one society, reckless in another, and insane in yet a third society. Currently this process is but vaguely understood. What is clear, at least to us, is the end result of this process. The end result is the creation of a strange "rule book," one that humans carry around inside their heads. The rule book states that in order to be (say) wise (a form of goodness) our actions should follow the form A, B, C; our speech should follow the form P, Q, R; and our emotions should follow the form X, Y, Z. Actually, this invisible rule book is much more complex than just described. For any given society, a demonstration of wisdom may vary with age, sex, and status of the person attempting to appear wise. Moreover, wisdom may have to be "shown" differently depending on audience, time, and place. Essentially, however, the following summarizes this aspect of the human condition: *We carry a rule book in our heads. The rule books tells us the correct or proper way to be something (e.g., good or wise) or to do something* (say, avoid drugs or mothers-in-law).

To say, "We carry culture in our heads," is too fuzzy a statement to present to modern students, who are critical people, raised on low-cholesterol food and high-information computers. Better, then, to say, "We carry a file in our heads labeled: '*How to be correct or proper.*'" The file, which Freilich calls the Proper-File, has many subdivisions, including being proper in family life, in business dealings, in education, in religious, ritual life, and in social life. And each subdivision is itself subdivided. In short, the Proper File is a big file—chock-full of information. But it is information that is given to a human, it is not strings attached to a puppet. So where do erudite scholars get their inspiration to show us as dancing to the tunes and directions of a puppeteer? Their error seems to be an enormous exaggeration of the costs of avoiding the Proper-File. The costs—depending on the culture, the situation where the proper is avoided, and the style of avoidance—vary from a loss of esteem to receiving physical punishment. The costs, generally, are not so high that humans are forced to follow the instructions of the Proper-File.

Actually the Proper-File (P) competes for attention with two other files: the Smart File (S) and the Personal File (Z). The reason for the existence of other files is simple: the Proper-File is an old file; a set of information that some call "tradition." The Proper-File has information which, among other benefits, provides us with roots. But humans cannot live by roots alone. Minimally, we need to solve problems of survival; maximally, many of us want comfort and power.

The Proper-File (with P-information) provides some help for solving survival problems, and for getting comfort, and power. However, for issues of survival, comfort or power, the Smart-File, generally, is more useful. Data from the Smart-File (S-information) are more up to date, more practical, more localized and more specialized to solve day-to-day problems. S-information, collected by and shared among members of small interaction units, often replaces P-information as the guidance system that monitors human action.

At times humans reject P-information and S-information. At times, each of us thinks, I want to do something "my way." As we sing the popular Sinatra song, we temporarily shut both the Proper- and Smart-Files, and open our Personal-File—a file filled with personal experiences; a file that focuses on personal preferences. This Personal-File (containing Z-information) puts us at odds with the larger society (which promotes P-information) and with members of various groups we belong to (who promote S-information). Yet, those like Frank Sinatra and "Dirty Harry," who regularly make decisions based on Z-information, are the ones who sometimes become culture heroes and role models.

SAPS, thus far, show humans as differentially utilizing three sets of information (P, S, Z) found, respectively, in three files: Proper, Smart, and Personal. Actually, our lives are yet more complicated. Human action includes two key ingredients: (1) a concern with where given actions are taking us—a focus on goals; and (2) a concern with how to reach goals—a focus on methods or means. How do we get the information that helps us to decide which goals to pursue, and what means to use in order to reach them? Following SAPS, such critical data come from the three files already discussed: Proper, Smart, and Personal.

SAPS, while indebted to Sophocles, presents us as being more than just cunning, artful, wise, good and evil. Additionally, we are expert jugglers of information. Since we can select goals from three files, since we can also select means from three files, and since we can mix and match our means and our goals, we actually have a choice of nine possible strategies. By using small letters for means, capitals for goals, and presenting means first, it is possible to present each strategy in a very simple manner. For example, sP = smart-means for Proper-goals; pS = proper-means for Smart-goals, and sZ = smart-means for Personal goals. In short, every type of human action, in any human society, can be presented as one of nine possible strategies-of-action. These universal action strategies are (1) pP, (2) sP, (3) zP, (4) pS, (5) sS, (6) zS, (7) pZ, (8) sZ and (9) zZ.

The development of SAPS is a story fully discussed elsewhere (Freilich 1992). In brief, it began with a simple dichotomy: the smart versus the proper. Smart and Proper Analysis (SPA) then grew into a four-box model called LOS: Law of Strategies. LOS, although useful in identifying and describing a strategy developed by young Trinidadian cricket players, had limited utility. When confronted with data on police discretion, LOS helped Freilich lose data rather than understand data better. Remember, a model provides no guarantee that it is the best model for the job; or even that it is an adequate model for the job. LOS, a thin model with only four categories, was replaced with CHAOS, an obese model with sixteen categories.

CHAOS was talented in a rather strange manner: its unique strength was to confuse everyone who tried to understand it. After CHAOS bombed at the 1983 Annual Meeting of the Academy of Criminal Justice, it was still utilized for data analysis. Somehow, the realization that CHAOS, rather than the audience, was dumb, seemed to escape Freilich. In his defense we note that there is a strong emotional tie between model builder and model. The model builder, therefore, moves around with a thought, which, from a scientific perspective is harmful. The thought is: "This beautiful model of mine is really great!" Absurd as it now must surely appear, CHAOS, along with novel data, was taken to the 1984 Annual Meeting of the Academy of Criminal Justice. After another disastrous presentation CHAOS was brought home and unceremoniously buried. Shortly thereafter CHAOS was replaced by SAPS.

The lesson here is very clear: Model builders must be fickle lovers of any given model. If a model does not obviously help research, and if additionally it confuses those who are trying to understand it, there must be a withdrawal of love. The model must be replaced by something better—at least something different that is given a chance to prove itself better.

In moving from SPA, to LOS, to CHAOS, to SAPS many marshlands were traversed and many shoulders were climbed upon. These experiences are well documented in Freilich's essay (Chapter 1). Special mention must be made of ideas borrowed from Robert Merton (1953) and from Albert Cohen (1966).

In a very real sense a model belongs to a community of scholars; it is part of a tradition of thinking about given problems. Generally one person receives acclaim when a model succeeds, or suffers pain when a model flounders. However, the model is actually the result of cooperative labors of a collectivity. Indeed, Freilich is still trying to "help" those half-wits who helped him construct CHAOS.

Hard versus Soft Deviance

The distinction between hard and soft deviance reflects three principal modeling assumptions. First, social behavior is best studied both at the macro-level at which institutions and aggregate phenomena are the units of analysis, and also at the micro-level where individuals make and act upon distinctions that are not institutionalized at the macro-level. Second, the types of social dynamics at work at both the micro- and macro-levels will vary with the scale of the social unit. Finally, the study of deviance can profit by treating divergent behavior as a socially constructed continuum rather than as a phenomenon that either exists or does not.

Levels

Those interested in normative social phenomena will find considerable utility in the study of deviance. The presence and nature of deviance illuminates cultural values, and the sanctions that pressure deviants to conform reveal both social and cultural dynamics. However, despite the promise of these insights, anthropology has been only slightly concerned with the study of deviance.

Although most anthropologists have done little to advance the study of deviance, those who have dealt with the subject adopted a relativistic approach congruent with their comparative perspective (cf. Malinowski 1964). Before 1950 anthropologists generally treated individuals as passive bearers of their culture, like so many Egyptian slaves hauling blocks of customary behavior under the firm direction of the overseer, culture. The anthropology of this period produced, not surprisingly, elegant, general models that displayed a symmetry of elements and a degree of harmonious integration that was often aesthetically, as well as intellectually, pleasing. Unfortunately, these models were so general and so "ideal" that there were frequently difficulties relating them to the reality they purported to describe. This was particularly true of situations involving change. Like symmetrical snowflakes, these formal sociocultural models achieved their elegance in part by treating their constituent elements as though they were frozen in place, timelessly related to one another. Here, again bowing to Blake, was yet another form of "fearful symmetry." Clearly a new perspective was desirable: one which could deal both with the stable enduring elements of culture and with those aspects that were unstable, changing, and often at variance with existing norms.

While sociology, mainly because of the efforts of members of the Chicago School, took an early interest in process and micro-level analysis, anthropology's concern with such matters was not an active one until the efforts of Raymond Firth in the early and mid-1950s (1961, 1964). For Firth, the correspondence of macro-level social structure with reality is problematic, largely because of the degree of abstraction involved in formulating the model. Social structure is derived from observations of regularities among people; yet, because it must include all such regularities, it can never be complete and is best seen as a conceptual rather than as a descriptive tool (Firth 1964:37-38). He addresses both shortcomings, the degree of abstraction and difficulty in treating change, by introducing a distinction between social structure and micro-level social organization:

One may think of social organization in terms of ordered action. It refers to concrete social activity . . . One may describe social organization, then, as the working arrangements of society. It is the processes of ordering of actions and of relations in reference to given social ends, *in terms of adjustments resulting from the exercise of choices by members of society.* (Firth 1964:45, emphasis added)

The approach employed in studying hard versus soft deviance reflects the importance of examining choices made by individuals, especially as members of small-scale social units.

Scale

In 1887 Ferdinand Tönnies, a German sociologist, made a useful and enduring distinction between *Gemeinschaft* and *Gesellschaft*. For Tönnies, *Gemeinschaft*, often translated as community, was a small-scale social entity, characterized by face-to-face relationships and utilizing kinship as a major organizing principle. In such a social unit, interpersonal relationships tend to be both intimate and very important owing, in part, to the interdependence of group members. *Gesellschaft*, best translated as society, was a large-scale social unit characterized by structured, often impersonal, relationships in which kinship bonds were subordinated to political, economic, and other broad social considerations.

Like a body comprised of cells, society is made up of communities. However, just as the processes that characterize cell activity differ significantly from those that describe gross physiological processes, communities and societies are characterized by markedly different social dynamics. Community involves individual and small-group behaviors reflecting a rich social context in which there is much tradition and little formalism. Society is concerned with large-scale aggregate behaviors occurring in a more impoverished social context in which there is little tradition and much formalism. Reflecting matters of scale, the reactions of members to deviance in these differing social units should contrast with each other.

Deviance: A Socially Constructed Continuum

Beginning with Durkheim, most of the significant contributions to the theory and study of deviance have come from sociologists. Many earlier sociological discussions of deviance described it as a metastatic cancer, symptomatic of problems in the social organism (cf. Edgerton 1976; Clinard 1974:11-14). However, some notable interpretations of deviance argued it was more like an occasionally troublesome liver, an integral part of society that could even function to increase the solidarity of most members of the social order (Durkheim 1938; Erikson 1966).

George Herbert Mead (1964) and others of the Chicago School were among the first sociologists to emphasize both social process and the role of individual perception in the construction of social life. Their influence is reflected in a recent, major treatment of deviance, namely, labeling theory, which is largely the work of Howard Becker (1963), Albert Cohen

(1965, 1966), John Kitsuse (1962), Edwin Lemert (1967, 1982), and David Matza (1969). Briefly, labeling theory asserts that deviance is socially constructed. The members of society decide what they mean by the term and then label individuals whose behavior is perceived as departing from accepted norms. The labelees, in turn, find themselves marginalized, prevented from engaging in certain forms of social participation, and encouraged to conceive of themselves as deviant.

Initially, there was little distinction drawn between the differing degrees of deviance assigned via labels. However, Robert Stebbins (1988) recently recommended recognizing a contrast between what he terms tolerable and intolerable deviance. These terms reflect the difference between deviance that involves a simple departure from the normative and deviance that places the social order in jeopardy. He argues that both abound in societies and that one can even find justifications for tolerable deviance as a leisure activity (Stebbins 1988:7-9). The distinction between hard and soft deviance parallels some of Stebbins' arguments, as Raybeck discusses in Chapter 2.

Raybeck is aware that a dichotomous distinction between hard and soft deviance oversimplifies the judgments of social members who are capable of making much finer discriminations. However, as is the case with any proposed model, the case to make is for utility rather than for truth. Social science must deal with units and distinctions that it can manage, and a dichotomous distinction is far easier to employ than one made up of an arbitrary number of gradients.

The test of these three modeling assumptions comes, not from arguments concerning their truth and beauty, but rather from an assessment of what they enable an investigator to accomplish. A delicious cake may appear quite unattractive compared to others, but the test of cakeness is in the eating, not in the appearance. It is hoped that the reader will find the assumptions invoked in the study of hard and soft deviance, at the least, palatable and perhaps capable of nourishing further research.

Staged Deviance

The meanings and functions of deviance are related to many cultural factors. As Raybeck shows, these include the scale of the society within which misconduct occurs, and the "hardness" or "softness" of the behavior at issue; and as Freilich's model indicates, it also involves the "smart" or "proper" ways in which rules are honored or violated. In Savishinsky's model of "staged deviance," he switches attention to a third dimension of culture, namely, the roles that audiences play in the creation and definition of deviance. His approach is built on the fact that in some situations, observers may not only watch the misbehavior of others, but they can also instigate and profit from it. He applies this perspective to field data he collected during research in the Arctic and the Bahamas, where people enjoyed "free shows and cheap thrills" by directing other individuals to act in deviant ways.

To understand this pattern of deviant conduct, Savishinsky draws on the kind of "symbolic interactionist" and dramaturgical approaches developed by sociologists such as George Herbert Mead (1934), Howard Becker (1963), Herbert Blumer (1969), and Erving Goffman (1959, 1963a, 1967). Their work shows that the public and self-image of people depends both on how others perceive them and how the actors themselves manipulate and feel about these perceptions. In particular, the symbolism of human interaction centers on the way individuals negotiate meanings and identities in various public arenas. Goffman develops this approach by arguing that the behaviors that occur in these settings often have the qualities of theater: people work "backstage" in order to prepare an act that will allow them to control the impression that they make on their public.

In his model of "staged deviance," Savishinsky explains certain types of misbehavior by shifting the focus from the actors to the public audience. During fieldwork in northern Canada and the Caribbean, he had been puzzled by the fact that adults took great pleasure in disapproving of behavior which they themselves had participated in or helped to promote. The normally controlled and nonviolent Hare Indians of Canada's Northwest Territories got drunks, pups, and young children to be aggressive instead of restrained. Native adults also mocked and mimicked movie actors for publicly showing affection on screen. He found a similar pattern among native people from communities on Cat Island in the eastern Bahamas. Usually constrained in their relations with one another, the Bahamians he lived with frequently manipulated and then disparaged the behavior of tourists whenever work or leisure brought these two groups together in a home, a hotel, or a bar. Bahamian men, for example, set white women up and came on to them sexually; they also treated white men with camaraderie to first put them at their ease, and then got them to play the fool by prompting them to speak or to joke in inappropriate ways. As an anthropologist who had gained access to the "backstage" areas where Bahamians talked openly about these outsiders, Savishinsky learned how they laughed at the boorish, often promiscuous, behavior of the tourists.

In both the Arctic and the Bahamas, whether on stage or on screen, human and nonhuman actors were being cast and conned into playing a variety of deviant roles. But what for? Why, Savishinsky wondered, did native people promote what they disparaged and then condemn their own creation? Building on the symbolic and dramaturgical theories noted above, he found a model—a way to answer this question—in the idea of staged deviance. The model came from the realization that, in the situations described, it was audience members who controlled and defined what actors did. The manipulations were subtle but always self-serving, and they fulfilled several functions. At the most basic level, native people simply enjoyed these "free shows." But part of their pleasure in staging what was variously ludicrous, violent, sexual and compromising was the opportunity it gave people to feel superior while in the very act of watching the forbidden. The staging of deviance brought other rewards as well. By putting improper insiders and outsiders in their place, it confirmed the virtues of those who conformed and fed their sense of solidarity. Virtue, in other words, was its own reward, but only if there was something deviant to compare it with.

Savishinsky's model explains the cultural creation of certain types of deviance, as well as the meanings that such deviance has for those who direct and those who perform it. He emphasizes the subtlety of these encounters, which derive their effectiveness from the fact that dogs, drunks, children, actors, and tourists are not aware of how others symbolically interpret their conduct. Their deviance is part of the plot in what could be called a theater of the unconscious.

Reflecting on the lessons that these small-scale communities might teach us about more complex societies, Savishinsky makes three comparative points. First, he notes the parallels between his Arctic and Bahamian data and both the "functionalist" and social conflict views of deviance articulated by Durkheim (1895), Cohen (1966), Sagarin and Kelly (1982), Taylor (1982), and others. That is, deviance can be used, or created, to enhance social unity among those who feel they are normal. Second, he argues that the dramatizing of deviance can also be a vehicle for promoting social change. He observes, for example, that "soft" forms of staged deviance—such as clothing fads, the open use of "soft" drugs, and the creation of new types of art—are often a harbinger of social and stylistic trends, especially when they are made "smart" and popular by the media (Rubington 1982; Freilich, Chapter 1). Finally, he notes that the staging of deviance has also been a favorite device for imposing repression. It has been used, for example, by "moral entrepreneurs" (Becker 1963) to enforce policy, power, and social control in the modern world. Referring to political events both in the United States and the USSR—ranging from the Moscow "show" trials of the 1930s to government infiltration of American protest movements—Savishinsky points out that leaders of modern states manufacture evidence, incite illegal acts, and force false confessions from their vocal opponents; they then destroy their competitors by dramatizing their deviance in public hearings and court-rooms. The moral of the tale is that deviance can be transformed into profitable theater—profitable, that is, from the perspective of those who remain in power and write the reviews after the show is over.

In summary, the model of "staged deviance" is built on the insights of several theoretical traditions, including functionalist, symbolic interactionist, and dramaturgical approaches. It seeks to make sense of four aspects of deviant conduct: (a) the promotion or enjoyment of deviance by spectators, (b) the role of deviance in the process of culture change, (c) the creation of deviance as a means for enhancing social solidarity, and (d) the invention of deviance as a political device to enforce conformity and suppress opposition. By showing that the staging of deviance occurs in both small-scale and complex societies, Savishinsky suggests that this model can help us understand a widespread feature of social and political life in the modern world.

Generally, we are arguing that the study of deviance provides another valuable means to study social life. Like biologists who seek to understand life through the study of anabolic processes, most social investigators seek to comprehend the order in social life through the study of structures and processes that promote order. However, as biologists can and do benefit from the study of catabolic processes, we argue that a concern with deviance and the forces that promote disorder enable social scientists to gain a better understanding of all social dynamics, including those that promote order. Indeed, we believe that a concern with deviance encourages development of a fresh perspective on many issues of social life. As many of the chapters in this volume demonstrate, the study of deviance not only can promote comparative studies, it can synthesize perspectives, insights, and data from a variety of disciplines. The result is a rich, contextually sensitive, and process-oriented approach to social life.

NOTES

1. Of the ninety-two volumes of *World Ethnography* edited by Sol Tax, not one includes the term *deviance* in its title, although anthropologists have done and are doing considerable work on deviance. Some good examples of existing efforts include

ethnographies which focus on deviance (Bohannon 1960; Malinowski 1966; Selby 1974; and Spradley 1979); works on legal anthropology (Collier 1973; Hollos 1976; Moore 1987a, 1987b; Nader & Todd 1978; and Starr 1978); examinations of child abuse (Korbin 1977, 1980, 1981), wife abuse (Erchak 1984), alcoholism (Marshall 1979; Singer & Borrero 1984) and suicide (Rubenstein 1983); discussions of deviance as it relates to such central anthropological concerns as symbolism (Douglas 1966; Turner 1969) and sorcery (Marwick 1967); and even some theoretical discussions of deviance (Edgerton 1976, 1986). Nonetheless, thus far anthropologists have lacked a central, institutionalized framework within which to share ideas and data, and through which to develop better integrated models.

2. Statements concerning paths of failure are often referred to as "postulates of impotence." A postulate of impotence, according to Sir Edmund Whittaker (1958:69), "is the assertion of a conviction that all attempts to do a certain thing, are bound to fail."

3. The generalization "human thought processes are largely metaphorical" is supported by works such as Lakoff 1987; Lakoff and Johnson 1980; and Lakoff and Turner 1989.

4. Those who want to know much more about models could hardly do better than begin with a marvelous essay by Roy Lachman (1960).

5. As the wise sociologist, Rolf Dahrendorf notes (1968:29): "*All the world's a stage* eminently anticipates the nature and potential of the category of social role, and thus illuminates many features of the sociological concept of role." This statement is part of an essay that *critizes* the sociological concept of role.

I   Models for Cross-Cultural Research

1   SMART RULES AND PROPER RULES: A JOURNEY THROUGH DEVIANCE

Morris Freilich

"Superstars," a mass-media congame, continues to fool many. Many, that is, sacrifice time and money for fake intimacy with the famous.[1] As played in the sciences, "superstars" leads to still greater losses. Behind the glitter and glamour of superstar-science sits a false and harmful message: "Ordinary humans cannot make significant scientific contributions." This message is usefully presented as an equation:

SUPERSTAR = GENIUS = BRINGER OF SCIENTIFIC BREAKTHROUGHS

"Three Princes of Serendip," Horace Walpole's (1754) amusing tale, is a valuable antidote to this depressing equation. Good fortune, Walpole teaches, often accompanies daring travelers and points them toward creative paths. And the decision to actually follow Luck's leads is more a matter of imagination than IQ, more a function of guts than of genius.

"Serendip" gave birth to "serendipity," luck seen and seized: not Blind Luck, sometimes involved in games of chance, but Masked Luck, sometimes involved in the knowledge game.[2] Masked Luck transforms herself into many and strange forms. For example, she visited Alexander Fleming, as a bit of dirt resting inside his experimental, staphylococcus culture. Once recognized, Masked Luck led Fleming to a path of discovery that contained a secret weapon against many bacteria: penicillin. Given that Masked Luck is often out and about it is necessary to reformulate the breakthrough problem. The question is not, Why do scientific breakthroughs sometimes occur? but rather, Why are they so rare? Why so often is Luck's labor lost?

John Ziman (1981) provides a persuasive answer to this peculiar problem. After luck is recognized, her gifts must be used as a new base from which to build a research path. The decision to follow a new path is risky. Current research may have to be deferred. The new research may be inconsistent with orders from employers, interests of colleagues, and one's self-definition as a given type of specialist. Moreover, work with payoffs that are unpredictable creates psychic pain, particularly so for scholars who are Apollonians—who are most comfortable with safe projects. And even risk-loving Dionysians, like myself, sometimes pass up novel opportunities for practical reasons (Szent-Gyorgyi 1972). Clearly, before luck can be fully exploited, economic, social, and psychological hurdles must be surmounted.

"Serendipity" hides a tricky time factor. To grab Luck and dance to her tune immediately is to take a double risk: first, that Luck will lead to progress; second, that the work Luck interrupted, essentially, was unimportant. Risks are reduced if Luck's gifts are set aside until conditions for using them are most favorable. This strategy, Luck embraced but her gifts placed on a back burner, worked for me in a manner to be fully discussed.

One hot afternoon, in September 1957, Luck and I met on a cricket field, in Anamat, Trinidad. Luck was disguised as friendly Hindu Indian boys who played cricket. By following Luck's lead, I entered a sociological domain. In the kingdom of Deviance I was a novice surrounded by experts. I assumed the role of the child in "The Emperor's New Clothes." Seeing much deviance data which was "naked," unclothed with theory, I said so. I then tried my hand at the "loom." My loom is Smart-Proper Analysis, a set of ideas. The weaving produced a formal model called Smart and Proper Strategies (SAPS). Both the loom and its production can help to improve deviance theory.

My belief that current theories of deviance are weak is not controversial (cf. Marx 1981). As three deviance scholars have put it, "the field is currently in a state of intellectual disarray. That state is the legacy of over two hundred years of mixing science with morals" (Rosenberg et al. 1982: 12). The degree of disarray is evident from even a cursory look at some of the work of three experts. Jack Gibbs (1981) presents a fair evaluation of the state of deviance theory. Among its essential flaws, Gibbs argues, is the attempt to link deviance to "norms." Norms, he says, cannot be defined in a scientifically useful manner. The concept must therefore be replaced by "normative properties." Deviance is explained by a theory that is linked to a model of social control. Gibbs's theory of deviance is so complex that he admits to being unable to present any more than its basic form. His model of social control is so cumbersome that after ninety pages of explanation its research utility still stays hidden.

Nanette Davis (1980), like Gibbs, attempts to ground deviance in a formal model of social control. Curiously, she both disavows the existence of deviance and attempts to define it—as a form of conflict. Edwin Lemert (1981, 1982), like Davis, takes an unusual approach toward the definition of basic concepts. Lemert suggests that "deviance" is best left as an undefined term. For purposes of research he would replace "deviance" with "deviance matters." Following his lead, empirical researchers would have the vague goal of understanding processes of differentiation, that is, how people become differentiated, and what moral significance attaches to their differences. Some might argue that an undefined, existent term is an advantage over a defined, nonexistent term. However, either approach to deviance is likely to confuse empirical researchers. Deviance theory, clearly, can use some help.

The help I provide stems from various sources. It comes from the idea-set called Smart-Proper Analysis, from the formal model called SAPS, and from data obtained as a gift from Luck. Historically, Luck's gift came first, so I will proceed in temporal sequence.

LUCK'S GIFT: PECULIAR PUJAH TRIPS

Mad dogs and cricketers play in the tropical sun. My folly enticed Masked Luck to visit Anamat, Trinidad, the site of my doctoral research (Freilich 1960). During what was planned as a short work break I walked to a nearby cricket field and watched some youths playing. Suddenly a cricket ball was hit in my vicinity. I caught it easily, and expertly threw it back to the bowler (pitcher). He threw back an admiring glance and asked me to join the game. Later, we all made plans to play again the next day. After several additional games I was invited to join one of the village teams.

After each game the players wandered off in several small cliques. The group I got to know well was a Hindu-Indian clique with a membership that fluctuated between nine and twelve boys. During one of many postgame conversations, some of the boys commented on my interest and regular attendance at local *pujahs*—Hindu prayer meetings.

They suggested that it would be useful for me to observe pujahs in communities other than Anamat. Moreover, they volunteered to take me to such. I was rather surprised to discover that these young Indians wanted more religion than their own community could provide. I agreed to take some of them in my car to a nearby pujah the following week. Thereafter, various members of this clique kept inviting me to pujahs outside of Anamat. I went whenever other work commitments permitted, and we always traveled in my car. After three pujah trips, I made a conscious decision to investigate further. The decision was made on the basis of what the boys did not do once we arrived at a given pujah site. They never actually participated in any of the rituals. As soon as we arrived at a given community, they introduced me to friends or relatives, arranged for us to meet at a given place and time, and left the area where the *pundit* (priest) was directing the ritual. Where they went and what they did, initially, was a mystery. Yet their presentation of themselves as religious was surely a lie.

After deciding to make time available for pujah trips with the boys, I discovered that I could go with them about once a month and still complete my planned "natural experiment" (Freilich 1960). The puzzle of the lie—the answer to why these boys are going to pujahs—was solved after reviewing data on the marriage practices of Indians in Anamat, and interviewing a number of members of this cricket-playing clique. Anamatian Indians arrange marriages in ways that differ minimally from the traditional practices of Hindus in India. An adult male finds a spouse for his son or daughter by adhering to the following rules: The spouse must belong to the caste of the father (caste endogamy) but must reside outside of his community (community exogamy). Spouse-finding activities are generally facilitated by information provided by local pundits.

A typical Hindu-Indian arranged marriage occurs as follows: A pundit discovers two teenagers who are permitted to marry. The pundit helps the boy's father make arrangements with the girl's father for a get-together; this meeting includes the two fathers and several of their male relatives. If the two families consider a marriage link to be mutually advantageous, a second meeting is planned. This time the boy's father brings his son along, so that the youth can be looked over by the males of the girl's family. If the boy is considered acceptable, he and the girl are allowed to spend several minutes alone together. The boy is then asked by his father, "Do you want to marry this girl?" The answer expected and almost invariably received is "Yes, I do!" Marriage plans are then finalized by the males of both groups.[3]

Shortly before my return to America, a member of the cricket-playing clique got engaged to a girl from one of the villages we had visited together. Finding the youth alone one day, I shook his hand, offered congratulations, and asked him some general questions about how his marriage was arranged. The questions made him nervous, and all I got were vague answers. I then began a grilling interview, one which challenged many of the interviewee's statements. The interview concluded with the following exchange.

MF: What did you and your future wife talk about when her father left you two alone for a few minutes?

Youth: I asked her if she likes me and if she would like to marry me. She said "Yes." Then she asked me the same questions, and I said "Yes."

MF: Are you sure this is the right girl for you? You have only spent a few minutes with her. How could you know so quickly?

Youth: My father looked into her family's background. . . . I am really attracted to her. . . . She is nice to be with. . . .

MF: Is this really the first time you met this girl?

Youth: No.

MF: Did you meet her when we went to a pujah at her village?

Youth: Yes.

MF: Did that meeting have anything to do with the fact that *this* marriage has been *arranged?*

My young friend could hold out no longer. He and the boys had arranged this marriage. It was all part of a game they had developed. They really cared very little for pujahs as religious experiences. They liked to go for social reasons: for the food that was served after the praying was finished; for the music that was played and sung; and, when held in other villages, for the opportunities afforded by a pujah to meet girls. At one pujah outside of Anamat he and some friends had met some girls they liked. They began to wonder how they could plan to see them again. Somehow, they jointly came to the conclusion that they ought to go to as many pujahs as they could get to, so that they could meet girls who might become their wives.

I later questioned other members of the clique, after first telling them what I knew and promising to say nothing to any member of their family. Those interviewed explained what they did in a manner that closely fits David Matza's (1964) discussion of neutralization. Their behavior was not wrong; they really did not lie to anyone. They did like pujahs. They harmed no one by getting people to take them, and they got rides from people (like myself) who wanted or needed to go. Why should the non-Hindu males of the village be allowed to choose their wives, while the Hindu-Indian boys had to marry someone picked for them? It was not fair.

The system developed had netted the boys one previous marriage, one future marriage, and several possible marriages still being worked on. The system was based on the following information and strategies: (1) Pujahs outside of Anamat provided good opportunities for meeting girls who could become wives; (2) pundits and others who travel around nearby communities must be asked about forthcoming pujahs; (3) people going to pujahs must be approached for rides; (4) people with cars must be encouraged to go to pujahs outside of Anamat; (5) appearing as religious will make it easier to get rides and to get permission to take pujah trips; (6) during a given pujah the boys must collect and share information with clique members about the caste, age, attractiveness, and availability of given girls met; (7) if a boy (B) finds a girl (G) whom he likes and who is of the proper caste for marriage, and if the girl likes him also, then B must get his family to arrange this marriage; (8) B is advised to speak to a friendly adult male—preferably a younger brother of his father—and tell him that he discovered that G (a very attractive girl in another village) was available as a marriage partner; (9) the friendly adult must then be prodded to push B's father to follow through in traditional ways: meet with the girl's father, bring the boy to the girl's father's house, and so forth.

The data on the pujah trips have remained unpublished for over twenty-five years. I was much involved with other projects and I had no idea that the data had any special value. After doing research with Mohawks, Trinidadian peasants, American hospitalized schizophrenics, and Hassidim in America and Israel, I was still unsure of precisely what I should be doing in "the field." I wondered if it were possible to develop a scientific approach to fieldwork. I convinced nine experienced cultural anthropologists to discuss two field projects, in essays that would go into one book. Along with two of my own projects, we had descriptions of twenty field projects published in *Marginal Natives: Anthropologists at Work* (Freilich 1970). In the concluding essay, "Toward a Formalization of Fieldwork," I developed a set of ideas that are relevant to research in deviance. Let us look at this idea-set, called Smart-Proper Analysis.

THE PROPER AND THE SMART: CULTURE AND SOCIETY

Smart-Proper Analysis proposes that the words *culture* and *society* refer to very different phenomena. Culture refers to ideas that are old.

In the aging process cultural ideas become infused with meaning and elevated in status. The prestige of cultural ideas is captured by the word *proper*. When we talk, act, feel, and think in ways taught by the culture, we are proper and our acts are proper. But often, proper ways are avoided for pragmatic reasons. Often the proper way does not lead to success. The problem is that the environment keeps changing. Society today is very different from society years ago. New adaptive modes are often crucial for survival. And these new, *social* adaptations require us to be smart rather than proper. The smart, the *socially* adaptive response is learned on the job, so to speak. In everyday experiences and interactions we notice that many of our co-workers, colleagues, and friends are avoiding given proper ways. We notice further that often they avoid the proper in similar ways, and they are not eager to discuss their smart behavior patterns with strangers. Given that the smart is more likely to be practical and effective than the proper, why do we still hold onto things proper? The question is complex and will be given a fuller answer later. For now let us note that life in the world of "properness" is a celebration of time. It is a recognition that time is our most valued possession. The scarcity of time, and our fears of what will happen to us after our time is over, makes it so. By living in the world of properness we give ourselves more time, albeit the time *behind us* rather than the time *ahead of us*. Yet this time behind us has qualities missing in the time ahead. Clearly, the time behind, or tradition, has certainty. Mystically, the time behind has strong sustaining powers. By focusing on the time behind, by remembering and giving honor to ancestors, we somehow get succor from our "roots." This is so because remembering is part of our very essence. We are what Alfred Korzybski (1933: 76) calls a "time-binding" animal. With "time-behind" pushing toward properness, and *survival-now* pushing toward smartness, we are more than just a time-binding animal. We are also an animal forever in conflict. Torn between being proper and being smart, we are, surely, a neurotic animal.

Whether these ideas are true and, if true, useful for social science, may be argumentative. What is obviously true is that I had hooked into a wide-ranging set of ideas. I forgot about the pujah trips. I had caught a tiger by the tail. The tiger, Smart-Proper Analysis, led me into many cultures, searching for various formulations of my smart rules. I first found smart rules in a negative form, that is, as patterns or established modes of avoiding proper rules. Let me present some examples.

Much ethnography exists showing people avoiding the proper in a similar manner. Typical of such is John Roberts and Thomas Gregor's discussion of sexual life among the Mehinaku, Arawaken-speaking

horticulturalists of central Brazil (1971: 207): "Most of the younger
Mehinaku conduct extramarital liaisons with everyone else of the opposite sex unless they are of different generations or are explicitly forbidden
from such a relation by the incest taboo." Patterns of avoiding culture
are equally evident in more complex systems. In modern India the
cultural ideal that women should stay at home and not run around town
is regularly avoided by many freedom-loving females. The pattern that
has developed is for women to form religious clubs. Since it is legitimate
for women to be involved with religion and these clubs are located away
from home, women both get out of the house and escape negative
sanctions (Nanda 1991).

Robin Williams, in a now classic text (1951:382), describes ten
patterns for getting around American ideals. These include bootlegging,
political graft, prostitution, nepotism, fee splitting, and false advertising.
The practical value of fudging the truth, and the patterned ways of doing
so in big business and big government, are well described by columnist
David Wilson (1981). The rules are to understate expected votes and the
cost of planned governmental programs and to overstate price hikes and
the cost of already appropriated programs. Patterned avoidance of
cultural ideals in the black ghettos has been documented by Elliot Liebow
(1967). There, a frequently broken cultural ideal is the notion that a
marriage should end only if a spouse dies. A second norm, the belief
that sooner or later the husband will be unable to support the wife, helps
women to reject the ideal. That is, "anticipation of failure" strongly
influences women to break marriage ties.

Those who avoid cultural rules in ways that fit in with the pattern are
generally not thought of as bad people by the other members of the social
system. Rather they are considered as regular or cool, people who know
the ropes. For example, as reported by Marvin Stone (1979:100), most
Americans do not consider tax dodgers as doing anything wrong. After
publishing an article on the persisting problem of tax cheating and its
patterned nature, Stone received an avalanche of letters from people
residing in twenty-four states. He was surprised to discover that "three
out of four people defended or sympathized with tax dodgers."

The patterns presented clearly are no accidents of nature or society.
They occur because many people know the same ropes and act accordingly. In the old sailing days, "the ropes" really were ropes, and knowing
them meant being an experienced sailor. Today, the ropes are but symbols
of experience. And today, the experience refers to being streetwise rather
than shipwise. The "street," moreover, is any setting where people
interact and exchange symbols, goods, and services. The street, that is,

can be a regular street, a center of business (like Wall Street), a branch of government, a hospital, a prison, a university, or a police precinct. In short, "knowing the ropes," for me, means knowing smart rules as well as proper rules. By this time, I had discovered the Rabbit Rule: *Once there are two, soon there will be more.* Following the Rabbit Rule, since two ways exist for discussing smart rules—as the ropes and street wisdom—there must be more ways. If I could find them, it would give extra proof that smart rules really are a different type of rules, and provide extra insights to the meaning and function of smart rules. I began a long literature search, long because I really did not know where to look.

I discovered that in order to find conceptualizations that function like smart rules I had to look for pairs of concepts similar to smart rules and proper rules. Let me present some examples of these findings.

Immanuel Kant (1966) distinguishes between hypothetical imperatives (action guides that are useful) and categorical imperatives (action guides that have intrinsic worth). George Santayana (1955) contrasts intellectual judgments with judgments of value. John Rawls's similar distinction (1955) is rules of a practice versus institutionalized rules. Building on the work of Rawls, John Searle (1964) distinguishes between regulatory rules and constitutive rules. These and other dualities coming out of philosophy (see Table 1.1) have parallels in the social sciences. For example, Emile Durkheim (1953) contrasts judgments of reality with value judgments. And Alfred Kroeber (1952) distinguishes between "reality culture" and "value culture." A careful study of these and very many similar dichotomies demonstrates that humans are guided by two distinctly different informational systems (see Table 1.1). Clearly that must be the case. How else can we explain essentially the same dichotomy developed by scholars from different disciplines, scholars unacquainted (generally) with each other's works? I go further and say: Smart versus proper is a dichotomy that is part of the base of human, social existence. Strangely, then, while many discuss these ideas with their own labels, the dichotomy has minimal influence on social science research. Even stranger, my pujah-trip data were sitting around and begging for a Smart-Proper Analysis. Yet, until Luck returned, I was blind to any connection between pujah trips and Smart-Proper Analysis.

LUCK'S RETURN AND DEVIANCE

Luck returned, masquerading as a letter from a publishing house, The New American Library. An editor from NAL asked me to edit a book of anthropological essays. The volume, *The Pleasures of Anthropology*

Table 1.1
Two-Informational Systems Comparable as Contrasts between the Proper and the Smart

Bailey (1968)	Normative Rules	Pragmatic Rules
Bittner (1983)	Legal Criteria	Workmanship Criteria
Bourdieu (1979)	Formal Rules	Habitus
Coser et al. (1983)	Official Norms	Counter Norms
Dexter (1981)	The Desirable	The Marketable
Diamond (1972)	Culture	Social Signals
Drabek (1968)	Established Norms	Emergent Norms
Durkheim (1953)	Value Judgments	Judgments of Reality
Good (1981)	Formal Rules	Practical Rules
Hall (1969)	Formal	Informal
Hocart (1970)	Cultural	Practical
Howard (1970)	Normative Decisions	Strategic Decisions
Hunn (1982)	Formal	Practical Significance
Hymes (1970)	Social	Empirical
Kant (1966)	Categorical Imperatives	Hypothetical Imperatives
Kroeber (1952, 1957)	Value Culture	Reality Culture
Leach (1954, 1961)	Ritual Formal Structure	Practical Informal Structure
Marcuse (1964)	Truth Value	Exchange Value
Page (1946-47)	Formal System	Informal System
Rawls (1955)	Rules of a "Practice"	Rules as Experience Summaries
Redfield (1953)	Moral Rules	Rules of Expedience
Reisman (1979)	Myth Systems	Operational Codes
Santayana (1955)	Judgments of Value	Judgments Intellectual
Searle (1964)	Institutionalized Rules	Regulatory Rules
Shils (1971)	"Traditional" Traditions	Rational, Empirical Traditions
Stoddard (1968)	Formalized Norms	Reference Group Norms
Turk (1969)	Cultural Norms	Social Norms
Weber (1947)	Wertrational	Zweckrational

(Freilich 1983a), had to be interesting, informative, and fun. After agreeing to edit such a text, I received a copy of NAL's first book in this "enjoy and learn" series, *The Pleasure of Sociology* (Coser 1980). As I skimmed through Lewis Coser's book, I soon was immersed in Erving Goffman's essay, "On Cooling Out the Mark." Goffman's analysis of con games took some fuzzy thoughts I had suppressed for decades and gave them clear consciousness. I was a "mark" in Trinidad. Joining me in this role of sucker were a number of adult Hindu-Indian males. And the group of Hindu-Indian youths were "operators," using trips to pujahs for personal, nonreligious ends. Yet to equate pujah trips with con games left some nagging questions unanswered: What did I lose? What did other marks lose? What was the crime that actually was committed?

Con games, as described by Goffman, are zero-sum games: there are losers, the marks, and there are winners, the operators. In a given con game the amount won is equal to the amount lost (hence the concept, zero-sum games). But in the con game invented by my young friends, there were no losers. Every player won. I won valuable data, and young Hindu-Indians won, by getting mates they knew and liked. Their fathers won by getting proper mates for their sons without much effort: without the traditional search for the right family, and without the usual resistance from their sons.[4] Moreover, Hindu-Indian social and cultural life could also be called "a winner." This con game helped Western ideas of marriage (presented in movie theaters, in nearby towns) gain peaceful entry into Anamat. Pujah-trip data, I realized, exemplified an appealing idea that merited its own label. I call it a victimless con game.

When pujah-trip data were reincarnated as a victimless con game, I also was transformed. I had gone from a somewhat deviant cultural anthropologist—someone without a specific culture-area who studied philosophy, sociology, and social anthropology—to a student of deviance in cross-cultural perspective. With the aid of colleagues and friends, I found a large literature on the sociology of deviance. A year's work with this deviance literature cannot be briefly summarized here, but I can focus on some readings that, initially, appeared relevant to the victimless con game. Like Richard Cloward and Lloyd Ohlin's model (1961), the victimless con game identifies behaviors that are neither legitimate nor illegitimate. However, those who exhibit "double failures," unlike my young friends, lack legitimate and illegitimate opportunities to reach valued goals. David Matza's (1964) "Drifting Delinquents," like the Anamat boys, move into norm manipulation gradually and through a first stage, which is unplanned. Unlike drifting delinquents, the boys freely chose to commit nonproper acts: acts that cannot be called crimes. While the boys were not part of the elite, their behavior had some similarities to that of the "deviant elite" (Simon and Eitzen 1982). That is, their behavior, while culturally wrong, was not illegal.

Robert Merton's (1957), model, "Social Structure and Anomie" (SSA), initially appeared relevant for my data. The model distinguishes five modes of adaptation (Figure 1.1). Each adaptive mode is a function of accepting or rejecting cultural goals or institutionalized means. SSA proved disappointing for analyzing my data. In the victimless con game the boys accepted cultural goals, but they rejected the institutionalized means. To call their behavior "innovation," as SSA requires, links them with criminals who pursue cultural goals by illegal means. In part, the boys are rebels, but unlike Mertonian "rebels" the boys only reject institutional means. Additionally, and making SSA still less useful, Merton's model includes premises with which many scholars disagree.

Figure 1.1
SSA: Merton's Model of Social Structure and Anomie

Modes of Adaptation	Cultural Goals	Institutionalized Means
I. Conformity	+	+
II. Innovation	+	−
III. Ritualism	−	+
IV. Retreatism	−	−
V. Rebellion	±	±

Key	"+" signifies acceptance while "-" signifies rejection. "±" signifies rejection of prevailing values and substitution of new ones

For example, deviants are not necessarily different and easily identified. And deviant behavior may not be pathological to the functioning of society.[5] Indeed some deviance is actually positive, a useful contribution to society.

POSITIVE DEVIANCE

In a section headed "Deviance in Support of Organization," Albert Cohen (1966:6-11) summarized much of the (then) existing literature on positive contributions made by deviants. Deviance, Cohen explained, need not be harmful. Indeed, it "may perform a 'safety valve' function, by preventing the excessive accumulation of discontent and by taking some of the strain off the legitimate order." Deviant behavior helps the group to clarify its common understanding of its norms. The deviant functions as a built-in sinner who helps to integrate the system "in much the same way as do witches, devils, and hostile foreign powers." The deviant may contribute to group integration by triggering activities in which the majority work together to bring the lost soul into the fold. Finally, the deviant identifies situations "in which conformity to the rules will defeat rather than implement the purposes of the organization."

In trying to integrate the contributions of Merton and Cohen, I translated some of Cohen's words into Mertonian language. Positive deviance seems to be the work of Merton's "innovator," someone who accepts cultural goals (whose work implements "the purposes of the organization") but who uses novel or innovative means. However, every innovator is not necessarily a positive deviant. For example, pimps and drug pushers may use innovative ideas in their work; moreover, they accept the American cultural goal: to make lots of money. But the means they use are both illegal and harmful to the total society.

This attempt to integrate ideas from Merton and Cohen gave me a better understanding of both the strengths and weaknesses of Merton's SSA model. Its strengths include a central, but formally unstated, proposition: It is essential to distinguish means from goals. The weaknesses in SSA include, first, using too many words. Models are supposed to be as simple as possible. But Merton uses two words which essentially mean the same thing: "cultural" and "institutionalized" both mean "proper." Second, while Merton overidentifies the proper, he underidentifies the nonproper. The nonproper is shown by minus signs (minus), which mean "rejecting the proper." Further, it is not clear whether a given rejection hurts the social system (negative deviance) or helps the social system (positive deviance). Put otherwise, Cohen's important insights on positive deviance cannot easily be linked to Merton's SSA model. I then realized that ideas found in Smart-Proper Analysis could incorporate and integrate some of the valuable contributions of both Merton and Cohen. What I needed to do was to add three propositions to Smart-Proper Analysis. Proposition 1, smart rules and proper rules help people select both means and goals. Propositon 2, any type of means (smart or proper) can be used to reach any type of goal (smart or proper). Proposition 3, some smart rules make positive contributions to the social life. Positive smart rules, therefore, must be distinguished from negative smart rules by empirical research. Propositions 1 and 2 are incorporated in a 2 × 2 matrix I call LOS: *Law of Strategies* (See Figure 1.2).

Figure 1.2
LOS: Law of Strategies

GOALS

MEANS	*Proper* ℙ	*Smart* 𝕊
Proper **p**	**p** ℙ 0	**p** 𝕊 2
Smart **s**	**s** ℙ 1	**s** 𝕊 3

Numbers refer to Deviance Scale

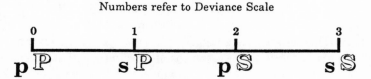

CON GAMES, TOLKACHI, AND OTHER
SP STRATEGISTS

The four strategies of action shown in LOS can be placed on a deviance scale. The scale is built with two assumptions in mind. First, the smart, whether positive or negative, always identifies deviance. Second, goals are considered more important than means. Therefore, those who avoid a proper goal are considered more deviant than those who avoid a proper means. On this deviance scale, 0 represents no deviance and 3 represents the highest level of deviance LOS can show.

LOS provides a descriptive set of terms, capable of making subtle distinctions. For example, the victimless con game played by the boys is an *sP*-game (one using smart means for proper goals). However, con games with victims, played by operators who are criminals, are an *sS*-game (one using smart means for smart goals). The smart goal of crooked operators is to fleece marks of their money. The proper goal of the boys is to get married to a girl of their caste who lives outside their village. The ability to describe subtle distinctions in strategies that superficially look alike is only part of LOS's talents. Among the other powers of LOS is to help identify similar strategies that do not look alike. Put otherwise, LOS can function as a scanner, seeking out strategies that are similar, but appear different to the naked eye—to the eye looking at the world without the aid of LOS. For example, without this model it is not obvious that the boys in Trinidad and the *tolkachi* ("fixers" and "expediters") in Russia have anything in common. Actually both use smart means for proper goals, the *sP*-strategy. Let me explain.

The *tolkach* (singular) is a modern, Russian Figaro. In an economy plagued by moronic mismanagement and systematized stupidity, tolkachi quickly move goods that officially take months to move. They find equipment that, officially, does not exist. And they exchange goods and services that, officially, cannot be exchanged. Tolkachi bribe and sweet-talk their way into the good graces of those with hands-on knowledge of scarce materials. In short, tolkachi know where to go, who to see, what to say, what gifts to present, and how to present them. Tolkachi know the smart means of getting things done. And the things they get done are the things that need doing. They are helping the Soviet Union to meet its planned, proper goals. The tolkachi are indeed *sP*-strategists (Berliner 1952). Let us listen in on a tolkach talking about his work, compliments of *Pravda* and the translators who work for *Current Digest of the Soviet Press* (vol. 35, no. 1):

An order of rolled metal was six months late. To re-order means sending forms through eleven offices, each of which will hold them for at least ten days and each of which may lose them. I packed my bag wondering if once again I would have to sleep in the lobby of some packed hotel, waiting for the right people. The bag I took with me had much "nail polish", for greasing the wheels. I rehearsed the rules I must follow. First, ask for more than you need, since you will always get less. Second, don't go to higher ups with each problem. Resolve it at the middle level. Third, move in with calculated doses of compliments, flattery and other signs of attentiveness and willingness to resign yourself to circumstances. Speak the way you would if you were asking for a reservation on a lower bunk on a train going south. Find a common language and the right facial expressions. Fourth, remember that what is written in the business office is not the law for the warehouse manager. Fifth, look up old cronies, good friends and not so good friends. Remember, with good contacts you can get even more than the authorized allocations.

Don't think I'm finished once I get promised the stuff I came for. I must deal with the transportation people; with the loaders; with those who run the railroad cars, and others. Everything has a little squeak; everything needs a little greasing. Keep the nail polish handy; that's my motto.[6]

Tolkachi meet with each other and share their experiences. From this shared information they develop smart rules, and use them for governmental or proper ends. As sP-strategists their work is much like that done by private investigators, police officers, and trial attorneys in modern American society. That private investigators bend the rules is well known; more of a secret is the rule bending done by police officers (cf. Freilich and Schubert 1989). The best-kept secret of all is that over 90 percent of criminal cases are actually adjudicated by plea bargaining: an sP-strategy.

After a brief flirtation with CHAOS (see p. 16), LOS was replaced with SAPS. Work with LOS led to a proposition and some research questions. The proposition, really a hypothesis that needs more testing, is one often presented as common sense: *Humans believe that, generally, the ends (goals) justify the means.* It may well be that here common sense and science share common insights. My linkage with this bit of common sense was due to the fact that I found the sP-strategy to be popular in very many different cultures. In asking myself why that should be so, it appeared reasonable to argue that, if the goal is proper and valuable, people will generally cast a blind eye to the means used.

The research questions also center around the sP-strategy. Many who use the sP-strategy want more "protection" than the probability that their smart means will be justified by their proper goals. Additionally, they use a clever hide-reveal strategy: They hide the deviant smart means and reveal the proper goal. However, this hide-reveal strategy is differentially used by different types of actors. Put otherwise, people who use the *sP*-strategy do not always try to keep their smart means secret. The boys in Trinidad operated at an extreme level of secrecy. The *tolkachi*, on the other hand, were so open about their smart means that their strategies found their way into *Pravda*. Somewhere in between the boys and the tolkachi sit the *sP*-strategies used by police officers, private investigators, and trial lawyers. Attempts to explain these and other differences in levels of secrecy can lead to interesting research projects.

SMART-PROPER ANALYSIS AND OFFSPRING

Those who grab a tiger by the tail are ever running and shouting, "Help." So it has been with me and my tiger, Smart-Proper Analysis. As colleagues, students, and friends will testify, hardly a day passes without some of them being confronted by this tiger. Comments from these encounters made me realize finally that sometimes I fudged on the meaning of *smart*. While I always defined smart as a strategy considered practical or worth doing, I was sometimes unclear as to who "owned" a given smart strategy (called *X*, for example). Who developed the *X*? Who defined *X* as practical and worth doing? Generally, the answers to these questions are clear; *X* is the property of a social unit, and the social unit defines *X* as practical or worth doing. For example, in the Trinidad case, the boys own information as to how to get their own wives, information which they define as smart. However, there were other times when I presented the owner and developer of a smart strategy as an individual. For example, at times, I use the fictional movie character "Dirty Harry" as an actor who uses the *sP*-strategy. But Harry uses his own, personal-smart means in pursuit of proper law enforcement goals. By using smart means, Harry has trouble with high-ranking police officers. The latter are angry that he did not use proper means. By using personal-smart means, Harry also had trouble with fellow police officers. His peers were angry because Harry did not use the means they used, "shared-smart." The compelling aspects of *Dirty Harry* movies are clearly revealed by these smart-proper ideas. Harry is performing an important public service; he successfully meets proper goals. But Harry remains a loner, an outcast. His sad social condition is the result of rejecting proper means (and making high-ranking officers angry) and rejecting shared-smart means (and making his peers angry). Angry peers do not help you hide evasions of the proper. Hence, Harry's personal-smart means, unlike his colleague's shared-smart means, are not protected by the veil of secrecy.

Given two smarts (personal and shared) and one proper, and given further that each of these three categories refers to means and to goals,

I had to bury LOS. LOS, a 2 × 2 matrix, was replaced by SAPS, a 3 × 3 matrix. Smart and Proper Strategies (see Figure 1.3) presents human activities in terms of nine possible strategies. It is worth noting that of these nine only one, proper means for proper goals (*pP*) is totally nondeviant. All the others deviate from the proper in some manner. Although all of these eight deviant strategies are not assumed to occur with the same frequency as the *pP*-strategy, common experience teaches us that the *pP*-strategy is not all that popular. With frequent evasions of the proper and with eight strategies of evasions, one is led to wonder why society is not more chaotic. Given the large amount of deviance (known from experience) and the many possible ways of deviating

Figure 1.3
SAPS: Smart and Proper Strategies

	GOALS		
	Proper Cultural Definitions $\mathbb{P}$	***Smart*** Social Definitions $\mathbb{S}$	Personal Definitions $\mathbb{Z}$
MEANS			
Proper Cultural Definitions **p**	**p**$\mathbb{P}$ 0	**p**$\mathbb{S}$ 3	**p**$\mathbb{Z}$ 6
Smart Social Definitions **s**	**s** $\mathbb{P}$ 1	**s** $\mathbb{S}$ 4	**s** $\mathbb{Z}$ 7
Smart Personal Definitions **z**	**z** $\mathbb{P}$ 2	**z** $\mathbb{S}$ 5	**z** $\mathbb{Z}$ 8

(known from experience and formalized by SAPS), how is it that some degree of order exists? What makes order possible? These and related questions, which suggest that deviance is the norm and order the problem, can lead to interesting research. Let me explain.

Smart-Proper Analysis rests on one proposition: Humans Struggle With a Terrible Conflict! The conflict is terrible because it is profound and cannot be solved in a satisfactory manner. The terrible conflict, or better the Human Dilemma, revolves around our two basic needs: survival and dignity. Survival we share with other members of the animal kingdom. To survive, we are ready to pay any costs, but we would prefer that the costs were low, so that we can live with ease and in comfort. To maximize chances of survival and minimize costs of survival humans must live smart. While the survival law for other animals is "Survival of the Fittest," for the human animal it is "Survival of the Smart." Put otherwise, for humans fitness equals smartness. Learning the smart is an important aspect of human social life. Our problems get clarified when we realize that living demands both more than and less than survival. In every human society humans are pressured to do more than just exist: Humans must live in a proper manner. While a peacock may naturally demonstrate that she is a peacock—her form and feathers prove it—it is otherwise with humans. The human form, by itself, suggests rather than proves that we are human. The proof comes from proper behavior: proper thought, proper communication, proper sentiment, and proper action. Humans are caught, not trapped, in a web of properness. Within the web, while behavior is proper, humans are assured the respect of community members. With respect comes the definition "real human being." The respect coming from others is internalized and transformed to self-respect or dignity. In the service of dignity humans sometimes sacrifice their lives. Such sacrifices prove that sometimes the purpose of human life is less than survival.

Survival versus dignity is the most extreme form of the human dilemma. At lower levels survival is changed to "life-style," the problem of maintaining creature comforts. Consider Q's problem—one that we all face in one form or another. Q has a high-paying job that provides many creature comforts. His boss directs Q to do something that is wrong. If Q refuses he may lose his job; if he agrees to do something that he knows is wrong, a bit of personal integrity is lost forever. How many times can Q afford to say no to directives that are morally or ethically wrong, before he loses his creature comforts? How many times can Q afford to say yes to these directives before he loses all dignity? Our big, high-quality brain is housed in a modified primate body. The latter pushes survival problems to the forefront. The art of human living, then, is to find some middle ground between mere survival—no matter how ugly life becomes—and beautiful living with dignity. "Beauty and the Beast" captures our existential dilemma.

Our dilemma can also be pictured as a charging bull. Move to the left and his right horn gets you. Move to the right and you are gored by his left horn. The classic solution of dilemmas is to try to slip between the horns. Many humans, I suggest, use the same strategy for slipping between the horns. That is, many grab the right horn (properness) with one hand, grab the left horn (smartness) with the other hand, and slide the body through the middle. In SAPS language, trying to slide through the middle is using a mixed strategy, one that mixes either a smart means with a proper goal, or a proper means with a smart goal. Why do some humans only use pure strategies: either pure-proper (pP), pure shared-smart (sS), or pure personal-smart (zZ)? There is much here that should be leisurely discussed and little space to do it in. I will conclude with a brief statement of how Smart-Proper Analysis can aid deviance research and theory.

RULES, DEVIANCE MODELS, AND SAPS

Stuck in a dilemma, humans twist and turn to avoid being gored by the bull. Some comfort seems to come from the thought that we are all in the same boat. Why "same-boat" thinking provides solace is hard to fathom. Easier to know is what same-boat thinking leads to. It leads to a desire for same-boat, or shared, solutions. A shared solution clearly is a social rule. We are fascinated with rules, I suggest, because rules put us even more in the same boat. Then we share the problem and the solution. Common sense, common experience, and much scholarship (Edgerton 1986) all lead to the same conclusion: rules form the basic building blocks of human society. With all this evidence it is curious that some scholars believe otherwise: some seem to be allergic to rules. Not being comfortable with rules, they "see" rules only rarely. Anti-rule writers, and these include some with superstar status are usefully subjected to careful scrutiny. Bronislaw Malinowski (1966: 120-27) proposes that cultural rules "are legal fictions" representing only the "fully conventionalized aspect of native attitude." The true problem, he suggests, "is not to study how human life submits to rules—it simply does not; the real problem is how rules become adapted to life."

Pierre Bourdieu, sympathetic to this model of reality, invents a number of fuzzy terms designed to prove that rules really are trivial forms. Conduct, Bourdieu argues, is in accord with "dispositions," organized by "schemes" and "strategies" that are all part of a "habitus:"

Talk of rules, a euphemized form of legalism, is never so fallacious than when applied to the most homogeneous societies . . . where most practices, including those seemingly most ritualized, can be abandoned to the *orchestrated improvisation of common dispositions*: the rule is never, in this case, more than a second best intended to make good the occasional misfiring of the collective enterprise. . . . (Bourdieu 1979: 17; emphasis added)

Bourdieu, with the aid of bewitching language, tries to make rules disappear. Translations, linked to SAPS, will break his spell. The collective enterprise (society), like a well-tuned motor, runs well (follows proper paths). Things are kept in order (apparently) by "habitus" and "common dispositions" (impossible to translate into meaningful language). Only occasionally do "misfirings" (deviance) occur. Rules then come in to "make good" (as a quick fix). As SAPS shows, misfirings occur all the time in eight variations; eight cells exist that are not totally proper. Bourdieu's model of society is then muddled, mystical, and, where translatable, lacking any fit with empirical reality.[7] The fact that many use his concepts leads to a sad conclusion: Well-chosen ethnographic examples can make any model appear useful. As a litmus test for models, SAPS says: If there are no rules, the model is too flawed to use. One more example of the validity of this test must suffice.

Harold Garfinkel investigated psychological autopsies done by the Los Angeles Suicide Prevention Center and the Medical Examiner's Office. Lawrence Wieder and Charles Wright (1982: 264) provide a short summary:

Garfinkel found that although the staff had been taught elaborate rules of correct procedure, and although they were trained in scientific procedure and scientific decision-making, all such rules and decision-making methods "in the actual situation were [known] to consist of recipes, proverbs, slogans, and partially formulated plans of action" (Garfinkel, 1967: 13).

So far so good. But immediately comes a partial truth wrapped in a misinterpretation: "It was the actual situation in its details, and not the rules of correct procedure to which the staff was primarily responsive." Having misunderstood one case study—because of a myopic view of rules as just rules of correct procedure—Weider and Wright then magnify their error with a false generalization (1982: 264-65):

There are no rules (or norms) that have the capacity to determine what medical examiners will understand as significant. . . . Indeed, not only is there no set of rules external to the examiner that cause his action, but there is no complete and determinate set of rules to which the examiner could simply refer to answer the questions he runs up against. . . .

Let us examine what Garfield actually said (with the aid of SAPS). The staff had rules of correct procedure (proper rules). But in the actual situation the rules and decision-making methods used consist of *recipes, proverbs, slogans*, and so forth. But the words italicized here are rules, not of correct procedure but of smart procedure—smart rules. As we learn from SAPS, a rule by any other name (say, recipe, proverb, or slogan) will "smell" the same; will function as a guide for behavior. A rule, whether proper, personal-smart, or shared-smart, is a guide to behavior with power coming from an "ought." At times the rule is difficult to see because the ought is hidden in recipes, proverbs, slogans, and metaphors (Lakoff and Johnson, 1980). Making matters yet more opaque "oughts" have powers that come from two different sources: properness and smartness. Put otherwise, sometimes the "ought" says: You ought to do X, because X is proper. At other times we are told: You ought to do Y because Y is smart. With the aid of these insights we can simply and accurately summarize Garfinkel's research: He discovered that medical examiners use proper rules for their goals (they seek the truth); but that very often they use shared-smart rules for means. Like the boys in Trinidad, tolkachi in Russia, and very many others (Freilich and Schubert 1989), much of the time medical examiners use the sP-strategy.

SAPS, along with its parental theory, Smart-Proper Analysis, has more than a litmus-test function for models. Additionally, they can act as mediators between types of models or paradigms. A useful point of departure is Jim Thomas' (1982) discussion, which fits deviance theory into three paradigms: social facts, social constructionist, and Marxian. For Thomas only the Marxian perspective is viable; my mediators prove otherwise. Social factist writings—with perspectives ranging from positivism and functionalism to anomie theory and conflict theory—have been criticized for treating rules as objective facts and rule breaking as nonproblematic. However, as the mediators show, some rules have an objective existence. Proper rules have achieved this concreteness by being allowed to age and thereby to pick up emotional appeal. These proper rules, what some refer to as tradition (Shils 1981), are not difficult to study. Breaking of proper rules is not problematic.

Social constructionist writings—whose perspectives include labeling theory, dramaturgical analysis, existential philosophy, and ethnomethodology—have been criticized (1) for underemphasizing the individual; (2) for perpetuating the status quo; (3) for dealing with such insignificant subjects as "nuts, sluts, and perverts"; and, among other things, (4) for not providing a theory of deviance, neither a body of well-confined and logically related hypotheses nor a set of causal explanations.[8] However, the contributions of this group are significant. Following Barry Glassner (1982: 72), their studies show that "deviance is not simply 'out in the world,' but persons are creating deviance through interactional processes." The mediators tell us additionally that social constructionists are teaching us that it is important to study new smart rules, and that such a study is difficult (or problematic) since smart rules are often hidden in recipes, slogans, proverbs, and metaphors. By focusing on practical reasoning, social constructionists are usefully steering us away from an oversocialized view of humans (Wrong 1961; Pollner 1974).

Marxian-perspective writings have been criticized for political and intellectual rigidity, and for seeing Marx's writings as sacred texts; for generally ignoring the fact that the abolition of private property is the basis of domination rather than emancipation; for rarely noticing that capitalists do not monopolize the production of inequality; and for tending to avoid rigorous analyses of the concept of classlessness. Reacting to such criticism, modern Marxists are busy reconstructing and transforming Marx's basic ideas. Such reconstructions and transformations rarely achieve consensual agreement. Hence any presentation of the Marxist paradigm is a political statement rather than a scholarly conclusion.[9] However, whatever else they share, modern Marxists do have a common concern with social justice. Such a concern switches the focus, away from rule breakers and toward the rules themselves. Smart-Proper Analysis and its model, SAPS, consider rules as the basic building blocks of society. These ideas should therefore be useful for those who continue to study deviance using the Marxist perspective.

My journey through deviance continues. So far I have picked up many ideas, including a victimless con game, more than two dozen dualities, the means-goals twins and nine universal strategies of action. Others are invited to bend, pick up these ideas, and use them for research. Those who stoop to conquer deviance with these tools are invited to share their findings with me, directly. Jointly we can sharpen, modify, or completely transform these tools. In short, I am still running after my tiger, Smart-Proper Analysis, and I am still shouting "Help."

NOTES

1. This is a much-expanded version of a paper delivered at the 1981 Annual Meeting of the Northeastern Anthropological Association, at Saratoga, New York. A longer version of the (1981) paper was presented at a deviance conference: "Deviance in Cross-Cultural Perspective," at the University of Waterloo, Waterloo, Ontario, Canada (June 2-5, 1984). This paper's many transformations were stimulated by valuable comments from Egon Bittner, Albert Cohen, Donald Cressey, Earl Rubington, Robert Stebbins, John Ziman, Mirjana Freilich, Harry Freilich, and John Gatewood.

2. Many examples of appearances of (what I call) Masked Luck are presented by John Ziman (1981).

3. Traditionally, and in India, the bride and the groom were not allowed to meet before the marriage ceremonies (see Basham 1959; Freilich 1960).

4. Boys who do not arrange their own marriages are generally reluctant to be married and thereby resist going to be looked over by their possible future in-laws. Although they generally follow their father's commands, they initially present arguments for not going. They present themselves as being too young for the added responsibilities (cf. Freilich 1960).

5. Among those who have noted that all is not well with anomie theory are H. Warren Dunham ("Anomie and Drug Addiction") and James S. Short ("Gang Delinquency and Anomie"), essays found in Clinard's edited volume (1964). See also Albert K. Cohen (1966) and Jack Douglas (1970).

6. I am indebted to colleague and friend Anthony Jones for directing me to literature on *tolkachi*.

7. Those who find me too critical of Bourdieu are invited to struggle with his *Outline of a Theory of Practice*. They will do well to realize that Bourdieu belongs to the FIT, the French intellectual tradition. FIT-followers find truth and beauty more in style than in content. Reviewing Bourdieu's book and concluding in a style which emulates its author, Gregory Acciaioli (1981: 7) artfully writes: "In the best French tradition he [Bourdieu] has presented a tantalizing menu of intellectual dishes combining new and old concepts prepared in new ways, all flavoured with a heavy sauce of *heartily unintelligible prose* that at times seems to deny the savour promised by the initial aromatic program."

8. Identified criticisms of social constructionist writings come, respectively, from J. Rogers and M. D. Buffalo (1974), Alvin Gouldner (1980), A. Liazos (1972), J. P. Gibbs (1966), and T. J. Scheff (1974).

9. Identified criticisms of the Marxist perspective come, respectively, from C. Wright Mills (1971), Alvin Gouldner (1980), Jim Thomas (1982), and Carmen Sirianni (1981). Additional confusion comes from attempts, by some, to reinterpret history so there is a better fit with Marxist theory. As Michael Burawoy has put it: "But as Marxists continually modify and sometimes even transform their theories to take into account unanticipated developments, it is also necessary to reinterpret the past in accordance with those transformed theories" (Burawoy and Skoepol 1982:8).

2 HARD VERSUS SOFT DEVIANCE: ANTHROPOLOGY AND LABELING THEORY

Douglas Raybeck

Most earlier sociological treatments of deviance focused principally on the macrolevel, but in the last twenty years sociologists have developed a new approach that melds concerns at both the micro and the macro levels. Labeling theory, a new sociological perspective on deviance, was developed in the 1960s by several sociologists (Becker 1963; Kitsuse 1962; Lemert 1967; Matza 1969). Labeling theory focuses on the manner in which society defines and creates deviance:

Social groups create deviance by making the rules whose infraction constitutes deviance, and by applying those rules to particular people and labeling them as "outsiders." From this point of view, deviance is not a quality of the act the person commits, but rather a consequence of the application by others of rules and sanctions to an offender. The deviant is one to whom that label has successfully been applied; deviant behavior is that people so label. (Becker 1963: 9)

This emphasis promotes an examination of how judgments of deviance are made by society's members and what the effect of the label *deviant* is apt to be on an individual.

Matza terms the process of labeling an act or actor deviant as "signification," and one of the principal concerns of Matza and others is with the interaction between the actor so labeled and those who label him (Becker 1963: 14; Kitsuse 1962: 253; Lemert 1967: Matza 1969).

One result of the labeling process is often to place deviants in the position of "outsiders" where their ability to interact with and influence the wider society is limited. The responses of society's members to a deviant act are not fixed but are influenced by such factors as who commits the act, the circumstances under which the act is committed, and, importantly, the degree to which the act is visible (Becker 1963: 11-14).

If society is viewed as capable of variable responses to deviants, depending on context, deviants themselves are also able to vary their behavior in different situations. Like hermit crabs selecting their shells, deviants are conceived of as actively engaged in the creation of their self-concepts and capable of selecting from among the reactions they encounter. Generally, however, theorists argue that the label *deviant* encourages persons who have committed deviant acts to become more marginal in response to the judgments of others (Clinard 1974: 14; Lemert 1967). As individuals accept and are influenced by the deviant label that others have applied to them, they are prone to engage in further acts that labeling theorists term "secondary deviance."

Although labeling theory has become the most popular of the current sociological approaches to the study of deviance, it has been criticized on several grounds. Glassner has noted that "labeling theory cannot explain primary deviance or what is taken to be a deviant act" (1982: 81). He also argues that the concern of labeling theorists with the individual labelee tends to obscure the phenomenon of categorical labeling, in which categories of people may be labeled as potentially or actually deviant, even though many members of the category may have done nothing to warrant this (Glassner 1982: 84-85). Nanette Davis has provided one of the more trenchant evaluations of labeling theory, observing that "the strength of the labeling formulation is apparent in its revised version of social order as itself problematic. *Its weakness is its failure to specify conditions under which official labeling works*" (1980: 199, emphasis added). One of my principal objectives is to address this weakness and to examine the contribution that anthropology, with its traditional emphasis on societies ranging from simple to complex, may make to our understanding of the operation of labeling theory in differing social contexts.

Although labeling theory was produced by theorists familiar with complex societies, it should be instructive to examine the process of labeling at lower levels of sociocultural integration. Ferdinand Tönnies, the seminal German sociologist, suggested in the late nineteenth century that there were significant dynamic and interactive differences between small-scale face-to-face social units and larger social entities (1967). His work influenced Durkheim's conceptions concerning the differences between organic and mechanical forms of solidarity (1964), and it was also to affect the thoughts and writings of Robert Redfield concerning the nature of peasant society and the differences between great and little traditions (1960).

Recently, several sociologists interested in labeling theory and the manner in which deviance elicits sanctions have noted the importance of such noninstitutionalized considerations as expectations (Birenbaum and Lesieur 1982), the importance of situational interests and commonsensical reasoning (Wieder and Wright 1982), and the evaluations and responses of individuals to varying behaviors (Lemert 1982). These concerns would seem to reflect an appreciation of processes relevant to the establishment and operation of deviant labels that occur in smaller face-to-face groups below the level of institutionalized patterning that characterizes large scale social units (e.g., Glassner 1982: 76).

Complex societies contain processes and phenomena not found at lower levels of sociocultural integration, but the concept of sociocultural integration also contains an assumption of additiveness in that social elements present at lower levels can also be found at higher ones (Steward 1973: 43). Thus an examination of labeling processes among simpler societies may well illuminate the conditions under which labeling works in complex societies.

Most social science approaches treat deviance like a light switch, as an on-off, either-or phenomenon. Either one has deviance or one has conformity without the possibility of interjacence. Although such a dichotomy possesses an admirable clarity, it involves a simplifying distortion of a more complex cultural continuum.

Believing that deviance is often a matter of degree, I wish to introduce a rheostat into the light switch and to distinguish between different degrees of deviance. In a promising treatment of this concern, Stebbins (1988) has recently posited a distinction between what he terms intolerable and tolerable deviance. His assumptions about the differences between these two forms of deviance parallel in some respects some of the distinctions I draw below between hard and soft deviance (Stebbins 1988: 2-5). However, his treatment differs from mine in that the definition of a deviant act is not seen as relative to the social situation but instead seems to involve classes of behavior. Thus, tolerated deviance is that which is not formally sanctioned by the state even though it may provoke civil sanctions. Further, unlike mine, his treatment of deviance is not linked to the size and complexity of the social unit.

The reactions of a society's members to deviance are generally predicated on their interest in maintaining cultural values and social order. Whether or not actors are labeled deviants, if their behavior departs from cultural norms and/or values in a fashion that hinders others' attempts to realize their ends, these others will be concerned with altering the discrepant behavior toward closer conformity with cultural ideals. However, the degree of people's concern and the form it takes can vary considerably. People are quite capable of discriminating between those who simply fail to manifest desired normative behavior (the overweight, the discourteous, the stingy) and those whose behavior actively threatens the social order (the violent, thieves, revolutionaries). Although I believe these discriminations form a continuum ranging from relatively inconsequential deviance to serious and substantial deviance, it is more manageable to invoke my own simplification (all models necessitate compromise) and to confine my distinctions to either end of the continuum. Thus I believe it is useful to distinguish between *soft deviance*, behavior that departs from social and cultural norms but does not actively threaten the social order, and *hard deviance*, which not only departs from the normative but also jeopardizes the social order.

SIMPLE VERSUS COMPLEX SOCIETIES

Relatively few researchers have compared the phenomenon of deviance in simple societies with deviance in complex societies, despite good arguments that much could be learned from doing so (see Clifford 1978). Those who have done so consistently emphasize the significance of informal controls in simple societies versus formal ones in complex, state-organized societies. Informal controls are found to be a superior means of avoiding and containing deviance for a variety of reasons (see Ball 1970; Clifford 1978; 71; J. Douglas 1970b; Pfohl 1981).

Steven Pfohl is the only researcher I have discovered who has provided a theoretical treatment of labeling processes in simple and complex societies. Pfohl argues that stateless societies are more apt than state societies to have effective "rituals of primary ordering" that prevent trouble by stabilizing the definition and nature of social life and by promoting a sense of shared social membership (1981: 75-78). Indeed, he argues that the very characteristics of state societies, especially their heterogeneity, increase the probability of social conflicts over ways of thinking and acting (pp. 74, 77-78).[1]

Pfohl also describes the differing responses of stateless and state societies when trouble occurs. In stateless societies the emphasis is on reconciliation of the offender to the group (pp. 80-84), whereas in the state societies reconciliation is more difficult to achieve, because of both the social and cultural heterogeneity, and the threat such reconciliation might pose to those in control (p. 87). Instead, "troublemakers become expendable and are ritualistically expended" (p. 84). While I agree with these assertions and the reasons he provides for them, I will shortly argue that Pfohl has omitted other important considerations that help to explain the emphasis on reconciliation in stateless societies and on exclusion in state societies.

I find much value in Pfohl's work, but I have serious reservations concerning his definition and treatment of the labeling concept. For Pfohl, "to label someone as a criminal is a highly ritualistic act. It can be performed only by duly authorized officials, acting within logically prescribed times and places, employing a code of specialized procedures" (p. 67). Obviously, the labeling ritual he describes would seem necessarily confined to state societies, and Pfohl asserts as much (p. 67). Further, he believes that this assertion is consonant with the labeling perspective (p. 67). While I would agree that the labeling ritual is by definition characteristic of state societies, I do not agree that such rituals are a necessary condition for labeling. If, as Becker and others argue, labeling requires that people be identified as deviants by social groups, it would seem reasonable that this be accomplished either by the formal rituals that Pfohl describes or by less structured informal means of the sort found in simple societies. The principal requirement would seem to be not ritual, but rather shared agreement on the identity of the deviant, the nature of the offense, and the deviant's resulting relationship to the wider social order. However, since labeling also involves placing deviants in the position of outsiders, where they are excluded from full social participation, there are reasons to expect that simple societies would engage in labeling far less frequently than would complex ones.

I would expect labeling to be far less common in simple societies for two basic reasons: Labeling seldom accomplishes social benefits of the sort that can be argued for the complex ones, and it usually involves social costs that are higher for simple societies than for complex ones.

Arguably, one of the functions of labeling individuals, whether positively (hero) or negatively (villain), is to increase the predictability of social life by adding information to the social context (one should not leave a thief alone with the family silver). Other researchers have emphasized that simple societies are characterized by a shared, comparatively well-integrated set of values and relatively little status differentiation compared to complex societies. These qualities clarify the nature of social life and promote consistent patterns of behavior (Ball 1970; Clifford 1978; J. Douglas 1970b; Pfohl 1981). What these authors have not emphasized sufficiently is that the social units in simple societies tend to be small scale and characterized by a number of cross-cutting interpersonal networks that promote a great deal of face-to-face interaction. In such social units there is a great deal of information about coresidents including their positions in the social order, their personality characteristics, and their past histories. In such circumstances the elements of social life are highly predictable, and labeling individuals does little to enrich the social context. In addition, the multidimensional social familiarity co-residents have with one another would inhibit the employment of labels, a process that encourages simplified and one-dimensional social stereotypes.

Authorities agree that labeling individuals as deviant tends to exclude them from full social participation. However, the cost of such exclusion is greater in simple societies than in complex ones. In small-scale social units each participant makes a noticeable contribution to the social order. Further, because individuals are often linked to a significant number of coresidents through kinship and other interpersonal ties, attempts at labeling that result in social exclusion not only lose the contributions of the individual, they also risk social fragmentation and increased social conflict (Edgerton 1976: 109).

The preceding arguments suggest that the size and scale of the social unit strongly affect the likelihood of a group's employing labels. However, coresidents who may be loathe to label one another may readily employ labels for outsiders who share neither their social context nor their interpersonal network. Indeed, when social boundaries are crossed, it is not unusual to find outsiders labeled as less than human (Scott 1976: 612). Inside a society, labels can be employed to emphasize subcultural or ethnic distinctiveness, and their use for outsiders may actually reinforce cultural identity and integrity.

Ethnographic Examples

As various authorities have noted, there are very few ethnographic descriptions of deviance in non-Western societies (Edgerton 1976), and cross-cultural studies of deviance are equally rare (Tittle 1977).[2] Thus, despite the desirability of including here an extensive and representative sample of societies in which deviance is well described, this has not been practicable. Instead, societies have been chosen according to a simple criterion: the existence of good ethnographic descriptions of both deviance and societal reactions to it. What follows is a selective review of ethnographic literature bearing upon deviance, the sanctions it elicits, and the relevance of this material for labeling theory. Given the selective nature of this sample, these examples must necessarily be taken as suggestive and illustrative rather than as conclusive and definitive.

The material is arranged in order of increasing levels of sociocultural integration, with the expectation that processes encountered in small-scale social units in simpler societies may also be found in similarly sized social units in increasingly complex societies. This approach will, I hope, reveal both continuities and discontinuities in the labeling process as it exists at different levels of sociocultural integration.

Hunters and Gatherers

Colin Turnbull's description of the Pygmy BaMbuti (1961, 1976), a hunting and gathering society dwelling in the Ituri tropic rain forest of northeastern Zaire, provides one of the more useful ethnographic accounts of band-level deviance and related social reactions. Turnbull notes that not only are the BaMbuti acephalous, but authority is evenly distributed among members of the band, both male and female, and attempts by an individual to acquire authority are resisted and often ridiculed (1976: 182-85). As several authorities would expect of such small interdependent units (Clifford 1978; Edgerton 1976; McHugh 1970), social membership in and continued acceptance by the group is important to each individual and exerts a strong pressure for conformity. Indeed, Turnbull has asserted that "the two attitudes which disturb the pygmy most are contempt and ridicule" (1961: 114).

BaMbuti reactions to deviant behavior range from arguments among litigants to the expectation of supernatural sanctions (Turnbull 1961: 110), but most offenses are dealt with quickly, informally, and seem not to result in labeling. "There were few instances where anything resembling a general opinion was expressed, and even fewer where any positive action was taken" (Turnbull 1976: 190). Turnbull describes instances of theft, a technical violation of the incest taboo, and other offenses (1961: 109-25), and in each instance the malefactor was dealt with in a disciplinary fashion that did not involve prolonged exclusion from social participation. After its discovery, the technical incest violation, an example of soft deviance, resulted in the culprit fleeing the camp for a day, following which he returned to the group, was reaccepted without comment, and went on to become one of the most respected members of the band (Turnbull 1961: 114). The most serious instance of deviance Turnbull describes involved an individual who set up his net in front of his fellows' nets during a communal hunt (1961: 94-108). This act threatened to deprive others of good, an example of hard deviance, and the culprit was publicly denounced and ridiculed, and his meat and that of his relatives was taken in reparation. However, even though he was publicly labeled an "animal," the use of the label was not prolonged, and he too was quietly reaccepted into the social network in a matter of hours. Thus, as Pfohl (1981) would expect, the band-level BaMbuti consistently evidence a concern with the reconciliation and reintegration of the offender to the group; he quickly returns to the role of full social participant.

Although pygmies are loathe to label members of their band, they readily label and disparage their Bantu village neighbors (Turnbull 1976: 218-28). Indeed, the BaMbuti view these outsiders as a bad influence, and lying to or stealing from them is seen as permissible, even laudable, behavior. In line with my earlier suggestion, the insider-outsider distinction seems to provide the BaMbuti with a means of reaffirming their own cultural values and distinctiveness.

The !Kung Bushmen, a hunting and gathering society living in the Kalahari Desert of South Africa, have been studied by several anthropologists, who have commented upon patterns of soft deviance and related sanctions. Unlike the BaMbuti, the !Kung do have acknowledged leaders, although these lack formal authority (Lee 1979: 343-45). However, they do display a great concern with group acceptance. Their desire to avoid both hostility and rejection leads them to conform in high degree to the unspoken social laws. . . . Most !Kung cannot bear the sense of rejection that even mild disapproval makes them feel. If they do deviate, they usually yield readily to expressed group opinion and reform their ways" (L. Marshall 1976: 288).

E. M. Thomas (1959) has described the !Kung as extremely pacific in their interpersonal relations, but this description has been challenged by Lee (1979), who recorded twenty-two killings among the !Kung between 1920 and 1969, fifteen of which were part of blood feuds. Such behavior may reasonably be viewed as hard deviance, and in four known cases the killers were executed in a fashion that suggested collective agreement among band members (Lee 1979: 370-79). It is unclear from Lee's description whether the killers were labeled as such, but the coordinate, collective nature of this punishment would seem to make that likely. Certainly, they were excluded from future participation in the social order.

Shostak's (1983) well-written biography of Nisa, a !Kung woman, describes the existence of interpersonal conflicts in a band. These frictions result in arguments, insults, and name calling, but these seem to occur as individual acts and do not result in labeling, where a pejorative definition of an individual's persona is developed and shared by the group at large. Indeed, band leaders seem concerned to reduce the possibility of labeling where possible. After Nisa fought with a woman who had accused her (justly) of adultery, the elders intervened, saying, "Talk of having affairs is bad talk. This has to stop now." It did (Shostak 1983: 280-81).

However, the !Kung do engage in a minor variation of labeling through the assignment of nicknames to individuals. These nicknames may reflect positive or negative qualities, as in the case of "Lazy Kwi," who was a poor hunter (Thomas 1959: 167). Such nicknames can reduce the status of individuals but do not seem to reduce the degree of their social participation. For instances of soft deviance, labeling does not seem to occur. Thomas notes that adultery is strongly condemned, yet a woman who ran off with another man was readily reaccepted by her husband, and the affair was never mentioned again (1959: 85-86).

Hunting and gathering societies as described above consist almost exclusively of small social units—bands or camps—within which values are widely shared, interpersonal networks are prominent, and interdependence is high. The characteristic reactions to deviance emphasize the reconciliation of the offender to the group and seldom employ labeling, which is usually reserved for the most disruptive of actors whose continued participation threatens the well-being of the group. These patterns may be found in other hunting and gathering societies that are not described here (see Chance 1966: 65; Holmberg 1969: 150).

The Middle Range: Swidden-Based and Tribal Societies

Swidden-based societies are more complex than hunters and gatherers; yet, as in the case of the two following examples, they are usually acephalous. The Mehinaku, studied by Thomas Gregor, dwell in the tropical Xingu region of central Brazil. While there are no superordinate authorities, each village has a chief, an individual noted for his oratory and other cultural skills and for the degree to which he is adept at the Mehinaku social game. Both men and women are sensitive to the opinions of others, and disapprobation, both feared and real, exerts a significant influence on the behavior of village members (Gregor 1977: 220-22).

Gregor notes that the Mehinaku do label one another "as good men or as failures" (1977: 200) and that there are three classes of failures: the trash yard man, the freeloader, and the witch. The first two of these are not serious (soft deviance), in the sense that they do not seem to exclude the actor from social participation, nor do they reflect a serious challenge to social interaction. The last class of failure is seen as actively threatening the social order (hard deviance), and the matter of labeling carries more serious consequences. While an individual may be a suspected witch and quietly be accused by members of the village, little will happen unless his behavior leads to a consensus and the shared application of the label witch. If a person already suspected of practicing witchcraft is publicly denounced by relatives of the deceased, this may lead to collective punitive action, including assassination (Gregor 1977: 204-5). Gregor reports on four witch slayings over a thirty-year period and notes that the victims are usually "socially estranged and lack the protection of male kin" (1977: 207). This material supports my earlier suggestion that labels are more easily applied to people who lack an extensive network of kin and friends.

Although the Mehinaku can engage in labeling offenders, Gregor indicates that for most offenses they are very reluctant to do so. Extramarital sex is common though disapproved, and neither a husband nor a wife should make public accusations or even be too curious about a spouse's behavior (Gregor 1977: 140). Theft, although strongly disapproved, is fairly common, but it does not result in the labeling of the offender. Gregor's explanation for the absence of labeling in such instances is congruent with my earlier arguments concerning the interdependence of small-scale social units: "Because the thief has not been denounced by name, the social and economic bonds that unite him and the victim have not been severed. The Mehinaku community could not long endure gashes and wounds caused by frequent public denunciations" (1977: 125).

The Mehinaku also make a clear distinction between Mehinaku (insiders) and non-Xingu indians (outsiders), who are labeled as wild, unclean, and dangerous. Other Xingu indians who are not Mehinaku are still viewed as relative outsiders, and the Mehinaku, through disparaging the outsiders' speech and behavior, emphasize their own distinctiveness. Mehinaku, by threatening to label offenders as outsiders, also pressure their deviants to conform (Gregor 1977: 308).

The Semai, a swidden-based people noted for their nonviolence, live in the tropical interior of the Malay peninsula. Although traditional Semai settlements lacked formal leaders, they currently have headmen, an office imposed by external authorities (Dentan 1968: 67). Generally, while elders have significant influence, authority seems well diffused throughout the settlement. The Semai are extremely sensitive to the opinions of others (Dentan 1968: 69) and greatly fear endangering their membership in and acceptance by the community (Robarcheck 1979: 105).

The Semai appear very reluctant to label offenders. Indeed, once an offense or conflict has been resolved through the traditional procedure of talking it out, no one is supposed to raise the matter again, let alone to promote labeling (Robarchek 1979: 111). The reason for the avoidance of labeling is their strong emphasis on reconciliation, interdependence and mutual aid (Robarchek 1979: 113). Interestingly, socialization in nonviolent attitudes seems quite successful; Dentan was unable to document a single instance of murder, attempted murder, or even maiming among the Semai (1968: 58). It is apparent, however, that Semai make a sharp distinction between themselves and outsiders. During the Communist insurgency of the 1950s, the Semai proved quite capable of killing outsiders; Dentan describes the enthusiasm and "blood drunkenness" with which Semai slaughtered their enemies (1968: 58-59).

The Tonga are a Zambian tribal people who practice simple sedentary agriculture and limited pastoralism. Elizabeth Colson has described their precontact political system as one that lacked effective chiefs (1974). She notes that chiefs were imposed by colonial pressure but they never became strong and that most Tonga display little respect for authority (Colson 1974: 3). Instead Tonga behavior is strongly influenced by public opinion and interpersonal networks in the small sedentary villages in which they reside. Because social relationships are perceived as ongoing and important, Tonga are reluctant to engage in violence or in the behavior that would disrupt these relationships (Colson 1974: 38-40).

For deviant behavior the Tonga have a range of sanctions, the most serious including ostracism, exile, and death, but these sanctions are invoked to prevent what persons might do, rather than as a punishment for what they have done (Colson 1974: 53). Clearly the concern is for the integrity of the social order rather than with the wrongs that may have been suffered by an individual. Individuals who endanger the social order are labeled "bad characters," and it is this label that both reflects and reinforces the reduction in social participation of the labelee. A principal "bad character" among the Tonga is the sorcerer, but before someone is formally proclaimed to be a sorcerer there will be a variety of attempts to warn the offender to alter his behavior. An increase in gossip and reproach signals the individual and his kin that his position is becoming increasingly marginal and that, should action be taken against him, there will be no support for his relatives to avenge him (Colson 1974: 56). Here, as among the Mehinaku, labeling appears to be a public acknowledgment of an undesirable and dangerous situation that has developed over time. The labelee becomes increasingly marginal even before the label is applied.

The Tonga seem representative of other tribal societies, which generally place a good deal of emphasis upon in-group acceptance and the maintenance of order within the social unit (see Boram 1973; Brandt 1954; Edgerton 1976; Kupferer 1979; Scott 1976). Edel notes that among the Chiga, "A man who is a thief or a bully is none the less entitled to support and formal participation in group activities. Though he may be privately criticized and even when possible avoided, he must still play the appropriate role in weddings, or beer drinks and so forth. This is true even when his offenses are serious ones" (Edel 1960: 439).

Robert Scott, who has examined deviance and related sanctions in several tribal societies (the Nuer, Kikuyu, Arusha, Barotse, Tiv, and Kpelle), finds that within closely linked social units deviance and sanctions can promote social integration but that between distantly related social units deviance and sanctions reinforce social distance and animosities (1976: 604). This insider-outsider distinction also affects the attitudes of a social unit's members toward deviance. Insiders are required to exhibit a greater degree of conformity than outsiders (Scott 1976: 612; Colson 1974: 57-58), and outsiders are sanctioned more severely than insiders for the same offenses (Scott 1976: 617).

Peasant Societies

The following two examples that illustrate this level of sociocultural integration were chosen because they are in many aspects typical of peasant or folk societies and because there is good information available on their treatment of deviant behavior and deviants.

The Kelantanese are Islamic Malays with a bilateral social structure who practice intensive wet rice agriculture. The state of Kelantan in the northeast of the Malay peninsula, and the nation of Malaysia, have formal mechanisms for the control of deviance, including Islamic religious courts, police, and courts that are part of a British-influenced legal system. However, the great majority of Kelantanese have little contact with the state and national mechanisms; instead, they are concerned with and influenced by the informal controls that characterize the rural villages in which they reside. Indeed, Kelantanese place considerable emphasis on the maintenance of village harmony, and they often seek to limit the involvement of external authorities in village affairs (Raybeck 1986).

The importance of village membership and integrity is reflected in a distinction that Kelantanese make between *orang sini*, people of here, and *orang luar*, outsiders. *Orang sini*, co-residents who are tied to one another through a network of bilateral kindreds and other less structured associations, treat one another with respect and are very reluctant to label one another since they are viewed as valuable participants in village life and because villagers, their past history, their strengths and weaknesses, are well known to their fellows. Indeed, villagers seldom engage in dichotomous judgments of co-residents but instead tend to describe a fellow villager's failing or virtue as one aspect of a complex and three-dimensional person. *Orang luar*, however, are frequently subject to simplistic stereotyping and to labeling.

The emphasis on village integrity and the importance of village-level social life and values lead Kelantanese to take a relativistic position with regard to state definitions of deviance. The state regards certain acts as illegal and formally labels the actors as criminals; yet villagers may take a very different view of these matters, especially if they involve indigenous cultural behavior. Thus the state prohibits smuggling, bullfighting, cockfighting, and a variety of gambling activities, but Kelantanese villagers, far from viewing these pastimes as deviant, actually regard them as valued pursuits through which villagers may gain the respect of their fellows. These attitudes reflect and reinforce the pride that Kelantanese villagers take in their cultural distinctiveness.

If Kelantanese are rather cavalier about many behaviors that violate state and national laws, they are very concerned with behaviors that endanger the solidarity and harmony of the village, and threats to village welfare, especially acts of violence, are viewed as strongly deviant (Raybeck 1986). The responses of villagers to an act that threatens village harmony are complex. The initial reaction is to curb the deviant behavior by employing a variety of sanctions ranging from gossip and social pressure through increasing social exclusion to expulsion from village society. Mitigating the concern with conformity to village norms is an intense interest in maintaining functional interpersonal networks within the village. Villagers are aware that publicly labeling someone a deviant tends to place that individual at the periphery of or outside of village society and, because of the many cross-cutting kindred ties, this can have serious consequences for village solidarity. Thus villagers usually promote conformity in a fashion that does not permanently damage the social persona of an offender.

While Kelantanese are usually reluctant to label co-villagers as deviant, they will do so in certain circumstances. If individuals engage in deviant behaviors that are serious (hard deviance) and visible, and if they persist in these behaviors despite attempts of villagers to make them conform, then they become increasingly marginal within village society and are likely to be labeled as members of a deviant category. Unlike the labeling process that Becker (1963) describes by which the label essentially creates a social reality, Kelantanese labeling reflects a social reality that has gradually and increasingly become manifest. Once an individual is labeled a deviant, that person's participation in village social life is either terminated, as in threats to village harmony that result in expulsion, or diminished, as is more often the case. If a person labeled as a deviant remains resident, other villagers seldom treat that individual in the dichotomous fashion suggested by Becker (1963), Matza (1969), and other labeling theorists. Instead, there is often recognition of and expressed value for other statuses the individual occupies, and continuing efforts are often made to reincorporate the individual into the mainstream of village life (Raybeck 1986).

Henry Selby's monograph on the Zapotec (1974), a peasant people who grow corn and reside in the Oaxaca Valley of Mexico, is the only work I have encountered that deals specifically with labeling processes in a folk society. Many of the characteristics and processes of Zapotec village life parallel those I have described for the Kelantanese. For instance, although they are part of a centralized state and subject to its formal controls, Zapotecans are far more concerned with village membership and more affected by the informal mechanisms of control that operate at this level.

Selby notes that village reaction to deviants differs from that of the state. Zapotecans are more concerned with maintaining amicable relations within the village and often facilitate the reincorporation of deviants into village life. Selby describes how two men, having been convicted and labeled as murderers by the state, were able to return to their village, where, after reactivating their networks, they were "unlabeled" and proceeded to lead productive social lives (1974: 64). Indeed, one man later held village office and became a widely respected member of the community. Examples such as these support Selby's contention that individual Zapotecans do not accept labels. Thus, unlike the situation Becker and others describe for industrial societies, there is no secondary deviance resulting from social pressures to act out the deviant status or from the individual's incorporation of a deviant self-concept.

Like the Kelantanese, the Zapotecans make a strong distinction between insiders and outsiders. Insiders, coresidents linked through kinship or interpersonal ties, are expected to maintain the integrity of village social life by realizing the important values of humility, trust, and respect and by avoiding envy, which can lead to behavior that disrupts interdependence within the village (Selby 1974: 18-30). Institutionalized envy in the eyes of villagers leads to witchcraft, and witches are seen as the major threat to Zapotecans and their social life (Selby 1974: 106). Not surprisingly, witch candidates are mainly drawn from the ranks of outsiders, and gossip is the principal means of identifying them. Selby notes that "the process of witch labeling goes on constantly," and "it may take months or even years to produce a witch" (1974: 128). Gossip sensitizes people to seek increasing validation, and an insider who behaves in a deviant fashion may gradually be identified as a witch: "A final decision that a neighbor or kinsman is a witch means that the community as a whole has made the decision, and the person is universally labeled a witch" (p. 126). Persons so labeled are apt to be excluded, ostracized, and even endangered, but it is also clear that their peripheral position is one that has developed over time rather than simply being the product of the labeling process.

While there is not space here to describe the manner in which other peasant societies react to deviance, the observations of several researchers are consonant with the material I have presented on the Kelantanese and on the Zapotec. In particular, elements such as the comparative importance of village versus state membership, the significance of an insider-outsider distinction, and the reluctance of co-villagers to label one another can be found in June Starr's description of a Turkish village (1978), Jane Collier's work on Zinacantan (1973), and George Foster's treatment of the people of Tzintzuntzan (1967).

Industrial Societies

The sociological literature on deviance in industrial societies is extensive. Rather than attempt to review this work, I will simply note that much of it is consonant with the assertions of labeling theorists; indeed, some of it has been written by them (cf. Becker 1963; Goffman 1961, 1963; Matza 1969). Instead, I will focus on two treatments of deviance in small-scale social units that exist within industrial states, since it is principally at this level I anticipate finding concordance with labeling processes at lower levels of sociocultural integration.

Marida Hollos (1976) describes a small Norwegian mountain farming community that since 1970 has been increasingly subject to modernization pressures. Prior to 1979 the community was well integrated and maintained a strong consensus about behavioral norms and cultural values, especially the importance of egalitarianism (1976: 242). Problems involving conflict or deviance were rare, and most were resolved through informal mechanisms of control, particularly gossip and other forms of social pressure. In nineteen years only ten cases of disputes were reported to various external agencies, and the great majority of these involved an outsider as well as a local (1976: 247-48).

Hollos makes it apparent that locals were very concerned with maintaining in-group harmony, preserving the network of interpersonal cooperation, and retaining an offender as a functioning member of the community. "In case of breaking a norm, if indirect pressures and sanctioning resulted in a change of behavior, no further punishment or ostracism followed. On the contrary, the conforming individual was quietly reinstated into all his former relationships as an equal and the breach was never mentioned" (1976: 246). In such circumstances locals were reluctant to invoke formal mechanisms of control or to engage in labeling.

After 1970, the circumstances of the community changed with increasing industrialization. This gradually led to a schism between the more traditional farmers dwelling on the periphery of the community and the more centrally located modernists who engaged in a variety of occupations that promoted neither strong interpersonal cooperation nor dependence on kin ties (Hollos 1976: 244). Not surprisingly, the modernists relied more frequently on formal sanctions, even against other community members Hollos (1976: 250), and they engaged in labeling more readily. Hollos is quite clear about the reasons for these changes among the modernist members of the community: "Since economic or social interdependence is much less important, and people are now more mobile and able to get away from one another, the maintenance of peaceful relations and a united community is no longer necessary at all costs" (1976: 254). Industrialization has not only led to diminished agreement concerning social norms and cultural values, it has also reduced the importance of community membership which is a major factor inhibiting the application of labels.

Rock Island, a small fishing community of 314 people, is located off the Atlantic coast of an industrialized nation to which it is linked both economically and politically (Yngvesson 1976: 355). Community membership and maintaining an ethic of equality within the community are major emphases. Decisions concerning the community and disposition of community problems are made in a public forum by consensus of an elected Island Council, but there is "an absence of mechanisms through which private grievances can be formalized or ritualized" (Yngvesson 1976: 359). Instead, instances of conflict or deviance are generally handled through informal means, including a cooling off period during which the matter is not subject to a public forum, but is discussed by concerned community members who will seek to resolve the issue or to eliminate the deviant behavior (1976: 354). If they are successful, no public forum is involved, nor is labeling likely.

The islanders make a marked distinction between insiders and outsiders and, reflecting the importance of community membership, cooling off periods are employed for the former category:

The long "cooling off" period . . . was found only in island cases in which two people defined as "insiders" were involved. When a non-islander or other person defined as an outsider committed a grievance, the response period was sought rapidly. This difference in response pattern is consistent with the hypothesis that people involved in ongoing relationships which they wish to maintain will try to heal a breach in the relationship rather than punish the offender. (Yngvesson 1976: 354-55)

Islanders are sufficiently reluctant to label other insiders as deviants that they will consciously avoid the use of such labels even for serious offenses. Yngvesson notes that theft was the worst offense an islander could commit but, if the offender was an islander, it was termed "borrowing" and "the act remained unlabeled" (1976: 358). However, should an insider remain refactory and persist in serious patterns of deviance, that individual might progressively be excluded from the community and ultimately labeled an outsider (1976: 358).

Both Hollos' study of the Norwegian farming community and Yngvesson's description of the Atlantic islanders reveal similar treatments of deviance and a general reluctance to engage in the labeling of deviants. Further, these themes appear frequently in the earlier description of the treatment of deviance in small-scale social units at lower levels of sociocultural integration.

Discussion

If "social groups create deviance by making the rules whose infraction constitutes deviance, and by applying those rules to particular people and labeling them as 'outsiders' " (Becker 1963: 9), they also create norms in a similar fashion and label rule followers as "normal members." All social groups can be seen to engage in a process of labeling group members, though, as I will make clear, the nature of that process differs for small- versus large-scale social units, especially when it involves the labeling of deviants. Since small-scale units constitute essentially all of the social fabric of simple societies but only part of the context of complex societies, one should expect to find both similarities and differences in labeling processes between the two levels of sociocultural integration.

My review of treatments of deviance in small-scale social units from simple, stateless hunting and gathering societies through complex, state-organized, industrial societies has revealed some significant continuities. As Pfohl (1981) characterizes simple societies, there is considerable social and cultural integration, stressing the importance of group membership, and placing an emphasis on reconciliation of the offender to the group rather than on punishment and exclusion. However, as the preceding evidence attests, these characteristics are also true of small-scale social units in state societies. Similarly, Pfohl has also argued that formal labeling rituals, found only in state societies, are necessary for the labeling of a deviant, and that implies that stateless societies lack labeling processes. Yet, it is apparent that informal means of labeling are employed, although reluctantly, in small-scale social units in stateless and also in state societies. These continuities suggest that we should direct our attention to the size and complexity of social groups rather than just to the societies of which they are a part.

Differences in the labeling processes of simple versus complex societies reflect the fact that the latter contain both small- and large-scale social units whereas the former consist entirely, or in some cases mainly, of small-scale units. Differences in the size and complexity of the social units promote a series of contrasting characteristics relevant to labeling processes. Table 2.1 below presents a somewhat simplified summary of the more important of these contrasts.

The well-integrated values characteristic of small-scale social units stabilize the definition of social life in the fashion Pfohl suggests (1981: 75). The relatively poorly integrated values usually found in large-scale units cannot easily accomplish this; indeed, conflicts between values can provide a source of deviance.

The relative equality among the members of small-scale social units reduces the likelihood that the labeling of deviants will be associated with inequalities of power, as is often the case in large-scale social units (see Becker 1963; Kilbride 1979; Matza 1969). Inequalities and other sources of social differentiation also increase the probability of interpersonal misperceptions, conflicts, and recourse to labeling individuals as deviants.

The interdependence that characterizes social relations among members of small-scale units inhibits the labeling of individuals as deviants. A member is often a significant contributor to a small community and is usually linked to other constituents through a variety of interpersonal and kinship ties. To label such a member as a deviant reduces or eliminates that person's social participation and risks creating divisions and conflicts

Table 2.1
Deviance and Social Scale

<u>Small-Scale Social Units</u> (Camp, Band, Village, etc.)	<u>Large-Scale Social Units</u> (City, State, Nation, etc.)
Well Integrated and Consistent Values	Poorly Integrated and Often Conflicting Values
Relative Equality among Members	Marked Inequalities among Members
Interdependence of Members	Independence of Members
Information-Rich Social Context	Information-Poor Social Context
Labeling of Deviants Occurs Gradually and is Rare	Labeling of Deviants Occurs Abruptly and is Common
Tolerance of Soft Deviance	Intolerance of Soft Defiance
Secondary Deviance is Uncommon	Secondary Deviance is Common

within the social order. In contrast, the contributions of most members of large scale social units are comparatively less significant, and the relative independence of these individuals reflects the absence of cross-cutting social and kinship bonds. Here, labeling a person as a deviant costs the unit very little, either in terms of social contributions or of risks to social integrity. Indeed, it can be argued that the labeling of deviants in large scale social units actually enhances social integration by singling out some individuals as social misfits who, through contrast, emphasize the "fit" of others with the social order (see Savishinsky, Chapter 3).

In comparison to most members of large-scale social units, each member of a small-scale social unit generally has available a great deal of information on the personality, past history, and current behavior of other constituents. This situation tends to reduce the utility of labeling deviants, since the label does not provide substantial new information, and it also makes this type of labeling less likely. Members of small-scale social units know one another in a multidimensional fashion that inhibits the use of comparatively simple, one-dimensional stereotypes. This has been the case at the lower levels of sociocultural integration we have examined, and it also occurs in complex societies in instances where individuals know one another well. Storz studied the situations of women who were officially labeled mentally ill by medical institutions; that label did not affect their husbands' perceptions of these women, nor did the husbands accept the labels unless they had already made the determination themselves (1978: 49). This finding contrasts markedly with Rosenhan's (1973) well-known study of the influence of labels on the perceptions of medical personnel who knew little of the patients beyond their labels. In Rosenhan's investigation, he had normal individuals enter mental hospitals complaining of mild symptoms that elicited a label, mentally ill. Thereafter the individuals and their behavior were evaluated in a fashion that supported the inaccurate label.

One of my major theses has been that, compared to large-scale social units, the labeling of deviants in small-scale social units seldom occurs and that when it does happen it is a very gradual process. In large-scale social units the absence of good interpersonal information and bonds of interdependence plus the presence of conflicting values and inequalities all promote the abrupt labeling of an offender as a deviant. In particular, the absence of a rich social context increases the likelihood of clear dichotomies (normal versus deviant), as does a reliance on formal mechanisms of control. Thus rule breakers, through a process that Schur (1971) terms "role engulfment," may find that their entire persona is defined through their deviance. For contrasting reasons, members of small-scale social units are reluctant to lose a contributing constituent and they will employ a range of informal mechanisms of control, reserving labeling for those instances where the mechanisms have proven ineffective and the offender actively threatens the social order. The process of labeling a deviant is also gradual because, in the absence of formal mechanisms, it requires a shared evaluation of the offender and his relation to the unit. It takes both considerable time and communication to achieve that consensus (cf. Selby 1974).

I have distinguished between soft and hard deviance in the ethnographic description in order to emphasize an important characteristic of small-scale social units. The members of such units will tolerate a considerable range of less-than-ideal behavior (soft deviance) so long as it does not actively threaten the integrity of the unit. For instance, I and other researchers have noted that the mentally ill in small-scale social units are apt to be accepted as active participants in the social order if their behavior does not threaten others (Edgerton 1976: 61; Raybeck 1986), and they may not even be labeled (Selby 1974: 41-47). Labeling of an individual as a deviant and attendant sanctions, such as expulsion and/or death, are generally invoked as a last resort to protect the unit from those who actively threaten (hard deviance) its well-being. In contrast, large-scale social units that involve labeling more readily, usually tolerate far less soft deviance and often blur or omit the distinction between those who actively threaten the well-being of others (thieves, murderers) and those who do not (vagrants, gamblers).

The characteristics of small-scale social units reduce the likelihood of secondary deviance deriving from the individual's acceptance of the label and the social position it signifies. Even in some large-scale social units, individuals who have been labeled deviant can remain aware of the other components of their social persona through interacting with their interpersonal networks (see Kilbride 1979: 247). They also remain conscious of the importance of their remaining connections to these significant others and can continue to be subject to informal mechanisms of social control. Indeed, a deviant may gradually be unlabeled and reincorporated into the unit (Raybeck 1986; Selby 1974). In large-scale social units the label *deviant* can more easily define the relationship of the offender to other members, and it can encourage further, secondary deviance as a result.

Reviewing the preceding contrasts between small- and large-scale social units, it seems that this material can provide information concerning the "conditions under which official labeling works" (N. Davis 1980: 199). The description of the labeling process in large-scale social units supports the contention of labeling theorists that labeling helps to create and reinforce deviance. Others create deviants by reducing the social participation of offenders and invoking labels that encourage offenders to think of themselves as deviants and to act in deviant fashions. Thus the range of labels employed and the frequency of labeling should be proportional to the size and complexity of social units engaged in labeling.

In small-scale social units the labeling process is qualitatively different from the process characteristic of large-scale social units. Because of their multiple connections to, and extensive knowledge of, offenders, members of such units invoke labels only after exhausting other means of dealing with them, and even then they are often willing to unlabel and reincorporate them if circumstances permit. Here, labels, rather than

creating a deviant identity, are reluctantly employed to recognize one that
has gradually emerged.

NOTES

I wish to acknowledge the award of a Hamilton College Research Grant, which
supported the research for this paper. I also wish to thank Joel Savishinsky and Hy van
Luong for helpful comments that have, I hope, led to improvements. An earlier,
somewhat different version of this paper appeared in the December 1988 issue of
Ethos, Vol. 16, No. 4.

1. Other researchers have advanced arguments that support or complement Pfohl's
position, for example, Ball 1970; Clifford 1978; J. Douglas 1970b; Scott 1970.

2. Edgerton (1976) accounts for the paucity of anthropological studies dealing with
deviance with an argument similar to one that appears in the introduction. He argues
that anthropologists' searches for patterns and regularities have inhibited an active
concern with those individuals and groups whose behavior departs from the normative
and is not easily integrated into social and cultural generalizations. Similarly, Wallace
(1970) argues that early attempts to study culture and personality were characterized
by attempts to replicate uniformity rather than to seek principles for the organization
of diversity. The result was a series of studies in which there was a "near-perfect
correspondence" between culture and the individual (Wallace 1970: 22). Clearly such
approaches leave little room for those individuals who departed from the cultural
ideals.

3 FREE SHOWS AND CHEAP THRILLS: STAGED DEVIANCE IN THE ARCTIC AND THE BAHAMAS

Joel Savishinsky

INTRODUCTION

Deviance is often perceived as being private, covert, culturally disapproved of, and socially disruptive. In many societies, however, people are highly tolerant of certain mild or "soft" forms of deviance (Raybeck 1988; and Chapter 2). Such tolerance derives from the fact that mildly aberrant behavior poses no threat to the physical or social well-being of others and may sometimes privately profit those who publicly disparage it. Spectators can manipulate other individuals to act out improper behaviors, thereby producing a kind of staged deviance as a public event. This pattern can be illustrated in two small communities, one in the Canadian Arctic and one in the Bahamian Out Islands, where certain forms of deviance occur that are public, overt, culturally permissible, and socially cohesive for those who witness them. These behaviors are engaged in by drunks, children, dogs, nonnatives, tourists, and movie actors. Such characters act out types of aggressive, sexual, and emotionally intense behavior that are normally forbidden to indigenous adults. But the performers usually remain unconscious of the meanings that their actions have for spectators because the latter stage-manage or interpret their behavior in subtle ways.

In the Arctic and Bahamian situations to be described, deviant acts often take the form of a performance; this makes the use of symbolic

interactionist and dramaturgical models particularly appropriate in analyzing them (Mead 1934; Goffman 1959, 1963, 1967; Becker 1963;
Blumer 1969). The staging of deviance is accomplished in several ways.
Using verbal commands and physical gestures, for example, community
members in the Arctic get drunks, children, and dogs to engage in fights.
By means of ambiguous statements and their control of space, local
Bahamian people cast nonnatives and tourists in compromising roles and
positions. And by making movie-going an active experience in which
they vocally interpret the events shown on screen, Northern Indians
re-define the meaning of what actors have done. The circumstances in
which these deviant behaviors are acted out, then, involve elements of
staging, impression management, discrepant roles, and manipulation—
processes that Goffman (1959) has identified as part of the self-dramatizing theater of everyday life.

The importance of meaning to people's self-definition is at the heart
of the symbolic interactionist approach to behavior and deviance (Mead
1934). It applies, however, not just to "self" but to "other" as well: It
underlies the way we define who we are through the attribution of a
deviant identity to some of those we interact with. But the situations that
produce deviance in the two communities described here also add some
new twists to the daily dramatics of life. The most significant novel
quality of public deviance in these two cultures is that it is the audiences
that direct and manipulate the actors, rather than simply defining the
meaning of their actions as deviant (Erikson 1964: 11). In subtle and
overt ways, spectators take on the mantle of "moral entrepreneurs"
(Becker 1963); and as amateur but highly effective "functionalists," they
promote the deviance of others to affirm their sense of propriety and
solidarity (Durkheim 1964; Cohen 1966; Taylor 1982; Sagarin and Kelly
1982). These situations also illustrate Blumer's point that in "the flow of
group life there are innumerable points at which participants are re-de-
fining each other's acts" (1969: 67). Compared to other forms of social
drama, then, in which performers play with and play to the spectators,
the locus of control is here reversed. The result is not so much a theater
of the absurd, however, as a participatory kind of drama in which the
audience composes the script that the performers unwittingly follow.[1]

This paper briefly describes these types of deviance in the two
communities. It then offers answers to several questions that such deviant
behaviors raise: Who stages deviance and why? How do spectators and
actors feel about such behaviors? What are the consequences of such
deviance for performers and observers? And do comparable patterns
exist in other societies? Drawing on the insights of symbolic interaction-

ist, functionalist, and social conflict theories, it will be argued that staged deviance is an organized event which provides moral affirmations and a degree of vicarious pleasure for spectators. In its softer forms, it can also contribute to innovative social trends by transforming "smart" styles into "proper" culture. Finally, it will be shown that staged deviance also gives people who are in or out of power an opportunity to exercise subtle forms of control over others, and it can therefore be a potent element in the political process.

PATTERNS OF DEVIANCE: COMMUNITY CHARACTERISTICS

The communities under consideration differ significantly from one another in terms of both their ecosystems and their economies.[2] The Hare Indian village of Colville Lake lies within the harsh sub-Arctic forests of Canada's Northwest Territories. Its seventy native people lead a relatively isolated, seminomadic life centered on big-game hunting, fresh water fishing, and fur trapping. The sixty-five people of Bramley, by contrast, occupy a benign subtropical environment on Cat Island in the east central Bahamas. Their economy combines sheep and goat herding, slash-and-burn farming, occasional wage labor, and fishing in shoreline and coastal waters.

For all their obvious differences, Bramley and Colville Lake also share a number of significant qualities. They are both small, isolated, traditional, and subsistence-oriented communities whose members emphasize self-control in their daily lives. While they are affected by the national governments and economies of their countries, there are no police or political agencies in either settlement. Furthermore, the diminutive size, physical compactness, and measured pace of these villages give the behavior of their residents a particular kind of visibility and publicity. These factors tend to throw into sharp relief the deviance of certain actors, which will be illustrated here with examples drawn from the experience of drinkers, young children, domestic animals, nonnatives, and characters in films.

Drinking

Among the Hare and other sub-Arctic Indians, behavior is ideally characterized by restraint, the suppression of hostility, and noninterference in the lives of others (Honigmann 1981: 736-38). However, under some conditions, people can respond to or manipulate persons to increase their public deviance from these norms. Drunken individuals are highly susceptible in this way. When families return from their hunting and trapping camps for extended holiday periods at the village of Colville Lake, a considerable amount of brewing and drinking occurs. Alcohol consumption is a very visible, audible, and social event, one which publicizes the behavior of consumers. But not everyone in the community drinks, nor do all who indulge comport themselves as drunks. This leaves a sizable residue of the population to observe and comment on the actions of those who make homebrew and take alcohol. Some drinkers frequently engage in sexually flirtatious and provocative acts, as well as in verbally and physically aggressive ones. Their interactions at drinking parties, usually held in family cabins, often spill out into the open plaza of the village, where anyone may witness them.

When this occurs, spectators appear at the windows and doorways of their homes, shouting "free show!" across the central space of the village. The drunks themselves are also called out to by people, who yell at them with encouragement and advice about their fighting strategies and amorous advances. The suggestibility of drunks at such moments intensifies their hostile, ludicrous, and compromising behavior. It also enables spectators to exercise an unusual degree of intervention, manipulation, and control over the lives of others. Since drinking is perceived of as a "time out" state[3] in which individuals cannot be held responsible for their actions, deviance here has a peculiarly disembodied quality: it lies more in the eyes of the beholders than in the persons of the actors themselves.

In the Bahamian community of Bramley, drinking occurs both in the privacy of people's homes and as a public event at the local bar. Bahamians are well aware that the latter is a male dominated setting, and that unaccompanied women do not patronize it unless they are willing to be sexually approached. The modest number of white tourists who visit the island are usually not aware of this definition of the situation.[4] If white women enter a bar on their own initiative or, as sometimes happens, at the invitation of Bahamian men, they may be subjected to teasing and propositioning. This is reinforced by the reputation for sexual laxity that white females have in the opinion of some Bahamian men.

In such a setting, women are unwitting deviants. They have either set themselves up or have been set up by the men. If the women resist the sexual approaches, drunken men may respond with punitive forms of teasing and with the sharing of "in" jokes told at the women's expense. Such behavior may not win the men any of their sexual objectives, but it capitalizes on the women's deviance to reinforce male solidarity and to reassert male control over the bar as a masculine space. By manipulating white females, the men ensure that women who cannot be had can still "be had."

Children and Dogs

Deviance is not an adult or a human monopoly. The Hare, who avoid aggression and direct confrontation, often act out the unacceptable by using children and dogs as their surrogates. Men will sometimes induce young boys to wrestle and fight as a test of their strength and skill. But the adults do not always allow the contest to end when the boys grow bored or tired. By means of pushing, laughter, ridicule, teasing, and praise, they provoke the boys to escalate a friendly, nonhostile, and mildly competitive encounter into one characterized by aggression, anger, pain, taunting, and tears—a range of emotions that sober adults would never allow themselves to display publicly.

Grown-ups stage similar fights among young dogs with comparable results. Pups who are rolling together on the ground will be picked up and have their faces rubbed together in order to evoke hostility and get them to engage repeatedly and aggressively with one another. Adults, who make up an informal audience at such times, respond to the man-made fights of boys and pups with the same types of encouragement, laughter, and disparagement. A fight among grown canines, by contrast, would be stopped immediately because of the danger of serious injury to the dogs. And fights among sober adults are almost unheard of in this community, where members are bound together by ethics of kinship and restraint. But deviance in the case of pups or children can be safely created and enjoyed, since the actors are either young or nonhuman and their actions threaten neither valuable resources nor social cohesion. Innocence here also masks the deviance because the forbidden emotions appear under the guise of playfulness.

Movies

Movies provide a different type of medium through which to experience the deviant acts of others. Among the Hare, people are particularly interested in the emotional rather than the narrative content of films. Since many villagers lack sufficient command of English to follow dialogue or nuances of plot, their attention centers on the affective and nonverbal language of performers. Scenes of marital disputes, spouse slapping, fistfights, arguments, drunkenness, romantic embraces, and comic blundering are responded to by all members of the community with vehement laughter, shouts, cheering, and sympathetic sighs. Aggressiveness on the screen evokes the same outbursts of encouragement that greet real-life fights among drinkers, children, and dogs. Romantic or passionate affection provides a kind of enjoyable embarrassment, during which people in the audience elbow one another in a mutual acknowledgment of their mixed feelings.

The most deviant part of the movie, as an event, is that it turns what would ideally be private behavior into public occurrence. The actors may be conforming to Western norms in their roles, but their open display of aggressive, intimate, and provocative postures before the whole community is nevertheless at variance with how the Hare experience one another. Native viewers take on some of the creative license of the film critic, remaking the movie to fit their own criteria of good, bad, and deviant. The fact that the people behaving inappropriately on screen are usually white adds an extra element of vicariousness to the experience. For the residents of Colville Lake, as well as those of Bramley, knowledge of the compromising behavior of others, be they white or native, is most commonly spread by gossip, not by dramatic presentation. To see people "acting out" is a rare treat. Films are thus a staging of what the Hare try to hide.

Strangers and Tourists

The deviance of the stranger is another intrusive element in the life of Bramley. There are no white people living in the community itself; but five miles away, there is a new European enclave—a condominium complex being built by a group of Germans. A number of Bahamians work here as construction laborers, maids, cooks, maintenance personnel, and groundkeepers. But the people of Bramley express a strong antipathy for the Germans and identify two sources for this feeling. One is their historical consciousness of themselves as English-speaking British subjects who fought against Germany in World War II. More current and more to the point is their professed dislike of the Germans' personality, specifically their colonial brand of condescension and their authoritarian way of ordering Bahamians around.

Despite these feelings, both work and leisure bring the two groups together. On the job, Bahamians will sometimes provoke the Germans by failing to do work in the manner prescribed by their employers. Aware of how dependent the Germans are on them, the Bahamians are either confident of not being fired or indifferent to the possibility. What they relish are the explosive outbursts and temper tantrums they can elicit, a kind of impotent rage that they themselves would never publicly exhibit before others. Workers are also amused by the way German wives order their husbands around—a sharp deviation from the islanders' own domestic roles.

The Germans sometimes come to the bar at Bramley on weekends because it is one of the few diversions available to them. While there, they affect an air of camaraderie with the Bahamians. The latter play along with them, but also play on this. Their definition of the situation differs from that of the Germans, who do not seem to appreciate the dislike that lies behind the friendly masks. Across the room, Bahamians are often mimicking, gossiping about, and making fun of these foreigners, protected both by the physical space and the barrier of language. If tourists slum by frequenting native haunts, natives haunt tourists by conning, toying with, and putting them on. Unlike unaccompanied women, it is not only the presence of the Germans that is deviant but also their presumption of closeness in a setting full of distance. In native eyes, tourists are already deviant by definition. But the Germans take this one step further by playing the role of tourist itself in a deviant way.[5]

MANAGEMENT AND MANIPULATION OF DEVIANCE

The patterns of deviant behavior that have been described share three distinctive characteristics. First, responses to them are informal and not directly punitive. Second, community members exhibit a mixture of pleasure and disapproval when confronted with these situations. Finally, the deviant actors tend to be unaware of the social meaning that others attribute to their actions. These three qualities merit further elaboration.

Qualities of Staged Deviance

First, in regard to the informal nature of social responses, it should be noted that staged behaviors constitute only one type of deviance in the two communities under consideration. They elicit mild reactions because they are relatively nondisruptive for village life. In contrast to this, other people in these settlements occasionally violate norms in direct, non-manipulative, and more serious ways, and they are, accordingly, directly sanctioned for this. Individuals who engage in theft, repeated violence, or chronic stinginess, for example, may meet with social withdrawal or economic isolation. But the "soft" forms of deviance noted above are under the control of other community members and are consequently less threatening. They can be responded to with ridicule, disparagement, and other types of tolerant subtlety, a quality that Pfohl (1981), Rubington (1982), and Raybeck (1988) have shown to be especially characteristic of small-scale, kin-based societies, which lack formal institutions of social control and whose members are more concerned with the maintenance of social harmony than with punishment per se.

Second, staged deviance evokes a mixed emotional response. When deviant behavior is purposely manipulated, it lends a special flavor to aberrant conduct. It can be attractive and repulsive at one and the same time. "In the queerest way," as George Orwell once observed of Jonathan Swift's prose, "pleasure and disgust are linked together" (Steiner 1983: 178). Prus makes a similar point about deviance when he notes that a single audience can simultaneously judge an activity to be "deviant" and yet exciting, fun, worthwhile, and desirable (1983: 8). At Colville Lake and Bramley, people can enjoy witnessing some of the very behaviors they disapprove of because they are being exhibited by those who do not directly engage, confront, or compromise them.

A third feature of staged deviance is the low level of awareness that performers have about the way others regard their behavior. Performers are shielded from self-consciousness and stigma because they fall outside certain social categories. At Bramley and Colville Lake, children receive absolution because they are not adults, drunks because they are not responsible, whites because they are not natives, actors because they are not alive, and dogs because they are not human. Their inebriation, innocence, foreignness, or ignorance each yields a special kind of bliss. Within the geography of social life, they inhabit what Becker calls "structured areas of ignorance," places that are notable on the deviant landscape because their inhabitants display a "lack of awareness" (1963: 25-26). To some extent, such people are all proxies, providing others with a vicarious license to enjoy deviance at a safe distance (Savishinsky 1982). The social response to them exemplifies what American teenagers, in their infinite wisdom, refer to as "cheap thrills"—a process of "getting off" on other people's behavior.

Perceptions and Functions of Deviance:
Insiders, Outsiders, and Labels

Functional views of deviance abound in the literature, and the phenomenon of staged deviance lends them some support. Their basic thrust is that deviant individuals are like the God of Voltaire: if they did not exist, people would have to invent them. Voltaire's fellow countryman, Jean-Paul Sartre, has made a parallel argument about modern prejudice and the imaginary deviant: "If the Jew did not exist, the anti-Semite would invent him" (1965: 13). Without the negative example of the maligned, then, conformists would not know how good they truly are. By punishing the deviant, people reward themselves for their own proper behavior. In epigrammatic terms, if everyone was good, goodness would cease to exist.

The idea that real or imagined deviance by some can promote social solidarity among others goes back at least to Durkheim (1964), and has been elaborated by Cohen (1966) and others. But it is important to note that the role of the social misfit as a source of group cohesion has both "inside" and "outside" dimensions. Misbehavior by inside or indigenous members of a community affirms the values and righteousness of their compatriots (Birenbaum and Lesieur 1982: 110). Inappropriate acts by outsiders reinforce the identity of the community as a whole (Erikson 1964). Deviant insiders and outsiders thus have distinctive roles, but they each have their value. Bahamian and Arctic peoples demonstrate the outside dimension in their response to several categories of people, not just in their disapproval of how whites act. The Hare, for example, also criticize the morals and mock the speech of the neighboring Eskimo (Inuit), with whom they have periodically had hostile contacts from early historic down to modern times. In a similar vein, native Bahamians deride individuals from neighboring settlements, nearby islands, and other Caribbean nations; this is especially true of Haitians, whom they sometimes suspect of witchcraft (cf. Bregenzer 1982; LaFlamme 1985). Such outside individuals do not have to be separately labeled as deviant, for the mere designation of a person as an Eskimo, a German, a white, or a Haitian already suggests disapproved qualities. Racial and ethnic terms thus do double duty as stigmas.

These interethnic and interracial situations illustrate one dimension of group perception and prejudice in pluralistic societies. But the negativism can cut both ways; that is, the outsiders in such settings also have their own styles of stigmatizing insiders. While the Bahamians perceive the Germans as loud, crude, maritally aberrant, and suspect former enemies, the Germans reciprocate by describing Bahamians as unreliable, lazy, and libidinous. In the Arctic, some whites speak about native peoples as being improvident, unmotivated, and susceptible to drunkenness, while Indians criticize Euro-Canadians for being racially prejudiced and hypocritical in their own drinking behavior. The relationships between Germans and Bahamians, and Indians and whites, thus embrace a politics of mutual disrespect, echoing the kind of negative affinities that Turnbull (1961) notes between the Pygmy and the Bantu.[6]

Compared to the conduct of foreigners, misbehavior by indigenous members of a community usually requires a different set of responses since the in-group/out-group distinction cannot be applied in a neat, sanitary way. While being bad may have its social uses, deviance by compatriots needs to be domesticated if it is to be tolerated. Stage managing the disapproved behavior of other natives is one way of controlling and appropriating it. As indicated above, the use of such a subtle and informal method of management in communities with modest populations suggests that the size of a society may significantly affect the way it responds to the aberrant acts of its members. Small-scale, kinship-based, and close-knit communities, such as Colville Lake and Bramley, have a particular problem with deviants that large, socially differentiated societies do not. Specifically, they lack the police, the jails, and the professionals to deal with such people in a formal way, and they cannot risk the exclusion, conflict, and social disruption that harsh or formalized measures would entail (Raybeck 1988).

Furthermore, since the types of deviance described here are socially perceived in these settlements as lacking in serious consequences and as being performed by characters without a conscious sense of responsibility, they fail to fulfill several criteria that labeling theorists regard as requisites for the labeling process itself: consequences, consciousness, and responsibility (Prus 1983: 11). This adds to the impression that the people of Bramley and Colville Lake seem more interested in deviance than deviants; that is, in the content of behavior as contrasted with the identity of the actors. For them, it is the performance rather than the performer that embodies the moral lesson. "The play's the thing" in Hamlet's terms or, to borrow from Yeats (1926), there is no need for them to "know the dancer from the dance." Hence, it may be more effective and appropriate for residents of such communities to avoid permanently labeling or stigmatizing people as deviants, since those who act properly cannot afford to ostracize or institutionalize those who misbehave.[7]

Complex societies, however, can afford to remove, redefine, and confine disruptive people. They can label, isolate, or house a variety of deviant populations, such as criminals, delinquents, mental patients, alcoholics, drug abusers, the retarded, and the unemployable. In recent centuries, Western countries have adopted this type of approach, enacting what social historian Michel Foucault (1973) calls "the great confinement." In the process of establishing treatment centers, programs, and institutions, modern societies have also given birth to entire professions to variously help, maintain, or contain the troublesome and the marginal.

Thus we have social workers, jailers, psychiatrists, rehabilitators, and caretakers. Such occupations have an obvious investment in deviance, and they are sometimes accused by their critics of encouraging people to act out in ways that will ensure the continuity of case loads, funding, and jobs (cf. Hawkins and Tiedman 1975; Sagarin and Kelly 1982). Labeling and manipulating others, then, can become a form of self-employment.

Comparisons and Conclusions: Social and Political Models

The staging of deviance occurs in many types of societies. Often the forms that such deviance takes are so blatant or so covert that people do not recognize the aberrations for what they are. Yet these dramatic acts are highly effective and can occupy a central place in a culture's religion, art, style and politics. On the overt dimension, there is the self-promoting and self-dramatizing deviance of individuals who wish to draw attention to themselves or a cause, such as religious martyrs, drag queens, *berdaches*, or individuals who parade around with bizarre clothing or exotic pets.[8] For such people, the social disapproval or persecution that they risk is an acceptable price for the emotional, spiritual, or political rewards they seek. Their deviance is not only publicly staged, but in contrast to the cases given above, it is conscious, purposeful, individualistic in nature, and sometimes validated by a visionary or religious experience. Dramatized deviance can also be collective and ritualized. Ceremonially, for example, Mardi Gras, orgies, and other rituals of license allow people to temporarily suspend everyday norms, transforming some of them from placid citizens into patrons of the repressed (Erikson 1964: 20). An excellent example of collective and conscious deviance are the *hijra* of India, a religious cult of eunuchs, transvestites, transsexuals, and hermaphrodites who perform as dancers at various public rituals (see Chapter 7).

Movies, art, and literature also celebrate deviant individuals, providing viewers and readers with both titillation and moral lessons. The Marquis de Sade's characters spend at least as much time at their preaching as they do at their perversions. Their deviance becomes a vehicle for didacticism. Gothic villains and Frankenstein's monster also speak for the dark underside of the psyche, the dangerous, feral, or antisocial part of ourselves that we love to see acted out, but which then needs to be brought under control. Our fascination with Romantic artists expresses the same ambivalence: The self-destructive heroism of Byron, and the decadent aesthetics of Baudelaire and Rimbaud, celebrate the deviance that lies at the heart of creative genius.

The theatrical phenomenon of presenting other people's deviance as a live, public spectacle is even more manipulative than the carefully staged life style of the artist. The impresarios of circuses and sideshows reap their rewards by turning what might otherwise be a free show into a freak show.[9] When modern print and electronic media celebrate eccentricities in dress, music, "soft" drug use, hair style, and life style, they lend them immediate visibility and familiarity. Behavior once considered deviant thus has a very short life span, for publicity quickly turns it into an acceptable model for others to emulate (Rubington 1982: 51-53). "Smart" behavior thus becomes popular and "proper" overnight (Freilich 1983b; and Chapter 1), enabling media figures to greatly intensify the rate of stylistic change in culture. And since the models on view here—the artists, performers, and media personalities—are often no more than the creation of their managers, agents, and publicists, their conduct is a very carefully staged phenomenon.[10] Thus, ritual and religious drama, art and theater, and the vagaries of style, all reflect the social incorporation of deviance as staged behavior.[11] In summary, within the broad range of dramatic displays catalogued here, the deviant, the exotic, the eccentric, the creative, the pathetic, and the freakish can overlap with one another and be hard to separate.

An added value of recognizing how people stage deviance in other cultures is that it increases our awareness of its subtle role in our own political life. The political dimension of deviance and social control in Western societies is one of the critical insights developed by the "new criminologists" and social conflict theorists (e.g., Schur 1980; Sagarin and Kelly 1982; Taylor 1982; Birenbaum and Lesieur 1982; Pfohl 1985). On the side of the oppressed, they note the way some deviant groups engage in organized, public activities in order to destigmatize their cultural identity (Kitsuse 1980). But they also show how the same strategy of public display can be applied from the top down to create stigma and foster persecution. In the Moscow "show trials" of the 1930s, for example, Stalin effectively turned the confessions of deviants into a form of national theater. The defendants, whether self-proclaimed, accused, or manipulated into an admission of their political sins, were meant to serve as a lesson on the virtues of adherence to the party line (Connor 1972; Bergesen 1977). In the postwar decades, independent thinkers in the Soviet Union have been specifically labeled and punished as "deviationists"—a remarkably precise term for the language of modern politics. Some have been hospitalized as "insane" by Russian psychiatrists, who are "predisposed to equate deviance with pathology" (Fireside 1979: 39). Other dissenters have been put through trials that "take on the character of a performance staged by the KGB" (Ibid.: 69).[12]

In the United States, the federal government has also played the role of theatrical producer. Through the use of disinformation and *agents provocateurs*, it has illegally manipulated deviance in radical groups in order to publicly embarrass and then legally destroy them. During the 1950s and 1960s, for example, the civil rights and antiwar movements were infiltrated by government agents; one of their prime roles was to promote violent and illegal activities by these groups so that the Department of Justice could justifiably intervene with, prosecute, and ultimately suppress them (Halperin et al. 1976). Consciously or not, political operatives in such instances show themselves to be good Durkheimians: They stage events which provoke social disapproval in order to manufacture social solidarity and suppress conflict.

Staging and labeling deviance for the social good is not as isolated an event as the public may assume. Government or police "sting" programs entrap people by staging events in which unwitting individuals are seduced into breaking the law. When law-enforcement personnel pose as prostitutes, bribe-givers, and foreign spies in order to solicit money or information, it is because the government is in the business of inducing people to behave illegally in the interests of law and order.[13] As part of a different strategy, people in power can also label opposition movements as "deviant" in order to destroy their credibility. In a recent example of this the president of the United States described proponents of a nuclear weapons freeze to be the perpetrators of a "dangerous fraud" and the dupes of the "evil empire" of world communism (Smith 1983). Supporters and members of the disarmament movement have responded that, in their opinion, the ultimate staging of deviance is the U.S. government's own suicidal plan to produce a "theatre" nuclear war with Europe itself as the stage.[14]

Such modern forms of political labeling and rhetoric reveal the intersection of national policy with religious and secular ideologies. The opposition is variously portrayed as insane, sick, evil, or fraudulent. The older social models of deviance as demonic, evil, or immoral are thus sometimes replaced by the newer metaphor of pathology (Pfohl 1985). Both twentieth century governments and activists, for example, have used disease imagery to discredit their enemies: The labels "cancerous" and "syphilitic" have been applied to Jews by the Nazis, to Israel by certain Arabs, and to Stalinism by Trotsky (Sontag 1978: 82-84). Cancer is a good metaphor, Sontag notes, "for those who need to turn campaigns

into crusades" (1978: 86). Deviance and opposition are thereby trans-
muted into clinical pathology.[15]

When opponents of a political system are seen as evil or sick rather
than merely wrong, then politics becomes a mix of theology and
pseudoscience; the world is pictured as divided into camps of the good
and evil, the healthy and the sick; deviance becomes not just aberrant
but devilish and deformed. The truth can then take on a religious or a
scientific character as well as a political shape. The biology of Lysenko
in the Soviet Union and the purified language of "Newspeak" in *1984*,
were articles of faith that left no room for dissent or dialogue (Medvedev
1971; Orwell 1950). The fate of Russian geneticists and Orwell's Winston
Smith, whose confessions were staged for the public good, reflect the
modern tendency to treat dissent as deviation, and deviancy as heresy
(Dewey 1939: 90-92). The political dividend of understanding staged
deviance is that it helps us to recognize these threats to dissent and critical
opinion. The process also shows that power and meaning are often
exercised by individuals working backstage rather than by those appearing onstage. People who fail to recognize that they are either the audience
or the actors for someone else's political drama would do well to consider
Hamlet's insight about the play being the thing.

Conclusions

Diverse situations have been considered in this essay, ranging from
dog fights, childhood play, movie shows, and drinking to tourism,
politics, and issues of national security. Together, however, they illustrate
how the manipulation of people to act in deviant ways can be used to
serve a variety of different goals. It can provide amusement, vicarious
identification, emotional release, a sense of superiority and solidarity, a
pretext for abuse, and a prelude for persecution.

These phenomena have been described here at very different levels of
social analysis. Sub-Arctic and Bahamian communities constitute small
islands of life compared to the large nation-states that mediate the future
of our planet. The latter make more significant use of labeling as a
technique for creating and managing deviance, while smaller, close-knit
communities employ more informal and subtle means. Further, recasting
movies, toying with tourists, and playing with dogs do not have the
institutional supports or long-term effects on the individual that police
entrapment, political show trials, and artistic self-promotion do. Such
differences in dramatic content reflect differences of social scale. Beyond
content, however, all of these cases also share a common process, that

of staging behavior as a way of creating meaning and controlling deviance. For both large and small societies, this widespread cultural technique suggests a sobering lesson. Where deviance is concerned, there is a striking continuity between the politics of everyday life and the everyday life of politics.

NOTES

This paper is based, in part, on research conducted in the Northwest Territories of Canada in 1967, 1968, and 1971, and on fieldwork on Cat Island in the east central Bahamas during 1977. Work in the Arctic was sponsored by the National Science Foundation and the National Museums of Canada; the Bahamian research was supported by Ithaca College and the College Center of the Finger Lakes. The analysis of field data was facilitated by a postdoctoral grant from the National Endowment for the Humanities in 1979-80, and a Dana Fellowship from Ithaca College in 1981. Additional work on this essay was made possible by a research grant from Ithaca College's Faculty Development Fund in 1985. I would like to thank Douglas Raybeck, Morris Freilich, and Dorothy Owens for helpful comments on an earlier draft of this paper, and Garry Thomas for his assistance in planning the Bahamian research.

1. The history, strengths, and limits of the symbolic interactionist and dramaturgical approaches are discussed by Davis (1980), Wilshire (1982), Pfohl (1985), and Collins (1985).

2. Anthropological descriptions of the two communities are provided in Savishinsky (1974, 1977, 1978, 1982, 1990). These sources include material on the patterns of drinking, tourism, child rearing, leisure activity, and human-animal relations discussed here. The ethnographic "present" for Colville Lake applies to the period 1967-71; Bramley is described as it existed in 1977.

3. See also MacAndrew and Edgerton (1969). As Edgerton (1976: 59) notes, alcohol in some cultures provides occasion for "socially sanctioned misbehavior."

4. For material on tourism and drinking on Cat Island, see the essays by Gelda (1978), Greenberg (1978), and Katzenstein (1978). The male dominance of bars as public spaces is also found in other Bahamian communities (Hayes 1974: 163-64).

5. MacCannell (1976) describes the difficulties of tourists who try to "go native." He documents how sightseers take in, and get taken in by, "the sights," though he does not dwell on situations where natives play on the credulity of tourists. In the history of the Bahamas, tourism has succeeded slavery, agriculture, and colonialism as the dominant dimension of the islands' economy. While the transition to tourism has been a relatively rapid and smooth one, the situation incorporates many of the elements of dependency, staged authenticity (MacCannell 1976: 91 ff.), and the uneven distribution of wealth that are found in other Caribbean countries. Thomas and his students (Thomas, ed., 1974, 1976), and LaFlamme (1985), have described the way natives and tourists perceive and treat one another on three other Bahamian islands.

6. Current political confrontations between Canadian native peoples and whites can bring out some of the same qualities and dynamics. Broch (1983: 184-93) applies Goffman's frontstage/backstage distinction to the way Northern Indians and whites

handled a community dispute at "Fort Sunset," a predominantly native settlement in the same region as Colville Lake.

7. Their approach, therefore, also differs from those small, traditional societies, such as the Ojibwa and the Navaho, who rely on witchcraft accusations and anxiety about illness as methods of social control (Hallowell 1941; Kluckhohn 1967).

8. For the role of berdaches in Sioux society, see Erikson (1963: Chapter 3). The use of exotic pets as a status device is discussed in Szasz (1969) and Savishinsky (1983).

9. See Fiedler (1978). As Fiedler demonstrates, the freakish deviant is as likely to become a subject for art and literature as a candidate for the circus. Velaquez' painting *Las Meninas* is a classic example of the interplay among deviance, art, and power.

10. Edgerton (1976: 95-99) suggests that people who deviate may themselves often be seeking variety, stimulation, contrast, or an escape from boredom. He and Durkheim (1964: 71) also point out that deviance can be a source of social innovation and change by providing new or alternative models for conduct.

11. Deviance as theater has a venerable history in Western society. From the early sixteenth to the early nineteenth century, the Bethlem Hospital in London, better known as Bedlam, was "one of the great tourist attractions" of that city (Stone 1982: 28). Some 96,000 people a year came to see it. It was a bit like visiting a zoo. "To contemporaries, madmen were reduced to the level of animals, since they had lost the power of reason and thus of their soul" (Stone 1982: 35).

12. The novels of George Orwell (1946, 1950) and Arthur Koestler (1941) describe how totalitarian regimes employ methods of melodrama and manipulation to create deviants and then use their invented behavior for political profit. Zhores and Roy Medvedev (1971), Bloch and Reddaway (1977), and Fireside (1979) detail the way that contemporary Soviet authorities stage psychiatric interviews in order to turn political dissidents into mental deviants.

13. For a recent moral critique of such practices, see Bok (1983).

14. See, for example, the "Resolution on Nuclear Disarmament" adopted by the American Association of Suicidology (1982), which describes "the current nuclear threat to the world as suicidal." Students of history are quick to point out how rulers and politicians cement their positions of power by distracting people with imaginary enemies, bogus threats, and concocted crises (Taylor 1962: 131-39).

15. While cancer, tuberculosis, and syphilis are universally seen as illnesses, the medical labeling of some other "deviant" conditions has also changed with the temper and mores of the times. A good example of this is the removal of homosexuality from the American Psychiatric Association's list of diseases in the 1968 edition of its *Diagnostic and Statistical Manual of Mental Disorders*. Such a change reflects the labile nature of labeling, and the way in which social activism by organized groups can lead to a change in their social identity (Sagarin and Kelly 1982).

II Ethnographic Essays

INTRODUCTION

Deviants often act out what others only dream of. The dreams may be nightmares or pleasant fantasy, but whatever their emotional content, they challenge people's tolerance and understanding of others. This test is there for teachers as well as students, for model-builders as well as the gatekeepers of society. The challenge to our tolerance, and the chance to learn from it, are especially strong when we look at deviance in other cultures because they provide different kinds of opportunities for people to dream and act, to plot and play. The ethnographic essays in this part of the book demonstrate this diversity by exploring how people from Africa, India, China, Europe, the Middle East, and other areas deal with violence, homosexuality, prostitution, child abuse, servitude, gossip, begging, and bravado. These essays also provide the reader with a chance to test the models of deviance we have proposed, and to rethink certain American assumptions about the nature of deviance as a human experience.

Witchcraft is one of the most controversial forms of deviance, and a great many interpretations have been proposed by historians and social scientists to account for beliefs and accusations in various cultures. Laurel Rose's chapter "Swaziland: Witchcraft and Deviance," examines the situation of an African people who must act upon their customary beliefs in the context of a European-imposed legal system. Using Freilich's SAPS model, she shows that the Swazi now have to choose among several options for dealing with suspected cases of witchcraft. Certain customary responses, such as community murder of a witch, are now impermissible in the European system, while traditional chiefs and present-day courts concur in stressing the avoidance of witches, or the private settlement of disputes, as proper means. Because the Swazi's traditional ability to try and sanction accused witches is now restricted, they often resort to "smart" behaviors, most of which are defined as deviant by European law. In many cases, the ironic result is that "witchcraft victims rather than suspected witches are more likely to be labelled 'deviant' by both Swazi and European-style courts, and [they are] subsequently sanctioned." Changing legal mores have thus made the "victims" of witches into victims of the legal system.

In the chapter on infanticide in modern Kenya, Philip Kilbride argues that changing social values can also affect the likelihood that certain people will engage in deviant behavior. Focusing on the situation among Baganda women, he notes that child abuse was very rare in the past; in the traditional extended families in which people used to live, wives were valued for their fertility and their agricultural labor, just as children were seen as a source of economic security for aging parents and grandparents. The modernization of the economy and the value system, however, has contributed to the powerlessness of women and the vulnerability of children. Men are taking less responsibility for their offspring, especially those born to unwed mothers. The latter thus bear a burden of greater stigma and parental responsibility. Without the support of extended families, they find themselves more socially isolated, which in turn makes them more prone to neglect or abandon their infants. Kilbride suggests that this process can help us to understand the social conditions that also foster child abuse in Western societies, and that it can sensitize us to the value of providing parents with better social support systems in order to reduce the risks to their children.

While some deviants commit abuse, in other cases they themselves are used and abused for a variety of ends and with a variety of means. Steven Caton amplifies this theme in "The 'Voice' of the Despicable: Deviance, Speaking, and Power in Yemeni Tribal Society." The *khaddaam*, a Yemeni servant group, are forbidden to own land, carry weapons, or work at jobs with status. They are forced to survive by serving as town criers, messengers, and public speakers for more respected people. They are also expected to show their deviant status by their speech patterns. The khaddaam are supposed to use language that is emotional and passionate, and which lacks the measured, poetic quality of the speech of truly honorable people. While the khaddaam have the license to mock and criticize public figures, they must do so in tones and cadences that are reserved for their own, socially inferior group. Their work and their speech regularly betray their lowly position in society. Khaddaam speech, for Caton, is actually a "symbolic representation of the person," reflecting the kind of power that others can exercise over these despised people.

In the chapter "The *Hijra* of India," Serena Nanda describes people who have turned their deviance—in this case sexual deviance—into a life-long career. The hijra are Indian eunuchs, transvestites, transsexuals, hermaphrodites, and homosexuals who adopt female clothing and behavior, and who live in organized, hierarchical communities under the leadership of gurus. They support themselves by prostitution, by begging, and by fulfilling a religious role; as the vehicles of Bahuchara Mata, the mother goddess, they perform at family rituals, bestowing blessings on newborns and newlyweds. While hijra are sometimes subjected to ridicule, abuse, and stigma by the public, their communal life also gives them a strong sense of security and identity. In this sense their deviant careers are very different from those of American street hustlers, whose rootless mobility reflects their culture's emphasis on individualism and freedom. Nanda argues that the life-styles people build around their deviance are thus an ironic reflection of the values of the larger society within which they operate.

Thomas Shaw's chapter, "Taiwan: Gangsters or Good Guys?", takes us to another part of Asia and moves us from the realm of sexuality to the world of gangsters. In urban China, male groups of *liumang* (hooligans) control small neighborhoods that are often only a few square blocks in size. While these men are criminals to the police and politicians, they embody core values that most Chinese have long revered. These include courage, manliness, loyalty to leaders, martial skills, and adherence to a personal code of justice. In the same way that organized groups of bandits once protected and exploited rural villages in the past, urban gangs now defend and live off the people of their neighborhood; they keep out other gangsters while running protection and extortion rackets, and offer their services to settle local disputes. Rather than creating conflict themselves, the liumang thrive on the quarrels of others by acting as mediators and enforcers. Their form of justice is swifter and often less corrupt than that offered by the courts. The gangsters perceive themselves, and they are seen by many others, as a heroic bulwark of traditional virtues in the face of modernization, bureaucracy, and the indifference or inefficiency of officialdom. Shaw argues that their deviance is, therefore, ironically conservative; they regularly press the limits of the moral order and thereby reestablish that order.

While witches, child abusers, transvestites, and gangsters are rare in most societies, there are other kinds of deviants whose behavior is commonplace in certain cultures. Dennis Gaffin found this to be true in Koppbøur, a small village in the Faeroe Islands of the north Atlantic. Virtually every person in this community was the subject of tales that others told about their failings and indiscretions. Gaffin shows how all members of this community were seen as being deviant to some degree. In the village's strong oral tradition, the invention of stories, nicknames, and *taettir*—satirical ballads—served as a way of highlighting people's adultery, laziness, drinking, arrogance, and eccentricity. Gaffin argues that the Koppbingar were not overly concerned that the facts of life did not always justify a person's reputation; of much greater importance to them was that the celebration of people's deviance was a highly effective "leveling technique" that maintained social equality. The village was an intimate, egalitarian, and virtually crime-free world, one in which all individuals were visible and familiar to everyone else. It was the deviant content of daily talk—what Gaffin calls "the community's continuing narrative"—that kept people in their proper place.

The chapters in this section have both intrinsic and comparative interest. First, they look at gossip, gangsterism, servitude, child abuse, witchcraft, and homosexuality in several societies. Through a consideration of the motives, attitudes, and reactions that accompany these patterns, they place these deviant behaviors in their cultural context. Furthermore, to explain these various experiences in Asia, Africa, Europe, the Middle East, and the Americas, the chapters also apply one or more of the models of deviance that were developed in Part I. The authors consider the strategies, the severity, the social scale, or the staging of deviance as part of their analyses. Their descriptions and explanations thus constitute a "test" of the general utility of the models that have been proposed.

Finally, these chapters also have relevance on the home front. Each of the controversial issues they address is and has been part of American culture. The questions they raise therefore provide opportunities to reexamine our own society's experience of deviance. Confronting other cultures thus becomes an encounter with our own ideas and concerns. It will lead, one hopes, to culture shock in reverse—enabling us to see the familiar as both strange and worthy of reexamination.

4 SWAZILAND: WITCHCRAFT AND DEVIANCE

Laurel Rose

INTRODUCTION

Blood-curdling tales of witchcraft have long filled the literature on Africa. Colonial administrators and missionaries, acting in response to a climate of disdain in Europe and fear in Africa, attempted to suppress witchcraft beliefs and practices as undesirably "deviant." Despite their efforts, witchcraft continues to exert considerable influence within African societies, and anthropologists continue to discover fascinating witchcraft cases during the course of their fieldwork.

In this chapter I review several major themes in the anthropological literature on African witchcraft. Subsequently, I analyze my field data on Swazi witchcraft within the framework of Morris Freilich's SAPS Model. Smart and Proper Strategies (Chapter 1) is well-suited to a study of the sociology of deviance in witchcraft; it aids in clarifying and graphically illustrating the range of possible behaviors in witchcraft cases.

THE PROBLEM

Anthropologists have argued for a definition of "deviant" behavior which is culturally relative. Kai Erikson, a professor of sociology, has

offered a classic definition of *deviant behavior* which the members of a
group

consider so dangerous or embarrassing or irritating that they bring special sanctions to
bear against the persons who exhibit it. Deviance is not a property inherent in any
particular kind of behavior; it is a property conferred upon that behavior by the people
who come into direct or indirect contact with it. The only way an observer can tell
whether or not a given style of behavior is deviant, then, is to learn something about
the standards of the audience which responds to it. (1966: 6).

The problem with Erikson's definition is that the "audience" responding to behaviors may comprise different groups or classes within the same
society—each of which has a different interpretation of deviance. In the
context of witchcraft behaviors in Africa, the belief in witchcraft, as a
cultural phenomenon, does not represent a deviation from accepted
religious and moral ideas; to the contrary, any one of a number of
behaviors may be defined as deviant in the context of each kinship group,
social class, or national legal/political structure (see Mair 1969). Therefore there are few, if any, objective properties that all deviant acts can
be said to share within a given group, much less, across groups and
cultures.

Witches' "deviant" attributes are diverse within and across African
societies; many categories of persons (kin, neighbors, foreigners) with
numerous personal characteristics (envy, malice, spite) are said to
become different kinds of witches (night or day, good or bad). Witches
may be deviant in a positive sense (economically successful and politically powerful) or deviant in a negative sense (physically undesirable
[e.g., ugly, deformed, or dirty], uncooperative, negligent of obligations,
bad tempered, eccentric, envious, selfish, nonconforming, or foreign).

African witches' "deviant" behaviors are also reportedly diverse. They
are believed to travel great distances, to turn into leopards, to go out in
spirit at night and kill victims, to remove corpses from graves, to dance
naked at night, to commit incest, to use familiars such as baboons, and
to cause misfortunes of others (death, illness, miscarriages, sterility,
difficult childbirths, poor crops, sickly livestock and poultry, loss of
articles, bad luck in hunting, and lack of rain).[1] A witch bewitches others
out of revenge, ill will, jealousy, or desire for power. He performs his
activities at night, often learning from and participating with other
witches (Beattie 1963; Beidelman 1963; Mair 1969).[2]

As dissimilar as witches' attributes and behaviors may be in each
society, witches almost universally represent the opposition between
deviant and normal behavior. Thus, witchcraft beliefs clarify values in

each society by contrasting the undesirable bad, wrong, improper, or sinful behavior of the deviant witch with the desirable good, right, proper, and righteous behavior of the "normal" person. Such beliefs also clarify the boundaries of group membership by opposing deviant outsiders with normal insiders: the opposition between "us" and "them," between in-group and out-group, and between allies and foes. Ultimately, the witch, in the process of being symbolically contrasted with the normal person who adheres to ideal values, becomes the ultimate representation of deviance, "the standardized nightmare of a group" (Wilson 1951: 313).

In analyzing the deviance of African witchcraft, anthropologists have generally focused upon the personality of the witch rather than the victim.[3] Some anthropologists comment that more needs to be known about the victim, whose accusation is important to an understanding of the sociology of witchcraft; he reacts to real social tensions, although not necessarily to real acts of witchcraft (see Marwick 1950, 1970 and Wilson 1951). In fact, few victims of witchcraft even make accusations; they are constrained by community interests in social unity. As Raybeck's model (Chapter 2) suggests, the scale of the society, and people's sensitivity to social roles, limits their reaction to provocative, deviant acts. A potential accuser realizes that his witchcraft accusation may be viewed as an individual, socially disruptive act that in itself might be sanctioned as deviant. The potential accuser bases his decision to react upon his need to assign responsibility for a disaster and remove its cause, among other things (Mair 1969). A victim of witchcraft can rely upon several types of behavioral responses: ignoring the problem; personal and informal arbitration; legal and formal machinery; and performance of public ritual (see Turner 1957). Moreover, the victim's responses can take different forms in a single case, be directed against various sources, and change regularly. In effect, the victim's range of possible behavioral responses is as important, if not more important, to the development of a sociology of deviance in witchcraft behaviors than the routine description and categorization of a witch's alleged attributes and behavior.

Victims' responses to perceived witchcraft acts may be categorized in two basic types: individual and group. An individual victim may respond privately to protect himself before witchcraft is used against him. Some methods are unobtrusive and therefore unlikely to be sanctioned under either customary or introduced European law. For example, a victim may wear animal teeth or hair charms for personal protection when traveling or hunting, or he may use charms to protect his gardens. Or he may try to appease, cure, or avoid the witch. After an act of witchcraft is believed to have been committed, a victimized person is more likely to resort to drastic and public measures that may not be sanctioned under customary law but are likely to be sanctioned under introduced European law if detected and reported to state officials. For example, a victim may consult an oracle or diviner to identify the witch (relying upon trance, medicines, water gazing, or consulting the dead), hire a professional sorcerer to counteract the witch's magic, hire a witch-smeller to ferret out the witchcraft articles in his house, or bring a case against the suspected witch.

A group responds collectively to protect itself before witchcraft is used against it. Again, some methods are unobtrusive and therefore unlikely to be sanctioned under either customary or introduced European law. For example, the group uses charms to protect houses, compounds, fields, and villages, or it relies upon ostracism (naming, ridiculing, or gossiping). After an act of witchcraft is believed to have been committed, a group relies on public measures that, if detected, are likely to be sanctioned under introduced European law. For example, it uses the ordeal, public trial, or beats the suspected witch to death. In accord with Savishinsky's model (Chapter 3), the private act of witchcraft is here dealt with by staging a highly visible, dramatic response. Mbiti (1969: 203), like others, writes that in the past communities periodically smelled out sorcerers and witches, punishing them, "cooling them off," curing them, and counteracting their activities; such activities were believed to purge communities of mounting tensions.[4]

European legal intervention significantly altered customary individual and group responses to witchcraft. Following the arrival of Europeans, suppression of witches was prohibited and disgruntled people were forced to devise new defenses against witches—such as cross-country witch-finding tours, local witchcraft hearings, and antiwitchcraft rituals of churches that had broken away from Christian churches. LeVine (1963: 231-33) argues that group actions against witches became more rare, while individual measures became more common than they once were. But even when public witchcraft accusations were made, courts hesitated to convict all members of the group. Because legal intervention dislocated control of suspected witches from the community to the victim, indigenous definitions and interpretations of deviance in witchcraft arguably became more idiosyncratically diverse and less cultural.[5]

Just as Africans' definitions of witchcraft are diverse, so too are scholars' definitions. Marwick (1970: 16) delineates three basic theories about witchcraft: historical or ethnological, psychological (e.g.,

Kluckhohn 1967; Krige 1947; and Malinowski 1970), and sociological (e.g., Middleton and Winter 1963). Psychological theories of witchcraft, which focus on the "deviant" witch or accuser, hypothesize that witchcraft beliefs serve the psychological needs of both the victim and the suspected witch: The victim adheres to witchcraft beliefs in order to explain events or attribute his failures to others, whereas the witch adheres to such beliefs in order to find achievement in spite of his undesirable personal attributes (Krige 1947: 21).[6] Sociological theories of witchcraft, which focus on the social groups to which the witch and his accuser belong, look for the structural logic of witchcraft beliefs and accusations, rather than patterns of individual antisocial conduct. Such theories hypothesize that witches are blamed according to the political structure of the community, the structure of the extended family, and the position of married women (LeVine 1963). Sociological theories interpret witchcraft accusations as mechanisms that either produce (dysfunctional) or release (functional) tensions in particular social relationships (e.g., jealous co-wives or unmarried rivals for a person's love).[7]

Several anthropologists have criticized the major theoretical approaches as methodologically and analytically narrow. One critique suggests that witchcraft beliefs have been emphasized at the expense of actual behaviors (see Beidelman 1963; LaFontaine 1963). A second, related critique argues that witchcraft situations have been undesirably studied through written case reports or interviews rather than observed over lengthy periods of time and reported in the extended case format (see Crawford 1967; Marwick 1970; and Turner 1964). A third critique argues that witchcraft beliefs and practices have been pigeonholed in narrow, descriptive categories (see Reynolds 1963 and Parrinder 1976) and that analytic concepts of witchcraft have been narrowly dichotomized (e.g., functional and dysfunctional) (see Turner 1964). A fourth critique proposes that witchcraft accusations have not been sufficiently studied within the widest possible field of social interaction—alliances and rivalries between witches, their accusers, and other community members (see Marwick 1970 and Turner 1964).

In an effort to accommodate critiques of witchcraft studies, when possible I collected my case material according to the extended case method. In my written analysis, I examine beliefs and actual behaviors of a wide range of actors in witchcraft cases, although I particularly focus upon the often neglected victim. I organize hypothetical cases (based on interview data) within the SAPS model and thereafter organize actual observed/reported cases in case summaries. The hypothetical and actual cases describe the nature of accusations leveled by individuals or groups against suspected witches, and show how these accusations were dealt with by customary and European officials. When actual cases are compared with hypothetical cases, it becomes clearer how beliefs translate into a wide range of behaviors in real life. My approach views deviance as much in terms of the individual actors' behaviors as the larger social structural framework.

SETTING OF STUDY

The Swazi are a Bantu-speaking people who settled in present-day Swaziland during the mid-eighteenth century. In terms of legal development, which is important in this analysis of legal interpretations of witchcraft,[8] the arrival of European settlers in the late nineteenth century was critical. After that time a dual legal system gradually developed: currently, one side of the system consists of Swazi customary law administered by the king, his councillors, and territorial chiefs in customary courts, whereas the other side consists of Roman-Dutch law administered by magistrates and judges in European-style courts.[9] There is some overlap between court systems in terms of jurisdiction over persons and causes, but the courts functioning according to Roman-Dutch law have wider jurisdiction (e.g., over serious criminal cases involving assault and murder) (Nhlapo 1982). (See Figure 4.1, which illustrates the dualistic Swazi court system.)

In Swaziland, as in other African countries formerly administered by the British, a so-called repugnancy clause was inserted into customary court legislation (Crawford 1969/1970). This clause states that the customary courts may not administer any Swazi law or custom that is " . . . repugnant to natural justice or morality. . . ." Witchcraft legislation prohibits the practice of witchcraft, the employment of a witch doctor or witch finder, accusations of witchcraft, and advice on how to bewitch. At the same time, the legislation prohibits public courts from trying people for witchcraft or using criminal sanctions against supposed witches. It does allow criminal conviction of a person for fraud, assault, or murder in connection with witchcraft. In any case, because European lawmakers were confused about the nature of witchcraft acts and the methods of witch finding, witchcraft legislation created problems of legal interpretation and enforcement.

Witchcraft is currently handled differently in the European-style courts as opposed to the customary courts. The two court systems diverge more strongly in attitudes about morality and justice in witchcraft cases than in most other types of case, although officials of both systems condemn

Figure 4.1
Swaziland Court Structure

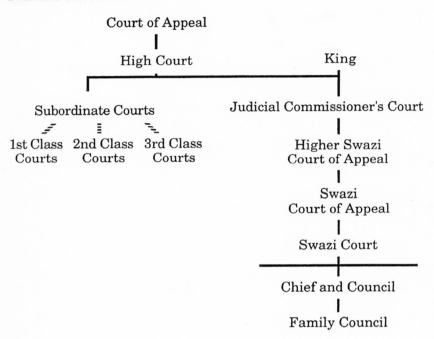

cases in which violence is used for personal gain (e.g., acquisition of human flesh for medicine). In the high court (European-style court), a person's belief in witchcraft may be used to mitigate a sentence in a murder trial, when the defendant has defensively killed a person whom he believes is killing his close kin through witchcraft. An important consideration for mitigation is whether the defendant can reasonably understand the law and whether the defendant could reasonably believe in witchcraft. Reasonableness is based upon the defendant's age, education, and life style (see Aremu 1971: 129).

In the customary courts of precontact days, a person who suspected that he was the victim of witchcraft could lawfully attempt to counteract the witch. He could bring a witchcraft case before the chiefdom officials and present divination results as evidence. Today, a person cannot bring a witchcraft complaint before the Swazi customary courts, and he is limited in what he can do against witches through diviners and private enlistment of chiefdom officials. Sometimes witchcraft accusations arise in the chiefs' courts during litigation over other matters. These accusations are not dealt with as part of the court record. If the concerned parties cannot be calmed, the chief may encourage private reconciliation. Most often, the person who suspects bewitchment must attempt to persuade the witch to undo the effects of the witchcraft, or he must attempt to counteract the witchcraft through use of his own magic. As in other parts of Africa, witch hunts have become largely private, and the cathartic public witch hunts of the past have disappeared.

It is unclear whether witchcraft beliefs and practices in Swaziland have expanded, contracted, or held their own in association with modern developments. On the one hand, some observers argue that European contact brought about economic and social changes through, for example, industrialization, urbanization, introduction of schools, reduction of land areas, and encouragement of population migration. They argue that these changes increased Swazi fears, frustrations, and jealousies about work promotion and school examination, among other things—with the result that people increasingly performed personal acts of witchcraft or privately resorted to the witch doctor for medicine to counteract the witchcraft of others. On the other hand, some observers argue that changes that were brought about through European contact improved standards of health and education—with the result that Swazis were decreasingly interested in witchcraft.[10]

SAPS ANALYSIS OF SWAZI WITCHCRAFT

As indicated, my analysis of Swazi witchcraft beliefs and behaviors is aided by the SAPS (Smart and Proper Strategies) model (see Figure 4.2). Morris Freilich (1985) describes how SAPS aids in categorization of a range of human behavioral responses. He writes that his model formulates three options that a person has to choose from in responding to a situation: (1) act according to ideal, cultural rules regarding good and moral behavior ("proper"), (2) use the problem-solving strategies of some group or network (group "smart"), and (3) develop private or personal problem-solving strategies (personal "smart").

Freilich further defines the proper, group smart, and individual smart within a means-and-goals matrix. The means are the routes taken by actors for the purpose of achieving behavioral goals. The goals are the outcomes actors wish to accomplish through behavioral strategies. When means and goals are paired with proper and smart behavioral strategies, nine behavioral styles result. In effect, there are means that are proper, socially smart, and personally smart, and there are goals that are also proper, socially smart, and personally smart. Means and goals are proper

Figure 4.2
Smart and Proper Strategies

MEANS	GOALS		
	Proper Cultural Definitions $\mathbb{P}$	**Smart**	
		Social Definitions $\mathbb{S}$	Personal Definitions $\mathbb{Z}$
Proper Cultural Definitions **p**	p$\mathbb{P}$ 0	p$\mathbb{S}$ 3	p$\mathbb{Z}$ 6
Smart Social Definitions **s**	s$\mathbb{P}$ 1	s$\mathbb{S}$ 4	s$\mathbb{Z}$ 7
Smart Personal Definitions **z**	z$\mathbb{P}$ 2	z$\mathbb{S}$ 5	z$\mathbb{Z}$ 8

Proper: Correct, right, good, moral (P or p).
Smart: Practical, effective, doable, useful.
Shared Smart: Smart as defined by a social unit (S or s).
Personal Smart: Smart as defined by an individual (Z or z).

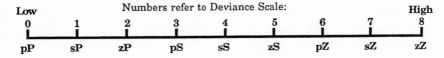

Numbers refer to Deviance Scale:

Low   High
0   1   2   3   4   5   6   7   8
pP   sP   zP   pS   sS   zS   pZ   sZ   zZ

when they are part of the cultural inventory. They are socially smart when they are openly developed by a group or subgroup to satisfy immediate social needs (sometimes an individual acts alone in a socially smart way). They are personally smart when they are secretly developed by an individual to satisfy personal needs or interests.

Freilich proposes that the propriety of proper rules, the efficiency of group smart rules, and the impropriety of individual smart rules must be empirically verified. He further challenges other anthropologists to analyze their own field data according to his nine "behavioral cocktails," i.e. the SAPS model. This paper takes up his challenge by proposing nine hypothetical Swazi witchcraft cases (one for each cell of the SAPS matrix), and then comparing nine actual Swazi witchcraft cases.

As a variation to Freilich's presentation of SAPS, I rely upon SAPS to demonstrate the diversity of behavioral responses to witchcraft in a pluralistic society. Therefore my presentation of witchcraft cases in the broad, multidimensional SAPS framework demonstrates the variety of ways in which individuals living under the jurisdiction of Swaziland's dual legal system can respond to perceived witchcraft. SAPS effectively integrates individual deviant witchcraft acts within a social structural framework.

When hypothetical Swazi responses to perceived acts of witchcraft are categorized within the SAPS matrix, nine behavioral combinations result (see Figure 4.3 which illustrates my SAPS matrix of witchcraft behaviors). Within each cell of the matrix, means and goals of witchcraft "victims" are described: the means primarily concern the use/nonuse of legal forums (reliance upon religious leaders or traditional healers is not discussed), whereas the goals concern the sanction aimed at. The means and goals in each cell are differentiated in order to demonstrate the convergence and divergence between customary and European interpretations of properness, social smartness, and personal smartness. Text in italics represents Swazi interpretations of behavioral propriety, whereas plain text represents both European and Swazi interpretations.

The model depicts three coexisting levels of legal interpretation: customary, European, and shared. For example, customary law permits a community to ostracize or banish a suspected witch. European law negates some customary responses (e.g., community murder of suspected witch) and imposes restrictions on other responses (e.g., chief may be consulted but may not advocate a violent response). Both customary and European law advocate either restraint in response or avoidance of a suspected witch.

Figure 4.3
SAPS: Witchcraft in Swaziland

M E A N S	Shared	GOALS		Nonshared	GOALS
	Cultural		Social		Personal
	$\mathbb{P}$		$\mathbb{S}$		$\mathbb{Z}$
p	**p $\mathbb{P}$** M: suppress fears of suspected witch or distance oneself from suspected witch p: Sw & W G: eliminate fear of suspected witch before personal or group action taken P: Sw & W 0		**p $\mathbb{S}$** M: *ostracize suspected witch after discussion between aggrieved parties fails* p: Sw G: *sanction suspected witch through public action* S: Sw 3		**p $\mathbb{Z}$** M: *ostracize suspected witch without confrontation about charges* p: Sw G: sanction suspected witch through personal action Z: Sw & W 6
s	**s $\mathbb{P}$** M: report suspected witch to chief on witchcraft or non-witchcraft related charges s: Sw & W G: eliminate fear of suspected witch through conciliatory efforts by customary authorities P: Sw & W 1		**s $\mathbb{S}$** M: *report suspected witch to customary legal agency (Swazi Court) on non-witchcraft related charges* s: Sw G: *sanction suspected witch by customary agency on non-witchcraft related charges* S: Sw 4		**s $\mathbb{Z}$** M: report suspected witch to Western legal agency on non-witchcraft related charges s: Sw & W G: *sanction suspected witch by Western agency on non-witchcraft related charges (ignore witchcraft)* Z: Sw 7
z	**z $\mathbb{P}$** M: forcibly drive suspect witch from community without public hearing z: Sw & W G: eliminate fear of suspected witch before personal or group action taken P: Sw & W 2		**z $\mathbb{S}$** M: assault suspected witch, thereby engaging customary legal agency z: Sw & W G: *sanction suspected witch by personal action which forces recognition by Swazi authorities* S: Sw 5		**z $\mathbb{Z}$** M: kill suspected witch, thereby engaging Western legal agency (community uninvolved) z: Sw & W G: sanction suspected witch by personal action which forces recognition of problem by Western authorities Z: Sw & W 8

KEY:
P = proper   S = social smart   Z = personal smart
Sw = means or goals in Swazi Customary legal system
W = means or goals in Western-style legal system
M = means (use or non/use of forum)   G = goals (sanctions aimed for)
Interpretation Code: Western & Swazi - Plain Text;   Swazi - *Italics*

As a whole, the SAPS witchcraft matrix reflects the assumption, as stated by both customary and European authorities in Swaziland, that legally proper means and goals, that is, ideal behavior, involves denying witchcraft and avoiding a suspected witch (Cell 0). The Swazi system allows the socially smart means of reporting a suspected witch to the customary authorities (Cell 1), but it prohibits the personal smart means of using force (Cells 2, 5, 8). The customary system also defines means and goals as socially smart and even proper when a suspected witch is ostracized, publicly condemned, and sanctioned by customary authorities on "other" pretenses (Cells 3, 4, 6); the European system does not define such means and goals as socially smart but does not legally disallow them as privately smart. The customary system further defines means as socially smart when a witch is reported to European legal authorities on a charge related to witchcraft (Cell 7), but indicates that a personal smart goal is incurred if the witchcraft issue is ignored. Both customary and European authorities assert that means and goals are personally smart, in fact illegal, when a suspected witch is assaulted or murdered (Cell 8). In effect, means and goals are generally proper when chiefs and other customary officials are manipulated, and are personally smart when customary officials are ignored and secretive, violent measures are taken.

When goals (sanctions) and means (use/nonuse of forums) are viewed separately, significant convergence between Swazi customary and European legal interpretations is evident regarding proper goals (Cells 0, 1, 2) paired with any means, and regarding personal smart means (Cells 2, 5, 8) when not paired with social smart goals (Cell 5). The greatest divergence between interpretations occurs regarding social smart goals (Cells 3, 4, 5) when not paired with personal smart means (Cell 5). Therefore, Swazis and Europeans agree most about proper goal combinations but agree less about some smart goal combinations. In effect, because Swazis' ability to try and sanction accused witches was restricted by European legal intervention, they resort to smart behaviors to deal with witchcraft situations.

Swazi and European witchcraft beliefs represented in the hypothetical SAPS model will become clearer in the actual case studies that follow.

CASE STUDIES OF SWAZI WITCHCRAFT

The following nine summaries of actual Swazi witchcraft cases demonstrate the hypothetical interpretations of Swazi witchcraft depicted in the nine cells of the SAPS matrix (Figure 4.3). I present the sequence of events in each case summary chronologically. After each case summary,

I explain why I interpret behavioral responses to perceived witchcraft as proper, socially smart, or personally smart, and thus why each case represents a particular cell in the matrix. My interpretations are based upon informant statements made in interviews and court sessions. Place names are omitted from case descriptions, but fictional clan names of the most important characters are provided.

Case 1 (Cell 0) (Proper Means for Proper Goals)

A woman, Simelane, marries and goes to live at her husband's homestead with his parents and four wives. After some time, she becomes ill and blames her problems on the local climate and the presumed witchcraft of her in-laws and co-wives. Simelane decides that the best solution is to persuade her husband to take her to another region and request land from the chief for a new homestead. When her husband agrees, her problems are eliminated.

Simelane's proper means for dealing with her fears of witchcraft, according to both customary and European legal interpretations, was to distance herself from the suspected witch. Simelane's proper goal, according to both customary and European standards, was to take private, evasive action.

Case 2 (Cell 1) (Social Smart Means for Proper Goals)

A man, Mamba, chops down a tree that his brother, Lukhele, claims belongs to him. When Lukhele confronts Mamba about the matter, Mamba denies Lukhele's ownership. Lukhele becomes furious and says that Mamba chopped down the tree because of jealousy in being childless. Lukhele further accuses Mamba of witchcraft and subsequently reports the tree incident to the chief.

When the brothers are called before the chief's council, Mamba utters a counterwitchcraft accusation against Lukhele. The chief becomes furious about this implied threat and comments angrily that Mamba will be fined if he repeats his accusation. Mamba is also told that he will be held (legally) responsible if sickness or death should befall Lukhele. Mamba tells Lukhele to admit that he made the first witchcraft accusation privately, but Lukhele remains silent. The chief tells the brothers to settle their problems at home.

Lukhele's smart means, according to customary legal interpretations, for dealing with his fear of Mamba's witchcraft was to accuse him privately of witchcraft and bring a case about an unrelated matter (tree) before the chief's council. His means were smart because they allowed him to inform Mamba of his individual interests, while ensuring that his adversary would be publicly sanctioned in the customary legal system for an unrelated matter. Lukhele's proper goals, according to both customary and European interpretations, was to involve the customary authorities in a problem related to witchcraft, but without publicly making forbidden (imposed European law) witchcraft accusations.

Mamba's goal of countering Lukhele's witchcraft accusation was socially smart, but his personal means, making counter witchcraft accusations against Lukhele before the chief's council, was merely individually smart. His behavior brought him severe public reprimand.

Case 3 (Cell 2) (Personal Smart Means for Proper Goals)

After a man dies, the community gossips that a particular man, Dlamini, has caused his death through witchcraft. Community members say bad things about him, causing Dlamini to fear for his personal safety. He reports his problems to the chief. The chief advises Dlamini to leave the community before some individual or group brings public action against him. The chief also explains that it is to everyone's advantage if Dlamini leaves, since people who are on bad terms with one another should not be neighbors. Dlamini follows the chief's advice and moves to another area. Dlamini's action serves to ensure his own and his family's safety as well as avoid official banishment by the community. Banishment would have hindered his attempts to obtain land in another chiefdom.

The chief relied on the personal smart means of advising a suspected witch to leave the community. Thereafter, the community's fear subsided and no personal or group action was taken against him—a proper goal.

Case 4 (Cell 3) (Proper Means for Social Smart Goals)

A chief's deputy dies, and many people suspect that the death was caused by Matsebula, a generally unpopular member of the community. They keep their distance from him and watch his movements until they can organize an expedition to a diviner. When the diviner is consulted, he cuts a lock of hair from Matsebula, who is present in the group. This indicates that he believes Matsebula is the witch. The community then informs the chief about the diviner's findings, and Matsebula is banished from the area. The community relied on the proper means of ostracizing Matsebula after public action (resort to diviner) identified him as the witch. The community's goals are socially smart because they result in consensual sanctioning of a suspected witch, without bringing the European-style or Swazi courts into play.

Case 5 (Cell 4) (Social Smart Means for Social Smart Goals)

A man, Shongwe, took out a bank loan so that he could buy seed, manure and equipment for planting maize and beans. After harvest, he sells most of his crop in order to repay his loan. He gives a small portion of the harvest as tribute to the chief but virtually nothing to his unsuccessful neighbors. People start gossiping that he is using "spooks" to enrich his fields. They also tell the chief that he gave only a small portion of his crop to him since he thinks that the chief is lazy and merits nothing more. The chief doesn't summon Shongwe to answer in his own defense, but notes privately among his councillors that Shongwe has assumed increasingly arrogant and disrespectful ways. Apparently, a history of bad relations between Shongwe and his community has culminated in current formal grievances. The chief's council banishes Shongwe on the ground of disrespect, but witchcraft is believed to be the main reason for banishment.

The community took socially smart means against a suspected witch in that they brought nonwitchcraft-related complaints against him. Such actions ensured that community members would not be condemned for illegally (European imposed law) naming a suspected witch. The community's goals were also socially smart because they resulted in banishment of the suspected witch on formal grounds other than witchcraft. The chief's council knew that suspected witchcraft was behind the charges of political insubordination and greed, but it did not have to confront openly problematic witchcraft charges.

Case 6 (Cell 5) (Personal Smart Means for Social Smart Goals)

A woman, Zwane, notices that her child is displaying the typical symptoms of a witch's spell. She goes to Motsa, a diviner, and asks Motsa to treat her child. Motsa refuses, saying that she is busy. Zwane then attacks Motsa with a bush knife because she believes that Motsa's refusal to help must mean that she is the source of witchcraft. Before injury is inflicted, the women are separated and the chief's messenger is called to help the women negotiate.

When the messenger's efforts fail, the case is reported to the Swazi court. The court president asks Zwane why she didn't report the case to the chief rather than attack Motsa. Zwane does not respond clearly. A witness called on behalf of Zwane argues that Zwane's child had been bewitched three times and therefore Zwane legitimately set out to attack the suspected witch. The court president then relates his own experiences with witchcraft, while also admonishing the court that only the matter of assault and not the witchcraft accusation may be legally entertained.

The court president fines Zwane for assault. Zwane leaves the courtroom shouting that justice was not served and that she will take care of the suspected witch herself.

Zwane's personal smart means for dealing with her fear of witchcraft was to assault the suspected witch. Zwane's socially smart goal, however, according to Swazi standards, was to seek private redress. Her goal failed because her personal smart means forced the customary authorities, who operate within the legislative constraints imposed on Swazi courts (colonial "repugnancy clause"), to ignore her witchcraft complaint and deal only with the assault. Had she approached the chief informally (socially smart means), her witchcraft complaint could have been dealt with.

Case 7 (Cell 6) (Proper Means for Personal Smart Goals)

A man, Sukati, drinks frequently and quarrels thereafter with people, telling them that he will kill them. Sometimes it happens that people in the community die after he has threatened to kill them. His neighbors begin to suspect that he is a witch and is making medicines to kill them. People avoid him, hoping that he will discontinue his actions. When the deaths continue, they consider approaching him about his assumed witchcraft activities, but before they can, he dies.

Community members who fear the suspected witchcraft of Sukati use the legally and socially proper means of ostracizing and avoiding him. Their action constitutes a personal smart goal of individualized action against Sukati. This case might have developed to constitute a case of the type in Cell 2 or 4 if Sukati had not died before public, concerted action could be taken against him.

Case 8 (Cell 7) (Social Smart Means for Personal Smart Goals)

A foreign man (African) is murdered ritualistically. When his body is discovered, the organs have been removed, presumably for the purpose of making "medicine." Some community residents suspect a community elder, Masuku, who had been anxious to enhance his prestige and political power. They assume that he needed the medicine to strengthen himself ritually. After an investigation is made, Masuku, is identified as the murderer and is reported to the police. Thereafter a case against Masuku is brought before the high court. Masuku is sentenced to prison for the murder. Community residents gossip that Masuku has been sentenced by the high court for murder but that his primary crime is that of being a witch.

The community relies on the socially smart means of reporting a suspected witch to legal authorities in a European-style court on the basis of a charge unrelated to witchcraft (murder). Their action ensures that they will not be legally sanctioned for making charges against a suspected witch. Their goals are personally rather than socially smart because they have made use of a legal system which is not founded on Swazi cultural standards. Their goals are also personally smart because they have not openly dealt with the real source of their grievances.

Case 9 (Cell 8) (Personal Smart Means for Personal Smart Goals)

One of three brothers, Tsela, whose father and daughter have died consults a diviner. The diviner tells him that a particular old man caused the deaths through witchcraft. Tsela and his brothers secretly plan to kill the suspected witch. Late one night the brothers steal into the home occupied by the old man, his wife, and a young boy. They beat and burn them to death.

When the case is brought before the high court, Tsela requests that his sentence be mitigated on the basis of a genuine belief in witchcraft. His request is denied. The court reasons that mitigation is uncalled for, since Tsela killed innocent co-residents of the suspected witch and since he appears too young and well educated to reasonably believe in witchcraft. Tsela is also condemned for falsifying evidence and appearing nonrepentant in court. He is sentenced to death.

Tsela's means and goals in handling a suspected witch were personally smart according to both customary and European standards. Roman-Dutch law severely sanctions murder, as does Swazi customary law. In the past, chiefs and public opinion occasionally condoned the murder of a suspected witch, but imposed European law transformed a customary proper means for dealing with witchcraft into a personal smart means. In the case at hand, Swazi assessors to the high court judge indicated that mitigation of Tsela's sentence might have been recommended had Tsela been socially smart, that is, had he consulted the customary authorities for advice. However, because he had taken personal smart measures that were detected, that is, private, violent actions, and because he had demonstrated contempt for European-style court authorities, he was sentenced to death.

The nine cases point to a wide range of possible perceptions about and responses to "deviance" in witchcraft; witchcraft victims may respond to witches in many ways, and different courts may respond to victims in many ways. This variation greatly complicates interpretation of "deviant" behavior. The SAPS model, which graphically illustrates the means/goal combinations according to which European or Swazis will attach a label of "deviant" to a particular actor and subsequently levy a sanction, is a useful analytic tool.

In the nine cases described above, victims respond to witchcraft with means according to which they avoided a suspected witch (Case 1), insulted a suspected witch and approached the chief's court (Case 2), assaulted a suspected witch (Case 6), and murdered a suspected witch (Case 9). In some of these nine cases, officials and courts responded with goals according to which they reprimanded a witchcraft victim (Case 2), fined a victim (Case 6), sentenced a victim to death (Case 9), as well as ostracized a suspected witch (Case 3), evicted a suspected witch (Cases 4 and 5), and imprisoned a suspected witch (Case 8).

Many Swazis complain that witchcraft has increased because Swaziland's courts cannot sanction suspected witches. In fact, as Cases 6 and 9 demonstrate, witchcraft victims rather than suspected witches are more likely to be labeled "deviant" by both Swazi and European-style courts and subsequently sanctioned. However, Swazi customary officials and courts attempt to handle witchcraft problems privately (informal settlement or recourse to diviners) as in Cases 2, 3, 4, 5, 7. They attach the deviant label to a witch or victim in connection with forum use (means)—when a witchcraft problem is reported to a Swazi court outside the jurisdiction of the chiefdom (Case 6). The European officials attach the deviant label to a victim in connection with a sanction (goal)—when violence is used against a suspected witch. For this reason, I would supplement Freilich's statement that social superiors "champion proper rules" and levy negative sanctions against "deviant" users, with the statement that authorities in juxtaposed legal systems in a heterogeneous society dissimilarly interpret and sanction deviance.

CONCLUSIONS

When Europeans arrived in Africa, they introduced a legal system that imposed new definitions upon traditional African notions of deviance. In the case of witchcraft, they labeled customary beliefs and behaviors "repugnant" and "deviant," with the result that customary forums and officials were denied full powers to hear and sanction witchcraft cases. Customary officials obligingly conveyed the European labels of deviance in their sentencing practices but abided by their own notions of deviance in courtroom rhetoric (see Case 6).

In an effort to understand witchcraft beliefs and behaviors, scholars have developed numerous definitions and concepts. They have defined the roles of individuals and groups in witchcraft scenarios and have devised psychological and sociological theories to explain the behaviors of these individuals and groups. Their theories have tended to dichotomize concepts regarding individual witches' and victims' behaviors ("normal" versus "deviant") and societies' structural formulations of witchcraft behaviors ("functional" versus "dysfunctional"). The SAPS model, as a contrast, depicts a wide range of individuals' behaviors (witches' acts and victims' responses) within a total social structural framework.

In this paper I used my interview data to construct a SAPS matrix of Swazi and European beliefs regarding hypothetical witchcraft behaviors (forum use and sanction). I then filled in the cells of this matrix with case data regarding actual Swazi witchcraft behaviors. My case-by-case analysis demonstrates how a multiplicity of variables combine in each case to produce particular patterns. For instance, when witchcraft victims avoid the suspected witches, they will be ignored by both customary and European officials; when these victims react as individuals or groups in a violent manner, they will be sanctioned by both customary and European officials; when customary authorities promote private settlement or banishment, officials of the European-style courts will not react.

The SAPS matrix sheds light on witchcraft in modern Swaziland, but it also points to changes that witchcraft behaviors have undergone as a result of the imposition of European law upon Swazi customary law. It does this by demonstrating points of convergence and divergence between Swazi and European beliefs about witchcraft, particularly the types of customary behaviors (legal interpretations) that were compelled to change after the Europeans' arrival. Some Swazi customary proper behaviors (e.g., murder of witch) became the personal smart (prohibited), whereas other customary proper behaviors (e.g., community

ostracism and banishment of accused witch) became socially smart
(hidden). At the same time, no known customary smart behaviors became
culturally proper in the dual legal system, although new socially smart
behaviors were promoted (e.g., through formal institutionalization by
legislation of Swazi and European-style courts that can deal peripherally
with witchcraft matters). In essence, European law defined all witchcraft
beliefs as personally smart (i.e., deviant) but allowed the customary legal
system some autonomy except when personal smart means (e.g., individual violence) were paired with either socially smart or personal smart
goals (e.g., private sanction that incurred the intervention of Swazi or
European-style courts (Cells 5 and 8).

Freilich suggests that social smartness as a means and properness as
a goal (Cell 1) is the most common behavioral combination. I would
state, based on my Swaziland witchcraft data, that Cells 0, 1, and 2
represent the most desirable but not necessarily the most common
combination. These cells probably represent the most "desirable" combinations since they incur the greatest convergence, and thus agreement
about the propriety or "deviance" of means and goals in handling
witchcraft, between juxtaposed legal systems.

Other students of witchcraft may be inspired to use Freilich's SAPS
matrix to test these and other assumptions with their own data.

NOTES

The research on which this chapter is based was carried out in Swaziland between
January 1985 and July 1986 with the support of grants from the Wenner-Gren
Foundation for Anthropological Research and the Fulbright I.I.E. program. I wish to
thank Morris Freilich and Robert Pratt for encouraging me to write about witchcraft
in Swaziland.

1. For an analysis of "inversion" theory which hypothesizes that witches reverse
physical, social, and moral normality, see Beidelman (1963), Buxton (1963), and
Gluckman (1965).
   2. For reasons of convenience, the masculine pronoun will be used throughout the
text, although both men and women may be witches and victims of witchcraft.
   3. The designation victim refers to a person's perceived, not necessarily actual,
victimization in an act of witchcraft.
   4. On the topic of individual and group responses to perceived witchcraft, see
Bloomhill (1962), Crawford (1967), LeVine (1963), Middleton (1969), and Parrinder
(1976).
   5. For more information about the impact of European legal intervention, see
Beidelman (1963), Bloomhill (1962), LeVine (1963), Mair (1969), Marwick (1950),
Mayer (1954), Parrinder (1976), Richards (1935), and Vansina (1969).

6. For more information about "expressive" theories of witchcraft, see Mair (1969), and about "instrumental" theories, see Beattie (1963), Crawford (1967), Marwick (1970), Nadel (1952), Reynolds (1963), and Turner (1957).

7. For a more in-depth description of functional and dysfunctional theories, see Beidelman (1963), Buxton (1963), Douglas (1963), Evans-Pritchard (1937), Gluckman (1944), La Fontaine (1963), Mair (1969), Marwick (1964, 1965, 1970), Middleton (1969), Parrinder (1976), and Turner (1957, 1964).

8. Although witchcraft in Swaziland has been discussed by Kuper (1947), Marwick (1940), and Deutsch et al. (1982), their discussions define witchcraft more in terms of magic, religion, medicine, and social structure than law.

9. I refer to these courts as "European-style" courts because they operate according to introduced European law and procedure. They currently have jurisdiction over the general population.

10. For an analysis of changes in witchcraft beliefs and practices in Africa, see Beidelman (1963), Crawford (1967), Gelfand (1967), La Fontaine (1963), LeVine (1963), Marwick (1965), Parrinder (1976), Reynolds (1963), Richards (1935), and Vansina (1969).

5 FEMALE VIOLENCE AGAINST RELATED CHILDREN: CHILD ABUSE AS A MODERN FORM OF DEVIANCE IN KENYA

Philip L. Kilbride

One of the most striking social problems in the United States is the high rate of child abuse. Behaviors that are harmful or injurious to a child, such as battering, burning, or starving, have become common enough to be of concern to a wide lay and professional public. In the social sciences, it is sometimes argued that psychopathological or other causes at the individual level are most important in understanding the etiology of child abuse. For example, the abuser is seen as having a personal history of being abused, inaccurate knowledge of child development, poor impulse control, and often alcohol or drug problems. Other researchers advocate a "social systems" position, with such factors as unemployment or isolation from potentially supportive kin or neighbor networks seen as constituting significant antecedents to child abuse. Those unable to decide on theoretical priorities seemingly advocate theoretical eclecticism (Garbarino 1977; Korbin 1981; Gelles and Cornell 1985).

Disagreement also exists on the present rate of child abuse (Segal 1979). Nevertheless, whether or not the rate is increasing in the United States, it is clear that child abuse is a form of statistically deviant or nonnormative behavior. Moreover, child abuse as a behavioral category is disapproved of by the general public and so can be said to constitute what represents a deviant or "troublesome violation of a socially accepted rule" (Edgerton 1980). Therefore, in both a statistical and evaluative sense, child abuse constitutes a form of deviant behavior (see Thio 1978 for approaches to and operational definitions of deviance), and in Raybeck's model (Chapter 2) it qualifies as hard deviance. Surprisingly however, theoretical work on deviance and on child abuse rarely to my knowledge converges, a shortcoming that this essay seeks to address along lines indicated below.

The discipline of anthropology has not established a strong empirical or theoretical research tradition in the domain of deviance (Edgerton 1980), although some recent anthropological work has been directed at child abuse in other cultures (Korbin 1981; Fraser and Kilbride 1981). This work emphasizes the need to define child abuse for cross-cultural application. Should culturally appropriate but painful initiation ceremonies in New Guinea be called abusive (Langness 1981)? Although it is often socially approved, is joint parent-child suicide in Japan abusive (Wagatsuma 1981)? On the whole, anthropological work would seem to support relativistically inclined child abuse theorists. Such an approach would define child abuse as occurring "when the child suffers non-accidental physical injury as a result of acts—or omissions—on the part of his parents or guardians that violate the community standards concerning the treatment of children" (Segal 1979: 580). Anthropologists have shown that in some societies there is little or no child abuse as this concept is understood in the West (for traditional Africa see LeVine and LeVine 1981; for hunting societies see Rohner 1975). It also has been documented that modernization seems to increase child abuse in Africa (Fraser and Kilbride 1981) but to decrease the rates in China (Korbin 1981). In summary, anthropology in the child abuse field emphasizes that child abuse (and by extension other forms of deviance) can be understood only in terms of social context. For this reason, the social systems approach mentioned above is highly recommended by previous work in anthropology.

My own material from Kenya would suggest that the social deviance perspective best suited for interpreting child abuse in this non-Western context is that of labeling theory (cf. Thio 1978; Becker 1963; Rubington and Weinberg 1968). This is because labeling theory is fundamentally social and relativistic along the lines emphasized by the anthropologists referred to above. For example, it recognizes that social rules are context-dependent, and their violation is open to negotiation through social interaction. An action is only troublesome from the perspective of individuals or societies who create, maintain, or construct a deviant label (such as rapist, murderer, thief, or child abuser). In an often-cited passage, Howard Becker remarks, "social groups create deviance by making the rules whose infraction constitutes deviance, and by applying those rules to particular people and labeling them as outsiders. From this point of view, deviance is not a quality of the act the person commits, but rather a consequence of the application by others of rules and sanctions to an offender. The deviant is one to whom that label has successfully been applied; deviant behavior is behavior that people so label" (1963: 9).

In labeling theory, therefore, attention is clearly focused on the manner in which society defines deviance. It would seem from the theoretical material that an emphasis on social causation provides a common ground where social-oriented child abuse analysis can be further enhanced by insights drawn from the labeling theory. In particular we will show that rules pertaining to women's moral behavior are sometimes quite harsh in modern Kenya as compared to the precolonial scene or to men today (cf. Kilbride and Kilbride, 1990). One consequence of a comparatively powerless social position for modern Kenyan women is that no exceptions are made concerning the negative label she suffers should she even attempt, for example, infanticide. This is so even though such behavior is sometimes seemingly unavoidable and also was once considered permissible under proper circumstances. In Freilich's scheme (Chapter 1), what was once "proper" has become "smart" and invariably deviant.

We consider below why the social order once permitted some exceptions to condemnation of infanticide as compared to the present where no exceptions are made. Specifically, today a female who commits infanticide is universally harshly, labeled with little evidence of exceptional circumstances being evoked by community members to lessen her stigma or rehabilitate her social standing. As we show below, this can be so in spite of serious attempts by the labeled deviant and members of her family to negotiate a favorable social reevaluation. Therefore the theoretical position of "strategic interactionism," which emphasizes that all social rules are negotiable through strategic maneuvers, is not supported. Importantly, we urge here a refocusing on the idea of labeling, its social history, and consideration of a power dimension in label construction (Edgerton 1986).

CHILD ABUSE AND NEGLECT IN KENYA

Modern-defined child abuse is becoming an increasingly more obvious form of troublesome behavior throughout Kenya, particularly in Nairobi (Onyango and Kayongo-Male 1982). Some material drawn from admissions to Kenyatta National Hospital, Nairobi, and reports in the daily press, are useful indices of this pattern. But there is no way at present to construct actual rates for Kenya (or even the United States, where debate flourishes over this issue). Bwibo (1982: 11), a Kenyan pediatrician, states, "Recent figures show that in 1980 and 1981 twenty-one children with battered child syndrome were admitted to Kenyatta National Hospital, of whom five died." Of significance here, a frequent category of child abuse noted by Bwibo in his survey is "the babies of single mothers thrown along the road, dropped in pit latrines or dust bins" (1982: 11). Below we describe a case of attempted infanticide by a secondary school student who threw her newborn into a school pit latrine.

During much of 1984 and until late summer 1985 the author regularly monitored *The Standard* and the *Daily Nation*, two popular Kenyan papers, for accounts of child abuse reported throughout Kenya. Information on seventy-five cases of child abuse were obtained in this fashion. A common form of abuse reported in the press (and reported above by Bwibo) is abandonment (or attempted infanticide) and infanticide of a newborn or older infant, most often by the child's mother. The following list of sample headlines from Kenyan newspapers shows those cases reported in the media and recorded by the author:

BOY FOUND BURIED IN MOLE HOLE

2-MONTH-OLD GIRL ABANDONED AT BUS STOP

5-MONTH-OLD BOY RESCUED FROM A CHURCH LATRINE

BABY WRAPPED IN A PAPER BAG ABANDONED

2-MONTH-OLD GIRL ABANDONED IN HOSPITAL

UNWED TEENAGE MOTHER ABANDONED 4-MONTH-OLD BABY

2-YEAR-OLD BOY ABANDONED IS RESCUED FROM ANTS

2-DAY-OLD BOY RESCUED FROM DITCH

4-MONTH-OLD INFANT ABANDONED IN THE RAIN

INFANT DUMPED INTO TOILET PIT

NEWBORN BOY ABANDONED IN PRIMARY SCHOOL

5-DAY-OLD GIRL FOUND IN MAIZE PLANTATION

MOTHER ABANDONS 2-WEEK-OLD GIRL

8-MONTH-OLD INFANT FOUND IN SEWAGE

2-WEEK-OLD BABY IN PLASTIC BAG FOUND ON WAYSIDE

DOG DIGS OUT BABY'S BODY

MOTHER THROWS 3-YEAR-OLD BOY INTO LATRINE

1-YEAR-OLD BOY ABANDONED BY GRANDMOTHER

UNMARRIED MOTHER THROWS 2-DAY-OLD BABY INTO PIT LATRINE

We can see from the foregoing that both boys and girls are at risk and that the pit latrine is a common location to dispose of unwanted children. Although the present paper is confined to infanticide, it is pertinent to our analysis to acknowledge here the range of other forms of child abuse encountered in press reports, so that the reader can fully appreciate the degree to which children are at risk in modern Kenya. Press reports of child torture, burning, scalding, battering, prolonged confinement, and the like are frequent. Editorials are encountered with such titles as "Our Sad Problem of Battered Children" and "State Urged to Tighten Laws on Child Abuse."

METHOD

The Kenyan field material referred to in the present paper was collected during a year's fieldwork (July 1984-August 1985). During this period I primarily resided in Eldoret, Western Province, my home base for field research among Abaluyia living further west in the vicinity of Kitale (about forty kilometers from Eldoret, itself about 300 kilometers from Nairobi). The research topic was child abuse and neglect to be viewed within the context of family life and changing socioeconomic circumstances. The presence of my wife and one-year-old daughter in the field proved to be a valuable research asset, as I was viewed in the role of husband and father. Accordingly, discussions about topics pertaining to family life and childhood were often initiated spontaneously by our friends and informants. Two local young Abaluyia (a male of thirty and a female of twenty years) resided with us throughout the field stay while working in a variety of capacities such as cook, baby caretaker, and research assistant. Many cultural details about childhood, marriage, and modernization were brought to our attention by these observant (and participating) friends. Several community nurses living in the village context formally assisted the research inquiries, including those relevant to child abuse.

Child abuse, as is also true for many other forms of deviant behavior, is difficult to research through direct observation or survey methodology. Rather I relied on the informed judgment of my local nurse assistants to discover past or on-going episodes of child abuse. Over a period of about eight months only two cases of past child abuse, and no present cases of such behavior, were discovered through these assistants. Extensive household visiting and daily participant observation revealed only one instance of child abuse in a geographical area containing several thousand residents. That instance occurred on a day in May 1985 while I was

preparing to "bow out" or leave the field (Freilich 1970). Quite unex-
pectedly I observed a large crowd gathering at the local secondary school.
Joining the crowd, my wife and I arrived just in time to see a newborn
infant being lifted out of one of the school's pit latrines. The infant's
mother, who had attempted the infanticide, was being hustled into her
dormitory for interrogation by local officials and nurses while we
observed the proceedings and the crowd continued to gather outside. This
incident and its aftermath were followed for several weeks through
observation and interviews, sometimes with the assistance of a female
research assistant and/or my wife. This work occurred in the school,
hospital, jail, and home situations. Discussions were conducted with the
girl herself, various members of her family, police, school officials, and
many other members of the general public. It was during this time that
the relevance of labeling theory to the facts at hand occurred to me. It is
of methodological significance to note here that my experiences, beginning from the fortuitous opportunity to observe an actual case of
attempted infanticide through my subsequent awareness of the relevance
of labeling theory, all involved the effect of serendipity in deviance
research (see Freilich, Chapter 1).

This chapter constitutes a modest and preliminary attempt by a male
ethnographer to focus on phenomenological issues germane to the
women's world in Kenya.[1] My informants were both men and women,
but the social problem considered here, infanticide, was one that affects
almost exclusively women in Kenya. I am not aware that my gender
influenced the data in any way; however, my status as an outsider no
doubt influenced the flow of events to some extent. Nevertheless, it is
very likely that the materials presented below are generally representative
of what would have occurred in my absence.

FAMILY, WOMEN, AND CHILDREN: ETHNOGRAPHIC CONTEXT

I have worked among Abaluyia communities in western Kenya where
modern, rural life still retains many of the social features prevalent in
the precolonial era of about a century ago (Kilbride 1980, 1985; Wagner
1949, 1956). The majority of people continue to be oriented to an
agrarian life-style and depend on their own labor for subsistence foods
and cash crops. This includes women and children who are, as in the
past, the most important source of farm labor. For this reason large
families are still desired by both men and women, and polygamy is seen
as a means to increase family size and thus provide additional free labor.

In our research, for example, when asked, "What do you like most about your child?", most of the twenty-five mothers interviewed mentioned work activities, although "obedience" and "respect for elders" were not uncommon responses. For example, one mother said of her nine-year-old daughter, "She is very much willing to help me. She does not feel comfortable when she sees me working when she is playing; she has to come and help me." Another mother noted admiringly about her nine-year-old son, "He helps in planting and weeding flowers and vegetables; he can also wash things and sweep the home." Rural family life is still very much a collective enterprise constituting an interdependent system where kinship, age, and gender roles are clearly utilitarian and reciprocal (Kilbride 1985). It is probably for this reason that only a small number (three) of present or previous cases of child abuse were observed or came to my attention during a lengthy project devoted to the subject of child abuse and neglect. There were, however, many cases of neglect (Kilbride 1985). In general, children are highly valued, serve important economic roles in family life, and are the responsibility of extended family members in situations where parents are unable to provide care. That most mothers are conscientious in their child care responsibilities was revealed in our study mentioned above. All twenty-five mothers interviewed reported accurately where their children were and what they were doing, as confirmed by subsequent observational follow-ups by our research assistant.

The importance of the extended family as a support network in child care, especially in times of crisis, was revealed in two cases of child abuse briefly described now, and in a third case to be discussed in detail later. One ten-year-old girl now lives with her paternal grandmother, who has adopted her because the child's mother regularly beat her badly, leaving a permanent scar on her forehead. In another case, a woman's brother assumed support of his sister and her three young children after discovering that his brother-in-law regularly beat the children, resulting in a permanently withered hand for one of the boys, who was three at the time of his injury. Cases of neglected children are primarily those resulting from unplanned teenage pregnancies. Paternity is frequently denied and maternal grandparents (particularly grandmothers), sometimes reluctantly, assume caretaking responsibilities. Cases of child neglect appear to have been quite rare in the past. Wagner (1949, 1956), writing about the Abaluyia in the 1930s, noted the importance of having children for both men and women. So strong was fertility emphasized that a young girl could increase her chances of marriage by becoming pregnant. A man usually welcomed and adopted his illegitimate child, who was often thought by his siblings to be their father's favorite child. Infanticide, while rare, did sometimes occur in cases of maternal death during delivery. This was done through fear that without his mother the child would have no place in society. The general picture that emerges from Wagner's description is one in which women and men both enjoy prestige and have social power as a consequence of significant economic roles as producers of children and crops, and as performers of other instrumental activities. Men, however, actually owned the land and their children and controlled their wives, giving them greater power than females.

My impression is that the powerlessness of women and the vulnerability of children in rural Kenya today have resulted from "delocalization" (Kilbride and Kilbride, 1990). Poggie and Lynch (1977) believe that economic delocalization is a chain of complex events that results when food, energy resources, and services that had formerly been provided within the local setting are transferred into market exchange commodities, most of which originate from sources outside the local area. Pelto (1973), who first coined the term *delocalization*, showed how Skolt Lapp social organization was transformed as their reindeer energy resource was largely replaced by petrol-dependent snowmobiles. The new technology created, for example, the "haves" (the snowmobile owners) and the "have-nots" (those still dependent upon skis and reindeer for transport). Today in western Kenya (and elsewhere in East Africa) a cash economy, land shortage, and the migration of men have made a profound impact on family structure, female power, and the previous rationale for maximal biological reproduction. Modern delocalization of the economy has involved a shift from local crops grown exclusively by subsistence technology and largely through female labor, to a monetary, national economy based on cash crops grown for sale outside. This has made many women, particularly those without education, economically worse off than their counterparts in the past. Generally concomitant with socioeconomic delocalization are changes in values, morals, or ideological dimensions of cultural experience. In western Kenya, Wagner (1949) observed the early stages of cultural delocalization in the 1930s. He observed, for example, that traditionally eleusine was the most precious crop: it "tastes to the Africans like sugar to the Europeans." In comparison, however, young people and Christians preferred maize.

In modern Kenya the ethical role of "elders" as moral entrepreneurs (label creators) has declined through what can be called moral delocalization. Typically, Western-educated foreign and Kenyan church leaders, secular authorities, and teachers eschew many indigenous values in favor of those originating elsewhere.[2] For example, the Western province has the highest birth rate in the world and in Kenya 62 percent of the population is under eighteen years of age (Onyango and Kayongo-Male 1982). Nevertheless, some international institutions with moral authority in Kenya are opposed to the use of unnatural techniques of birth control there. Interestingly, the elders often decry the new economic and moral order, but they do not get a sympathetic ear from delocalized moral entrepreneurs. The traditional teacher of wisdom Baswala Kumuse, for example, is active as a funeral orator or singer for whom "the child-parent relationship is a pervasive theme. . . . Baswala Kumuse comment on the pervasive individualism of the present day Kenyan societies" (Wanjala 1985: 89).

INFANTICIDE: A MODERN FORM OF CHILD ABUSE

The normative or proper pattern of child care, with its reliance on the extended family for support, the value of children as sources of labor and future support, a subsistence economy with women as agriculturalists, and elders as moral leaders, persists today to a great extent. Yet a breakdown in this system is becoming apparent with the advent of a monetary economy through delocalization. It will be argued that physical aggression against related children, which is most often committed by women, is best understood by focusing on delocalization, which has caused a decrease in the woman's social power relative to the past, when physical aggression against children was also apparently quite rare. As we have seen, however, infanticide was in the past sometimes acceptable behavior. Nowadays, significantly, infanticide would seem to be an unnegotiable offense, one that confers essentially a permanent stigma on the offender.

AN ATTEMPTED INFANTICIDE

We now turn to a brief description of an extended case analysis of what turned out to be an attempted homicide by a young school girl. The narrative is reconstructed from field notes and observations. Pseudonyms are used throughout the following account.

Sara and her baby sat together in the cool darkness near the dormitory doorway. It was around 5:00 A.M., still quite early, although some of her fellow schoolmates would be awake. Where will I take this baby, she thought while rising and slowly starting to walk toward the pit latrine. Thirty minutes earlier she had delivered a baby boy, silently enough not to have aroused any students. Yes, there were no alternatives. She did not know precisely where the child's father was—after all Nairobi is a very big city. She had also considered the matter of her school fees. Her mother's brother had already paid her fees, which could under no circumstances be refunded. Somehow she must remain in school. Never in her sixteen years had she been so frightened.

Several hours later a curious and somewhat hostile crowd grew around the girl's dormitory in this small rural school in western Kenya. I had seen such crowd excitement on one other occasion, when "mob justice" was administered to a thief in Nairobi. Since traditional times thieves, along with witches, have evoked wide public anger.

Inside the dormitory a tall, large man who represented the chief's office was loudly asking questions in the midst of stern-looking observers. "Where do you come from?" "Who are your parents?" Sara sat quietly even though one man threatened to slap her for her silence. He eventually learned that the baby had been discovered by a student who had followed blood spots to the pit latrine. The chief's assistant had been summoned and had rescued the newborn from the latrine. Much to his surprise the infant was alive. Soon mother, child, and the chief's assistant were off to the district hospital about twenty kilometers away. Another official was dispatched to the nearest police headquarters since infanticide is always today, unlike premodern times, a criminal offense.

With anger in her face the senior nurse said, "How does she feel now? Will she not want help from that boy one day?" "Yes," responded the medical assistant, "in fact, how can she ever face the boy knowing that he knows what she had done?" The strong negative tone expressed by these two women was not unlike other accounts elicited from men and women as the community continued its appraisal of the morning's troublesome event. Negative appraisal was so much in evidence that on one occasion my research assistant commented, "That person would even torture Sara if given the chance."

For about ten days Sara and her baby remained in the district hospital under police guard. When the child's health was normal, Sara was released from the hospital, then detained for several days in a district police headquarters from which she was taken to Provincial Court. Since the survival of her baby seemed assured, Sara was not booked for murder, but was instead placed on court probation under the supervision of her mother for a period of three years.

"Well, Charles, what do you think about all of this?" I asked as I drove Sara's brother to collect Sara's mother and her mother's brother for still another visit to police headquarters. On this occasion the family wished to bring some food for Sara. He responded, "It is certainly expensive. As you can see, my uncle has already paid for medicine, transport to hospital, jails, and now he is worried where to get a thousand shillings for bond fees. There is nobody else who can help out. My father wrote in reply to our letter and said he has too many commitments to help. In fact, Sara's problems began when our parents were divorced. When she was five she went and lived with our father and our mother's co-wife. Our stepmother is barren and Sara would sometimes write and tell me that she was beaten by her for no reason, or given extra work to do. Yes, divorce was a cause of all of this . . . but, of equal importance is poverty. Where could Sara get school fees? I think she fell for some man, perhaps in hopes of getting some money from him."

"Yes," I replied, "she seemed to have known him for only a few days. According to my discussions with many other teenagers who have gotten pregnant, there is much misinformation about how one gets pregnant. Your sister told me she didn't even know she was pregnant until the seventh month."

"Anyway," Charles continued, "we want to get the entire matter resolved before it gets on the radio or newspaper. Our family's reputation will be affected. The whole matter could have been avoided if the police were not involved in the first place. After all, the baby did not die. Yes, the headmaster made it unnecessarily complicated. I want to get my sister out of jail as soon as possible. Moreover, so far, she has been slapped by the police only once but, overall, they have been fine."

"That's good," I concluded, "perhaps my presence has helped out in that regard. By the way, you believed the headmaster or matron should have known about your sister's pregnancy and thereby have prevented the incident. You will be pleased to know he was dismissed. Some powerful members of the school board have long suspected that he is not someone people can bring their problems to. It is alleged that he has sexual interest in young girls. Sara's matter was a kind of last straw. Some of them believe the blame should not be entirely on your sister. The new acting headmaster seems nice. He showed me your sister's grades and attendance records. You know, she is 'average' in everything recorded about her. Well, here we are at the jail."[3]

Sara's Troubles: A Theoretical Interpretation

Sara's troubles, although summarized here, do reveal some points of interpretive significance. First, it is clear that Sara's attempted homicide is troublesome and therefore deviant in the sense that "We know when the limits of acceptable behavior have been exceeded because the result is 'trouble' in the form of complaints, disputes, accusations, recriminations, and the like" (Edgerton 1980: 466). It should also be noted that not only verbal markers, but also affective ones such as anger, can also be evident in at least some forms of rule violation such as that described here. Research in anthropology has in fact recently witnessed a resurgent interest in affect or emotion as a culturally constituted experiential phenomenon (cf. Harkness and Kilbride 1983). It would prove theoretically useful, in the future, to pursue typological work on deviance in terms of affect. For instance, hard deviance (Raybeck, Chapter 2) with "high" public consequences (Thio 1978), such as murder, armed robbery, and cases of attempted infanticide such as Sara's, may evoke negative affect in other cross-cultural situations, too. The mob justice that Kenyans mete out to thieves and witches suggests another dimension to Savishinsky's model (see Chapter 3) of staged deviance—the public staging of outrage in response to covert deviant acts. Deviance and associated affective states, such as pity, anger, rage, and mirth, would warrant further cross-cultural study and comparison.

Significantly, however, not all members of Sara's audience offered hostile accounts of her behavior. This is, of course, a central point of labeling theory, which argues that judgments about deviance are relative and vary with the kind of audience making the appraisal. In general, the wider public considered Sara to be a serious criminal wrongdoer for whom punishment in some form was necessary. Her rule violation permitted no exceptions for special circumstance. For her family members, however, Sara's behavior was negotiable though troublesome in practical terms. Blame for the attempted infanticide was placed by family members not on Sara, but on others including the chief's office, school matron, and headmaster. The family, particularly her maternal kinsmen, worked collectively and rapidly to minimize Sara's, and therefore their own, stigma. It is quite clear that Sara's family perceived her situation, or at least the consequences of her wrongdoing, to be negotiable, and the faster the better. An important theoretical conclusion follows from this observation. We agree with Edgerton that deviance is essentially a social process that involves "creating an awareness of deviance as a property that is conferred upon an individual by others who disapprove of his actions or beliefs" (1980: 408). In fact, we could probably conclude that for Sara's family her behavior was not deviant at all. This interpretation would confirm Raybeck's argument that in small-scale societies that stress kin ties, there are fewer deviant roles and those that exist do not confer lifelong stigma. Raybeck believes that this follows from the multiroles and contexts within which individuals are normally enmeshed in small-scale societies.

Overall, our material strongly shows that labeling theory and strategic interactionism (the idea that labels are negotiable) provide a useful perspective to interpret the immediate interactional social conditions surrounding Sara's attempted infanticide. When our attention, however, focuses on the wider social order, we must shift our attention away from Sara's social context negotiations and must consider more directly the label itself. From this perspective the phrase "whose rules?" (Becker 1963), rather than the idea of potential negotiation of a rule violation, prompts one to ask, for example, why is infanticide something attempted almost exclusively by women, a troublesome behavior for which the wider society (Sara's "public" as opposed to her family) admits of no negotiation? In short, infanticide is a rule violation that is punishable without exception. Why, in Freilich's terms, has situationally "proper" behavior become universally "smart" and stigmatized? Young girls, for example, who commit infanticide (or attempt it) may never return to school. Such a nonnegotiable rule as this provides ethnographic support for the position that strategic interactionism, now so popular, is in need of a corrective revision, one that once again emphasizes theoretically the significance of social rules conceived of as "norms," sometimes without behavorial exception (Edgerton 1986). Accordingly, our interpretation of Sara's case would be incomplete without consideration of the context of social power (Thio 1978). It is a power dimension that will best account for Sara's nonnegotiable position *vis-à-vis* her wider public.

In Kenya, women are now more disadvantaged in social power relative to men today and women in the past. Such inequality is one kind of social context that cross-culturally often results in societies having rules with no exceptions, or rules whose violation is nonnegotiable. Edgerton, for example, writes, "Usually, however, it is the powerful who impose strict rules on others. In many societies, as we have seen, men use their social or religious dominance to hold women strictly liable for following certain rules" (1986: 227). Social inequality is an important social structural element in Sara's situation described above. She is without financial means to control her own affairs. Though her situation is by no means desperate (there are few job opportunities for teenagers), her family has had to struggle to provide school fees for her. Young women like Sara can no longer achieve social power solely through the reproduction of children and through their agricultural labor. The threat of "lack of school fees" is a most serious one in modern Kenya. One distinct disadvantage that renders women particularly powerless relative to men is their assumed culpability for bearing children out of wedlock.[4] Girls, not boys, are dismissed from school for getting pregnant. Girls are not permitted to return to school after cases of attempted infanticide. Many boys revealed to me that they did not acknowledge paternity in cases where they knew the child to be their own. In Sara's case not even one person from inside or outside her family considered the lover's behavior to be in any way problematic.

The refusal of the male to accept his illegitimate child, which was disapproved of in traditional times when paternity was welcome, is not problematic in the modern context. Such "smart" behavior has become tolerable. It has become so common that Sara did not view the father as a source of help for her and the baby—so much so that she did not even tell him she was pregnant or had delivered. This moral imbalance in modern gender roles represents historically an ethical delocalization. That is, local, traditional values more favorable to women have been replaced by standards from outside. In Kenya, the burden of childrearing now falls disproportionately on the shoulders of women, particularly in their role as mothers or grandmothers (Kilbride 1985). Kenyan men on the whole oppose birth control, often with the ethical support of powerful outside institutions. It was often acknowledged by male informants that women are no longer willing to bear children to capacity. This was exemplified by one informant, a medical doctor, who reported a strong preference among his married female patients for the pill as a birth control strategy. This was so that their husbands could be better deceived through secret use of the pill.

To conclude, our interpretation of Sara's empirical case is necessarily informed by several factors: consideration of social context including the modern Kenyan economy; social process, particularly the relativity of audience appraisal and subsequent negotiation; and social power, specifically the powerlessness of modern Kenyan women. It is important to note here that males also have less power than in the past because, as in the case of women, of changing economic circumstances associated with delocalization. For this reason, many men have no practical alternative but to avoid the burdens of expensive child care responsibilities. What is argued here is that the modern condition is particularly stressful for women, given that the gender imbalance in power is far more striking than in the past.

The present empirical ethnographic study builds upon an earlier one in East Africa where the author considered the disvalued occupation of barmaid among contemporary Baganda of Uganda. It was discovered that barmaids are negatively labeled by members of respectable Ugandan society. Kilbride (1979) established that Baganda barmaids conform to Goffman's (1963b) view of the stigmatized individual as one who is not accorded the respect and regard that the "uncontaminated" aspects of her social life would otherwise lead people to extend to her. Barmaid stigma results from a powerless position of the barmaid derived from her situation as an unmarried and marginally educated woman in a modernizing society. Wealth and authority in Uganda, like Kenya, is primarily in the hands of married men, and formal education is required for access to modern jobs. Married women are particularly hostile to barmaids, who frequently befriend married men. Barmaids are perceived as representing a threat to the wife's economic interests by being a drain on her husband's financial resources.

Theoretical interpretation of the barmaid materials employed labeling theory, but it also built on the "power" consideration of which Lofland (1978: 33) has written: "If it is possible to isolate a category of deviance . . . it is essential that there be involved at least a powerful minority, even if not a majority, who feel a strong sense of threat and fear." In premodern times in Buganda (a region where Baganda reside) it would appear that the only female role that was stigmatized was that of barren women (Roscoe 1911). The emergence of new categories of troublesome female behavior, such as that of the barmaid and prostitute, represents in Uganda an overall loss of female power and influence compared to the agrarian past. Previously most Baganda women enjoyed productive economic roles that were different from but symmetrical to those of men, and they enjoyed prestige for bearing children as well (Kilbride 1979).

The Uganda and Kenya situations are not unusual in the developing world, where women have generally experienced a loss of social power because of the colonial policies of recent times (Etienne and Leacock 1980). In fact, one good index of people's loss of power in modernization research could well be the frequency of deviant roles at various points in a society's modernization history. Similarly, temporal variation in a society's definition of "proper" behavior is precisely the sort of evidence needed to substantiate the social etiological assumption of labeling theory. That is, "deviant behavior is behavior that people so label" (Becker 1963: 9). Modern women, such as barmaids in Uganda and infanticidal mothers in Kenya, are now implicated in disvalued actions that were once not problematic for their grandparents' generation. As stated, Kenyans knew about but did not always disapprove of infanticide (Wagner 1949), and Baganda women traditionally served as beer brewers without stigma

(Robbins and Pollnac 1969). The modern disvalued roles are, therefore, clearly social constructions in Becker's (1963) sense.

A final theoretical point should be emphasized here. As noted, anthropology has yet to develop a theoretical perspective or body of comparative field data specifically concerned with deviance. It is hoped that this study will stimulate further theoretical work on deviance through an increased awareness of the modernizati·n process so often studied by anthropologists. This process provides a rich opportunity to test propositions now under consideration in the deviance literature. This is possible because, as noted by Poggie and Lynch (1974), modernization is a process of worldwide social, economic, and cultural transformation involving change from a traditional way of life to a technologically advanced mode of modern life. Such modernization often results, as we have seen here, in the emergence of new disvalued behavior. Modern social processes, such as delocalization, can be theoretically assessed for their potential significance in the interpretation of new forms of deviance. Such research can shed light, for example, on the significance of deviance as a labeling process and as a social construction.

CHILD ABUSE AS LABELED DEVIANCE: THEORETICAL AND APPLIED CONSIDERATIONS

In the context of modern Kenya, infanticide is a form of criminal child abuse. To consider this behavior as only a moral shortcoming worthy of jail, or as grounds for preclusion from reentry into school or respectable society, is to entirely miss the point. Child abuse in Kenya is best interpreted as a social form of constituted deviance, one that is informed by consideration of power and social context. In other countries, where social factors have been seen as the main cause of child abuse, practical efforts have proved effective in eliminating child abuse on a national scale. For the People's Republic of China, for example, Korbin reports that under the prerevolutionary ethic of filial "piety," children were considered the sole property of their parents. As such, they could be dealt with in whatever manner the parents chose, with little or no interference from outsiders. Severe beatings, female infanticide, child slavery, the selling of young girls in prostitution, child betrothal, and footbinding were common (1981: 167). Korbin believes that along with a modern transformation of the structure of Chinese society, the experience of childhood has also changed. Although no specific studies of child abuse exist and information from rural areas is scanty, Korbin's own impression, and that of other specialists who have also visited China or written about children there, are optimistic. These observers report "very few cases" (Korbin 1981) of abuse, which constitutes a striking contrast with the past. Korbin notes that "neighborhood vigilance concerning child welfare is well developed. Such watchfulness not only prevents child mistreatment, but it is built into the structure of a society whose members are all concerned with and responsible for the welfare of others" (1981: 171). In an observation that is central to the theoretical argument advanced here, she concludes, "Because of the nature of the community, intervention occurs before potential abuse or neglect reaches the level at which the child is damaged or the *parent labeled a child abuser*" (1981: 192 emphasis added).

Unlike the situation in many other modernizing societies, it appears that female power has increased with modernization in China. Women there, for example, are frequently employed, have maternity leave, and enjoy access to abortion services. These and other efforts in China to improve the status of women are no doubt associated with the apparent decline in child abuse there. In the United States, enhancing people's social support networks is also an effective measure for the prevention of child abuse. In Los Angeles, for example, a parent-aide program was established for abusive parents "to provide them with someone in the community who would fulfill the role of a good neighbor" (Kent 1979: 621). Salaried aides were recruited from among a pool of university students and unwed mothers. The program proved quite effective in relieving the stresses associated with babysitting, loneliness, or the participants' general social, physical, and economic isolation from other people. The parent-aide program is consistent with what Kent refers to as a "systems" approach, which "calls for radical change in those social conditions which predispose people to abuse, such as inequities in wealth, education, opportunities and quality of life. Proponents of the systems approach also advocate establishing widespread networks of supports for parents. . ." (1979: 628).

It would appear that child abuse can be greatly curtailed or even eliminated in societies where the collective moral responsibilities of the nation, family, or neighborhood are more heavily weighted than are individual responsibilities. Thus, child abuse is rare in traditional Africa in general (LeVine and LeVine 1981) and in rural Kenya in particular, where the extended family is important (Fraser and Kilbride 1981; Kilbride 1985). Even research in the United States, where kin or neighborhood bonds are comparatively weak, shows that families isolated from relatives and friends show higher rates of violence than do other families (Strauss and Gelles 1979). The present study of infanticide in Kenya has shown that this modern form of deviance can be best understood as the outcome of specific social circumstances. If this argument is valid, it points to obvious clues for the prevention and eventual elimination of infanticide and probably other forms of child abuse in Kenya. By theoretical extension, the analysis and prescription argued here for Kenya could be applied to the Western industrialized world as well.

NOTES

The field research for this chapter was supported by a grant from the National Science Foundation, United States of America. The Institute of African Studies, Nairobi University, Kenya, is thanked for the assistance during my tenure there (1984-85) as a research associate. Dr. Janet Kilbride provided assistance in data collection while in the field and editorial comment on this manuscript. An earlier version of this chapter was presented at the American Anthropological Association National Convention, Philadelphia, December 1986.

1. See, for example, Raybeck (1981), who examined women in Malay society, and Gregory (1984) for a position paper on male researchers working with female informants or issues.

2. Nevertheless, some churches have recently become critical of the modern economy. Some Bishops have advocated in print acceptance of polygamy.

3. When I returned to Kenya in 1990 Sara told me that her mother now fully supports her son. He does not know that Sara is his mother, and others where she now lives do not know about her concealed past.

4. In accordance with British-derived law, only mothers are legally responsible for supporting children born out of wedlock.

6 THE "VOICE" OF THE DESPICABLE: DEVIANCE, SPEAKING, AND POWER IN YEMENI TRIBAL SOCIETY

Steven C. Caton

Anthropologists have taken over their concept of deviance from the sociological literature. It is time, surely, to reconceptualize the analysis of deviance in terms more relevant to contemporary anthropological notions of culture (Freilich 1989a). Three points warrant analysis: First, deviance is not simply the violation of norms. It is a complex symbolic representation of the person understood as a social category or type. The theoretical point to be gleaned from this observation is that the analysis of deviance is as much a problem of symbolic representation—the cultural construction of persons—as with the violation of particular social norms.[1]

Second, this symbolic representation of the deviant person is imposed by the dominant group; it is a form of "symbolic violence" that damages the social persona of the individual (Bourdieu 1972: 190-97). Hence the classification, assignment, or labeling, as well as the actual taking on of deviance by the subordinate group or individuals, all have to do with power. Labeling theorists, to some extent, are sensitive to the fact that the categorization and assignment of deviance go hand in hand with power. Indeed, they ask the question "Whose norms form the yardstick against which deviance is measured?" (Becker 1963). However, for labeling theorists power is a secondary issue.[2] Yet it is precisely in light of power that one must try to explain the existence and nature of deviant labels.

Power, the capacity to make others do what one wants, remains a problematic concept. As Dumont (1977: 19) correctly suggests, one of the more complex and obscure aspects of power is its relationship to ideology and to social symbolic representation. However, Dumont's explication of the relationships between ideology and power is incomplete. As Pevin (1981: 501) reminds us, power is also interactionally determined. In concrete situations and interactions, even subordinate groups have a certain power over the dominant one. Therefore, those who receive a pejorative label, while disadvantaged, are not necessarily rendered entirely powerless. Humans have an uncanny ability to exploit even their own weaknesses to exert power over others.

Finally, symbolic domination serves to exclude nondominant groups or individuals from benefits in a particular political and economic system. Hence the "grounding" of symbolic representation and power in the system of ownership of the means of production cannot be neglected.[3] Moreover, concrete acts of production are themselves invested with symbolic meanings in the cultural system (Sahlins 1976). The result is that an act of economic production is never merely a means of earning a livelihood but simultaneously is an act of cultural construction of the person. In turn, this cultural construction reconfirms the status system and power relations of the society at large, a process that works in the interest of the dominant group (Bourdieu 1972; Bourdieu and Passeron 1977). The person labeled as deviant, therefore, often is forced by the dominant group into engaging in marginal economic activities, which are themselves laden with negative social meanings. These social connotations in turn reconfirm the deviant's subdominant status and hence his or her relative powerlessness in society. This vicious circle is closed when a subdominant status along with powerlessness become legitimate reasons in the eyes of the empowered group for labeling certain individuals as "deviant."

In short, while I analyze deviance from a perspective that has been anticipated by labeling theorists, my emphasis on certain aspects of symbolic representation, power, and economic relations seems to represent a new synthesis. I illustrate the utility of this synthesis by analyzing the situation of a North Yemeni servant group known as the *khaddaam*; with a special focus on khaddaam speech behavior, which the dominant group define as deviant.[4]

The khaddaam case is interesting for several reasons. First, the case illustrates a situation in which the imposed deviant label is so inclusive that it constitutes a symbolic representation of the whole person. Second, while this negative representation is imposed by the dominant (tribal) group, the servant group is able to exploit the deviant identity to achieve certain powers and alliances. Third, both the linguistic and the social roles of the khaddaam serve the power interests of the dominant tribal group. Finally, this case draws attention to the importance of studying language from the perspective of speech deviance per se.[5]

The last point needs some clarification. Servants engage in work (including crucial verbal tasks) for which they are rewarded in a direct and often substantial monetary form. This work, however, is labeled deviant by the dominant group and is therefore forbidden to the latter's members. As a consequence, certain individuals of the servant group can and do become wealthier than their tribal patrons. In what sense, then, can we be right in affirming that the imposition of deviant categories on the subdominant group serves the interests of the dominant group? If the consequence of this imposition is that the subdominant group can exploit an economic niche to its own advantage, how can we still argue that the subdominant group is being oppressed?

Part of the explanation for this apparent anomaly is historical. That is, it has only been in recent times, when the Arabian Peninsula as a whole has undergone extraordinary economic and social transformations as a result of oil production, that pariah groups like the servants have been able to accumulate large amounts of capital earned abroad or in low-status jobs inside the country. Because of their low status, these groups were not obliged to spend their capital on lavish entertainment or to support a hugely extended kin network. They have thereby become economically dominant over their tribal masters. External changes have thus produced a situation in which, perhaps for the first time, the subdominant group is in a position to challenge the dominant one.

The second explanation has to do with the way in which cultural systems reproduce in symbolically laden economic activities, the social status system. In other words, what the khaddaam do economically is financially rewarding but socially punitive. In fulfilling their role, then, they also recreate the power of the dominant group (Bourdieu and Passeron 1977). Furthermore, as we shall see, the dominant group prevents the deviantly defined one from transforming itself symbolically and thereby climbing to the top of the social hierarchy. I refer to this as the "hermetics" of the symbolic system that serves the interests of the dominant group.

ETHNOGRAPHY

North Yemen, located in the southwestern corner of the Arabian Peninsula, is a mountainous country flanked by an arid coastal strip to the west and the fringes of the vast interior desert known as the Empty Quarter to the east. It is the central highland region that concerns us here, which is inhabited by predominantly sedentary tribesmen cultivating terraced fields of sorghum, barley, wheat, corn, a variety of different vegetables, and the *qat* plant, a lucrative cash crop whose succulent leaves are chewed for their slightly narcotic effect. At one time considered to be the breadbasket of the Arabian Peninsula, these lands have seen an alarming shrinkage in agricultural production ever since young males have found it more profitable to work in the oil-producing countries rather than in their own gardens. Imported agricultural products are paid for out of income from remittance payments sent by immigrants to their relatives back home.

The social system of this rural area is composed of three main groups: the tribesmen (*qabaayil*, pl. of *qabiilah*); the religious elite, who claim legitimacy either by virtue of descent from the Prophet, in which case they are generally known as *saadah* (pl. of *sayyid*), or by virtue exclusively of their religious learning and piety, in which case they are also known as *qudhaa*, "judges" (pl. of *qaadhi*); and the khaddaam or servants to the tribes and the saadah. It is too simplistic to maintain that there is one agreed-upon social hierarchy, for the tribesmen see themselves as the privileged group, whereas the religious elite claim this distinction for themselves. There is much competition for power between them, but both consider the servants beneath them. The tribes and the servants will be described in greater detail below; given space limitations, I will not say anything more about the religious elite.

The North Yemeni tribes subscribe to the Zaidi sect of Shiᶜaa Islam (similar to the Iranian Shiᶜaa), but what is far more important is the ideology of history and honor by which they interpret action. They consider themselves to be descendants of the most ancient Arabs, namely the sons of Noah, who supposedly settled in the Yemeni highlands to found not only the capital Sanᶜaa but also the great kingdoms that arose 3,000 to 3,500 years ago along the spice and incense routes of southern Arabia. Ruins in which they read the testimony of their past greatness can be found everywhere, but particularly in the dam at Marib and the columns of monumental buildings located in its vicinity; these are impressive even to one who has seen Abu Simbel and Ninaveh. Present deeds are interpreted in light of past greatness; past greatness is confirmed by present glory. Hence a code of honor informs action that is supposed to replicate the heroism of the past. Land, for example, belongs to the tribe and must be defended from encroachment by other tribes or else honor is lost. Women become symbolic of male honor and must be protected and controlled for very much the same reason; that is why they are veiled, segregated from strange males, and kept in the private domain. In addition, a man must achieve honor through "glorious deeds" (Meeker 1976), which include lavish hospitality, valor in warfare, and oratory.

A man of honor is a man of his word, though "plain speaking" is not necessarily valued for its own sake as it is in our culture. The truth ought to be heard between the lines, and the ability to allude subtly is much prized. However, one ought to openly challenge another man's honor if one has been wronged by him, though the challenge should never be hurled in anger. It is delivered with control over one's passions, as shown by a loud though steady voice, a stylized though determined way of speaking, and an unflinching resolve. Above all, a tribesman embodies in himself the man of honor and power through his poetry, which he may be called upon on many occasions—public or private—to produce. Indeed, the most exalted way in which to honor another and to challenge him is through verse.

The servant category is the structural reverse of the tribal one. Within this category, a distinction is made between the *muzeyyin* (roughly translated as "one who embellishes or makes something appear pleasing," such as a barber or a musician), and the *dooshaan*, who is a kind of professional "town crier." The dooshaan on whom we will focus our attention is a man whose words are lacking in honor. The servant of either type lives with his family surrounded by tribesmen in the village. He is rarely found in separate quarters and almost never in separate settlements (except in the southeastern region of the country). He gains his livelihood by performing various tasks, disdained as "dishonorable" by the tribes, for which he is paid in agricultural products or cold cash. He is a minority both in numbers and in power.

Servant and Tribesman

The category of servant does not really represent anything positive so much as it does the absence of the meanings associated with the category of the tribesman. One of the commonly accepted origin myths of this category makes this absence dramatically clear. In the days of the ancient Yemeni kingdoms, there was constant warfare among the tribes who were vying for control of the lucrative spice trade. It is said that occasionally one of the sons of these kings would lose heart in battle and act despicably by fleeing from the enemy. How did the king respond to his son's cowardice? Not by execution, nor by incarceration, nor by any corporal punishment. Rather, he was stripped of his honor, lost his rights over tribal land, and was forced to become the servant of the tribe, doing all the work despised by men of honor. In return for his services the warrior-turned-servant would receive one-fifth of the war booty (hence, the epithet for this servant class as "the people of the fifth").

As the myth makes clear, servant and warrior come from the same stock. True, one can distinguish ancestors with different characters, heroic and nonheroic, and argue that the servant and the warrior trace their lines to these different types. But I suspect that this would be more our way of looking at the problem of descent than theirs, for what the origin myth emphasizes, and what is communicated in daily interaction, is that the servant is historically a tribesman manqué. It is almost a form of reverse Platonism, he has all the appearance of a tribesman with none of the essence. If one loses sight of the fact that it is really the absence of tribalness which marks the servant, one misses entirely the pathos of this culture: the tribesman sees in his servant an abject lesson (there, but for the grace of God, go I) and the servant sees the irony of his own situation in always appearing to be like a tribesman but fundamentally never being one.

How, then, is this symbolic relationship of tribesman and servant expressed in daily interaction? In the most obvious reflection of his status as tribesman manqué, the servant does not, indeed cannot, carry weapons, except perhaps for the largely ceremonial dagger known as the *jambiyyah*. He has no honor to defend. The tribesman, to the contrary, has and therefore keeps a weapon by his side, because his honor is always vulnerable to attack. The servant, like the Christian and the Jew, is *maskiin* (weak) and therefore under tribal protection, but no one protects the tribesman, for he and his kinsmen are independent and stand alone. This absence of a weapon on the servant's person is made all the more conspicuous by the fact that the dress of the servant and tribesman is otherwise indistinguishable. Both don the same cloth headgear—a loose kind of turban, both wear a jacket and undershirt, along with the pleated, knee-length skirt (*magtab*), and both sport leather sandals or plastic shoes. But what is crucially missing on the servant's shoulder is the rifle. The similarity between them extends physically to their skin color, which is the same light brown, and for this reason the servant (khaddaam) is most readily distinguishable from another servant in Yemem (called the *akhdaam*) whose color we would consider "black" or negroid.

It is their deeds, not their appearances, however, which really set the categories of tribesman and servant apart. The tribesman owns lands, one of the great symbols of his honor, and works it; the servant may not own land but can only rent it (at least in the tribal regions). Therefore he is not engaged in cultivation but usually receives his grains (like his cash) from the primary producers, the tribesmen, in payment for his menial services to the tribe. These services include the following: he butchers meat, circumcises young male children, acts as the village barber, runs errands between villages or within the village, acts as a master-of-ceremonies on ritual occasions such as weddings whose feasts and other celebrations he arranges, and he plays on the tambourine or a kazoo-like instrument or sings for the guests. Some of these activities are connected in other cultures with the notion of pollution, but in tribal Yemen I never found this a particularly useful concept to explain why they were negatively valued. The one exception may be music-making, which tribesmen occasionally deem to be sacrilegious because of a Prophetic *hadiith* that takes a dim view of it. It is important to note, however, that there are two culturally perceived ways of using the human voice, singing (*ghinaa*) and chanting (*sayhah*), and that only women and servants are thought to sing whereas tribesmen chant. The Arabic term for chanting is also used for the warrior's battle cry, another association with honor that would exclude the servant. The point is that the servant inhabits the economic-aesthetic space vacated by the honorable tribesmen.

Perhaps it is in the activity of speaking connected with a particular servant known as the dooshaan that the representation of the tribesman manqué is most interesting and at the same time most profound. The label comes from the Arabic *dooshah*, "palavar," which is sometimes used to describe loud and idle chatter. A tribal poet once said to me, "Why don't you come back to talk to me when the doosha*h* is over in here," referring scornfully to the conversational bedlam in his sitting room. Conversation, according to the tribal view, should be pointed and purposeful, not diffuse and idle. Silence is preferable to chitchat. A Yemeni proverb says: *laa takuun thartharan been an-naas*, "Don't be a chatterbox among the people." Precisely how the servant in question contravenes this norm of speaking will become clearer shortly.

The dooshaan performs a number of verbal tasks for the village and is paid for his services. For example, when the pilgrim (*haajji*) returns from Mecca, the dooshaan is hired by relatives of the haajji to greet the arrival loudly at the village entrance, a greeting overflowing with religious encomia. Or, during a particular moment of the groom's wedding ceremony, the dooshaan will enter the hall, seat himself in the middle of the assembly facing the groom, and then proceed to greet him, his family, and his friends with lavish praise. Should a major feast be held in the village, the dooshaan may be hired to climb onto the rooftop and laud the host's generosity and nobility at the top of his lungs. When important village proclamations have to be heard or when there is a major tribal gathering at which public announcements are to be made, the dooshaan will rise to the occasion as a sort of town crier. The more modern ones even use a battery-operated bullhorn for that purpose. In war he may carry messages between the enemies, since his protected status theoretically keeps him out of harm's way. A distinctive emotional tone is projected by the loud, brash, and exaggerated manner in which the town crier uses his voice. It contrasts with the more modulated, controlled, and economical style of speaking common to the tribesmen; it has the tone of a parody or a burlesque act. More significant still is the fact that when flattering the tribesman, the dooshaan cannot hope to receive praise in return because, not being a man of honor, he is therefore not praiseworthy. The only thing he receives is cash in exchange for his praise, money that the tribesman disdains.

Let us briefly examine one of these contexts in greater depth, namely the dooshaan's appearance at the groom's wedding *samrah* (an evening devoted to pleasant conversation and amusing games). The guests are assembled in a large hall, chewing the slightly narcotic *qat* leaf and conversing among themselves, when the dooshaan suddenly makes a dramatic entrance. He seats himself before the groom in the center of the hall and delivers a speech of about five minutes in length that honors the groom and particular members of his family. His language is rhythmic, alliterative, metaphorical, and highly formulaic. It employs greetings and other speech acts of *mujaamilah*, "flattery," reminiscent of what one commonly hears in tribal poetry, except that it appears even more effusive. I was, in fact, so struck by the similarity that I exclaimed to my neighbor at a wedding the first time I heard the speech, "By God, that's poetry!" He immediately denied it. When I asked him to explain why it wasn't, he could not or would not defend his position though he adamantly stuck to it. In subsequently examining the dooshaan's speeches, however, I found that the meter and rhyme schemes were highly irregular in comparison with the more complex and rigid forms tribal poets self-consciously compose in. Perhaps this fact explains my neighbor's reaction, for he took what I would have called "poetic prose" to be no more than doggerel. This was because of its irregularities of form, which signified to him the absence of tribalness. More specifically, this could be heard in the lack of control over passion as it flowed into form. In other words, we are left with the presumption that only tribesmen can be poets, and everyone else must fall short of this artistic pinnacle. What I heard was obviously not verse.

At the end of his speech, the dooshaan was openly given a purse of coins. This purse was not cordially handed to him, however, but thrown his way, almost contemptuously. Though the drama of the gesture made a deep impression, its explanation escaped me until much later. For what I learned was that according to tribal ideology, a true poet would not, indeed cannot, accept money for his verse (at least not publicly), and so the assembly was reminded in this way that the man to whom the purse was flung could not be a tribesman. In exchange for his words, a tribesman receives honor, not coin. A servant, if he is to receive anything, cannot receive honor, but only money or the products from lands owned by someone else. Thus the servant is a greater beneficiary in economic terms but a loser in symbolic transactions.

Although a dooshaan cannot be a poet in the tribesman's sense of the term, he is usually given the task of memorizing the tribesman's verse. If his voice is good, he may be commissioned to sing it publicly. I knew some singers who had memorized hundreds of poems, and the best of them could make a small fortune from their performances, especially nowadays when the sale of tape recordings more than triples their incomes. But in accordance with Bakhtin's concept of "voice" (Bakhtin 1981), they are only reporting the speech of the tribesman, and are unable to originate that speech themselves because the system forbids it. They are deprived of the power to originate discourse through which persons are able to create themselves as tribesmen.

Oppressed though the dooshaan may be, he is not in reality altogether powerless. His power lies in his vituperativeness, a sort of symbolic aggression that borders on insanity. Another Yemeni proverb says: *laa tasubb wa laa tizⁿal*, "Don't curse and don't get angry." In one sense, this is a religious injunction; that is, don't take the name of the Lord in vain. But it is more significantly frought with social sanctions. The ideal tribesman is able to master his or her passion, not by extirpating it like the aesthetic, but by channeling it into a creative social practice (e.g., a controlled challenge, a mediation of a dispute, a poem, etc.). The point is that he or she is in control of the emotion, not the other way around. Cursing, on the other hand, is culturally perceived as an act of weakness, where the speaker is out of control of his or her emotions. True, there is always a fine line between pure reference and vilification in "calling a spade a spade," but the tribesman should know how to walk that line and keep his balance. During the evening poetry performances at the groom's wedding ceremony mentioned above, for example, tribesmen will pair off in duel-like exchanges that border on cursing, but as soon as one of them is provoked to call the other a "horse's ass," he has lost the match.[6] Immediately an elder will step into the fray and bring order back to the performance. In an important sense, this little altercation is allegorical for the groom watching the proceedings; it is he who is about to assume adult responsibilities by marrying, setting up a household and supporting children, and he must know how to act the role of the tribesman. The dooshaan, on the contrary, can tongue-lash another, even a tribesman, cursing him for his stinginess or cowardice or falsehoods, and still remain immune from censure. People will say of him, "But he's just like the *johaal*" (children), meaning in effect that like immature beings the dooshaan is ignorant and undomesticated.

The victim of a dooshaan's curses is a tribesman, a man of power, who ironically cannot avenge himself on his verbal assassin, or at least not openly, for the aggressor is "weak" and must be protected according to the honor code. Now, the tribesman is not a random object of his cursing, but it is assumed by the audience that he deserves it because he has himself transgressed or deviated. In other words, it is assumed that the town crier is not acting on his own motives but has been put up to it by other tribesmen or is acting on behalf of the larger moral community. In terms of Savishinsky's model (Chapter 3), the publicly staged deviance of the dooshaan is used to expose the deviant acts of tribesmen. In reality, I was told, the dooshaan might be paid by an elder or even a jealous rival to attack someone who was irritating public sensibilities or threatening someone else's power, though I never could confirm this. Once again we see that he is no more than a "voice" who is reporting the gossip he has heard in the village. But he is a most convenient one, for if a tribesman were to accuse another tribesman of wrongdoing, a public challenge would probably ensue with a long and sometimes expensive and tedious litigation in its train. The dooshaan is excused, however, because he is just not honorable, not just right in his head, not quite an adult.

The power of the town crier lies, though, in this: that he can occasionally manipulate the dramatic situation to his own advantage because of the supposed anonymity of the slanderer. That is, he can act as if he had heard damning gossip about his victim but offer to keep quiet for a small fee. If the unnamed victim of the slander calls his bluff and the dooshaan talks maliciously about him in public, the tribesman seriously risks blemishing his reputation, for we all know very well that proof of wrong doing is not required to make people believe the worst of an enemy or an unpopular person. Also, in situations where the dooshaan is acting on behalf of someone else, the former can often obtain hush money from the latter by threatening to betray his identity to the victim. Thus, if the dooshaan is devious about his communicative deviance, he can make a little pocket money. A Yemeni proverb says, "Cut off the dooshaan's tongue with giving (gifts)."

The terrible irony of the dooshaan's power, however, is that by cursing another he is showing himself to be irrational or childlike; in other words, less than tribal, indeed less than adult. He is thus publicly confirming his lower status and his ultimate powerlessness. His actions generate his own socially demeaning categorization of self.

We have been concerned with the official or public situations in which tribesmen and servant interact with each other. Let us now turn to the unofficial ones where the servant might act "deviantly" with respect to the ideals of the dominant group. For example, a muzeyyin who would be carving up a newly butchered carcass (a job that his social status requires him to perform and which neither the *gabiili* nor the *sayyid* would dream of doing) starts to horse around with his higher-status observers, almost to the point where he seems voluntarily to become the butt of their jokes. He, not they, takes up pieces of raw meat and gnashes his teeth on them, pretending he is a famished dog (the most pariah of animals). Or he may obscenely dangle a sliver between his legs to the amusement of the audience. His gestures are overdrawn and slapstick, his face contorted in awful grimaces, his legs exaggeratedly bowed as if he could not walk steadily. In brief, his figure is that of the clown, except for the fact that there is no costume and makeup to conceal the identity of the actor. He is naked before his ridiculers. While in one sense the audience is laughing at the antics performed by the individual, on a deeper level they are clearly laughing at the absence of dignity his social person implies. He in turn pretends they are laughing only at his antics while being mortified at the deeper and more insidious implications of the jest. In any case, he is forced to condemn himself.

We have learned that the dooshaan is often loud and brash and some of them even have a reputation for being insane, a reputation that can be manipulated by the dominant group in certain social interactions. I was once in a market when a famous dooshaan strode onto the scene to make a grain purchase. The store owner teased him and egged him on, until the tall, imposing man obliged his importunings by acting the very part expected of him. He rolled his eyes, spoke in a booming "stage" voice, accosted me as though he were about to pummel me with his walking stick, and acted brashly toward the other customers as well. They all giggled and pointed at him in amusement and he seemed to laugh with them. Then, just as suddenly, he dropped the performance of the deranged fool, the idiot, and became an entirely changed man, seriously and cunningly haggling with the store owner over the price of his goods.

How does one analyze these scenes? The individual in the center of them is clearly playing a dramatic role in a command performance. It is "staged deviance" on center stage, and it is a role that not just anyone can assume. If a tribesman were to behave this way, his family would slit his throat. It is a role, in other words, that represents the despicableness of the individual playing it, but because the enactment takes place for the amusement of the upper-status tribesmen, it also serves to represent to them their social superiority. It is a role that only the low-status can play and it is also one they cannot voluntarily shed. They are coerced into playing it, even though they are made to appear to play their part voluntarily. The servant is condemned by the tribal system to deviance and, as such, to submission. And he is made to agree with the efficacy or rightness of the tribesman's imposition of that perspective on him by colluding in a performance of self-parody. It is the ultimate form of domination: the oppressed "voluntarily" represents himself as damned.

Certain culturally valued economic transactions are forbidden to the khaddaam, and it is precisely when one understands which economic activities he is allowed to engage in and which not that one also grasps the extent to which his oppression is symbolic. There was one khaddaam I knew well who was reputed by his covillagers to be a millionaire. It was said that he was fortunate in having had strong, intelligent, loyal, and hard-working sons who emigrated to Saudi Arabia during the height of the oil boom and made small fortunes which they sent back to their father. He invested the money shrewdly in large, earth-hauling equipment that his sons operated for an enormous fee to clients building houses in the area; it went into automobiles that his sons drove as taxis; and it was invested in stores he set up in the village market. Then, there came a time when he wanted to build a house on village-owned land and asked permission to buy a plot. Permission was denied on the ground that he was not a member of the status group and never could be; thus, owning land rather than renting it was unthinkable. In such an agricultural region land is, of course, at a premium, but was the motive to deny him permission purely or even essentially economic? Note the correlation between land and the concept of honor on the one hand, and the presumed despicableness of certain occupations on the other. The latter include selling one's labor to another (as in the case of taxi driver or tractor operator), or of engaging in the low-status occupation of trade. The khaddaam could become rich, and I knew some who were better off than many of their tribal or sayyid counterparts. But this did not happen in a way that would allow them to be a tribesman or a sayyid. Their oppression was not in having to remain poor but in remaining symbolically powerless. Furthermore, the very means by which the servant is allowed to earn his livelihood—labor which is denigrated by the culture—reinforces the symbolic representation of him as a subordinate in the system. It is only by leaving that system that he can escape this kind of symbolic bondage. And this is one of the reasons that many khaddaam leave the tribal regions for the cities. It is in the variable, changing, and relatively anonymous urban system that they can climb to the top of the power echelon. Some, in fact, have done this; for example, the first president of Yemen was of khaddaam status. Otherwise, they leave to work abroad.

CONCLUSION

Let me end on a discussion of the prosperous servant whose sons labored in Saudi Arabia. He was a renowned storyteller and jokester whose verbal skills would make an interesting study, and so I interviewed him. He suddenly dropped his jovial mood and asked me: "Is it true that blacks in America have equal rights?" Perhaps I was temporarily stunned by the suddenness of the question or else I hesitated to reply because of its complexity, but for a long time I didn't answer and then I basically said that they were still discriminated against. "But the law does uphold their rights?" he persisted. Then he told me that he had tried to buy land in the village for his house, but the villagers refused to permit the sale and he had no recourse but to accept their refusal. Domination in this case was not by economic means, for the old man was as wealthy as any villager, and, if the owner had been interested in selling it for such a substantial profit, he could have bought the land for ten times its market value. Rather, what was at stake was symbolic power: to be a landowner is to be a man of honor and thus to be confirmed as a legitimate "master" in the society. Money payment for services rendered often contradicts the code of honor: a man of honor receives honor for the services he renders the tribe; a man who lacks honor receives only money (or its equivalent)—that is, symbolically unmediated capital—for services he renders the tribe. In many ways, the symbolic world is the economic one reversed.

The point is that deviance, as a negative representation of the person, is imposed by the dominant group on the old servant in order to confirm its own superiority and to exclude him from status. It thereby also disbars him from empowering activities that depend on high status (e.g., leadership in the tribe). In the Yemeni case, the servant's deviance requires the violation of certain norms. The real insight is that what is constituted in their violation is a cultural construct of the person diametrically at odds with that of the tribesman, whose actions are ideally based on such honorable endeavors as fighting to defend one's honor, owning land, composing poetry, and in general maintaining control over one's passions. The servant in all cases represents the absence of honor, but no more so than in the patterns of his speaking. He may vilify the other in language in a manner that borders on insanity and get away with his transgression because he is deviant. On the other hand, he is not capable of exhibiting the sort of control tribesmen have over their complex verse forms and he will thus chop up his rhythms and rhymes. He is expected to tell jokes and is indeed expected to become the butt of them, as we have seen, because he has no dignity to uphold. But woe to him who should laugh at rather than with a tribesman. As a praise singer, the servant receives capital and not praise in payment, for he is not praiseworthy. And in general he is capable only of reporting the speech of others because his own voice is devoid of authority. His own assertions brand him a liar because he is devoid of honor.

As the case of the older servant reveals, it is almost impossible for servants to escape these negative valuations imposed on them by the tribe. In order to live, the servant obviously must labor, but the objective conditions of his labor are frought with symbolic meanings that only reconfirm his subordination and the tribal masters' dominance. The irony is that the more he labors and the more economic capital he accumulates, the more the value of his symbolic stock tumbles. So complete, so hermetically sealed is this closed system of the symbolic representation of the person that, at one and the same time, it classifies the products and practices of the economic world, which in turn replicate the symbolic order and the sociopolitical hierarchy. The servant is thus condemned to powerlessness unless the world is transformed radically by outside pressures or the servant leaves it for another.

As we have seen, the servant is not completely powerless. Quite the contrary is true. This can be seen in both his interaction with tribesmen, whom he can blackmail, and in his ability to accumulate capital. However, while some successful individuals may attempt to transform their circumstances and shed their stigmatized selves by moving or by buying their way into respectability, these efforts are very often frustrated. Like the damned, his deviance is irrevocable.

NOTES

I thank Margo MacLeod, Daniel Chambliss, Dennis Gilbert, and Douglas Raybeck for their helpful criticism of earlier drafts of this paper.

1. In this chapter I develop a notion of symbolic representation that owes much to the structuralist idea that conceptual categories are communicated through sign vehicles and are always in a system of relationships with other categories; but this essay also draws on the kind of symbolic interactionist approach pioneered by Mead.

2. That is, in the labeling approach it may be recognized that the assignment of deviance labels is used by some for the purpose of dominating others, but according to this view the existence of the labels is not to be explained in terms of power but in terms of a concept of society dependent upon moral or behavioral norms and their enforcement.

3. See Randall Collins (1982: 94-109) for an interesting attempt to synthesize a Durkheimian concern for symbolic representations with a Marxist analysis of class to account for the labeling of deviant behavior.

4. The notion of deviance I am talking about should not be confused with the term deviance as it is used in grammatical discussions. The latter concept has to do with violations of rules of grammar or the relatively context-free, semantico-referential system. The notion of deviance I invoke is related to norms of speaking serving a multitude of distinct communicative functions in variable contexts of use. If there are certain "ways of speaking" that can be said to be culturally preferred in the speech community, there are also other speech patterns that are considered "deviant" or "abnormal" in relation to these.

5. See, for example, E. Sapir (1915) and E. Lemert (1967). There are also works in related literatures that bear on the study of speech deviance. Erving Goffman (1981), has an interesting discussion of "talking to oneself" and he also shows how deviance can be employed by people as a way of "keying" social situations (1974). Keith H. Basso describes the way Western Apaches will imitate Anglo joking routines that deviate from Apache moral norms (1979). Remarks on the culturally perceived deviance of various American English accents such as Black Street English or Puerto Rican English can be culled from a vast sociolinguistic literature. To carve out, in a sense, a field of inquiry having to do with "speech deviance" would require a review of these literatures that this article does not presume to undertake.

6. For an example, see Caton (1985).

7   DEVIANT CAREERS: THE *HIJRAS* OF INDIA

Serena Nanda

My fate is written on my forehead.

—Salima

I make my living with my feet.

—Kamaladevi

Now that I am a mother-in-law and have a grandson, I get full respect.

—Sushila

Men come to us as they do to a woman. God made such people so that we, too, could earn a living.

—Mira

Salima, Kamaladevi, Sushila, and Mira are all *hijras*—members of a highly organized community and religious cult in India, made up of eunuchs, transvestites, transsexuals, hermaphrodites, and homosexuals. The cultural definition of hijra is that of intersexed, impotent men who undergo emasculation, wear female clothing, and adopt female behavior. They are viewed as neither male nor female, but "in between," containing elements of both sexes but not being fully either.[1] The hijra are thus a genuine example of an institutionalized, albeit deviant, alternative gender role.

Hijras are devotees of the goddess Bahuchara Mata, a version of the mother goddess worshipped all over India. In her name, as vehicles of her power to give blessings, the hijra traditionally earn their living by receiving alms and performing at weddings, at temple festivals, and at homes where a child, especially a male, has been born.

The *dharma* (religious obligation) of the hijra is emasculation, and the term *eunuch* is the most frequent translation of the word hijra. The emasculation operation is called *nirvan* or rebirth; only after the operation can hijras become vehicles of the goddess's power. Connected to the obligation to undergo emasculation (for those who are not born inter-sexed) is the hijra claim that they are other-worldly people. Impotent as men, and unable to reproduce as women, the hijra are like ascetics (*sanyasi*) in their separation from normal family life (*samsara*) and in their dependence on alms for their livelihood. This ascetic ideal links the hijra to their goddess and to other figures in the Indian religious tradition, such as Arjun, hero of the Hindu epic *Mahabharata* and through him Shiva; hijras also identify with Krishna and Ram (avatars, or incarnations, of Vishnu). These religiously sanctioned connections help legitimate the hijra role in Indian society (Nanda 1985).

Hijras are mainly found in north India, because in south India they do not have the traditional performance roles they have in the north. As hijras are not enumerated separately in the census, only the roughest estimates of their numbers is possible; about 5,000 hijras are estimated living in Bombay and Delhi, and perhaps a total of about 50,000 is spread throughout India (Bobb and Patel/*India Today* 1982). Although some hijras reside alone, most live in hijra communes of between five and twenty individuals.

The major principle of social organization in the hijra community is seniority, expressed in a hierarchy of *gurus* (seniors, literally teacher), and *chelas* (juniors, literally student or disciple). Every hijra has a guru, and initiation into the hijra community occurs only under the sponsorship of a senior hijra guru. At the initiation ritual, the initiate takes a female name, vows to obey the guru and the rules of the community, and is presented with some small gifts. An initiation fee (about 150 rupees, or $12) is paid by the new disciple, or by her guru on her behalf. This entitles her to earn a living as part of the group, under the leadership of the guru. Once begun, the guru/chela relationship is expected to be a lifelong bond of reciprocity, in which the guru is committed to taking care of the chela and the chela is committed to being loyal and obedient to the guru. The chela gives part of her income (this varies as to exact amounts) to the guru, and the emotional, social, and material dimensions of this relationship replicate in many aspects that of the Hindu extended joint family (Roland 1982). Beyond this principle of seniority, there are no formally significant social principles such as caste, religion, class, or ethnic distinctions that structure the hijra community.

Hijras are also tied together by a network of fictive kinship. Through rituals a hijra may take another as a daughter, and the daughters of the same mother regard themselves as sisters. The expansion of these relationships to aunt and grandmother follow the general pattern of the larger society and provide a mechanism for individual hijras to expand their social networks both within and beyond their local community. This foundation for the geographical mobility is characteristic of the community (especially its younger members) and useful as an element of economic adaptation. Another advantage of joining the hijra community is the economic security it provides: hijras who are old or ill can always find a place to stay and be cared for.

Another important social relationship for many hijras is having a husband. In the role of wife, a hijra has a long-term, sexually and emotionally satisfying, and economically complementary relationship with a man with whom she may or may not reside. Hijras with husbands do not break their ties with the hijra community. Having a husband is not incompatible with any other hijra occupation, including prostitution, and most hijras continue to work in hijra groups and maintain strong social ties with the community even while maintaining their marital relationships. Being a wife is a status many hijras, especially hijra prostitutes, look forward to. In Freilich's terms, it is a proper goal that they pursue by smart means. While Sinha's statement (1967) that hijras in Lucknow "all have husbands" seems something of an exaggeration, many hijras do have husbands and my impression is that many of those who do not would like to. Because having a husband is a source of both emotional and financial reward outside the hijra community, many gurus (who may themselves have husbands) appear threatened by it, and husbands can be a frequent source of conflict between guru and chela.

EARNING A LIVING

Hijras traditionally earn their living by receiving payments for bestowing blessings on newlyweds and newborns. After a marriage, when the bride has been brought to the home of the groom, the hijras shower the couple with blessings. When a child is born the hijras are called, or more likely appear at the house of the newborn, claiming their customary right to confer blessings of fertility and prosperity on the child and the family. This showering of blessings (*badhai*) is done as part of a performance that includes singing, dancing, clowning, and drumming. This public

acting out of the hijras' role fits Savishinsky's model of staged deviance.
The incorporation of their performance into domestic ritual also shows
how soft their deviance is in the eyes of the public. As payment for the
hijra, a fixed amount of money and goods are collected from the family
of the child or the married couple as well as small amounts spontaneously
given by the spectators. These programs are the work of the hijra
community, and their prerogative to perform on these occasions is
zealously guarded.

As in many Indian castes, however, not all hijras earn a living through
their traditional work. In the first place, there is simply not enough work
to go around. Hijras complain that opportunities for their traditional work
seem to be declining. People are having fewer children as they become
more urbanized, and the influence of Western values make ritual performers of all kinds less significant. Also, the elaborateness of weddings
has declined, and many of the festivities previously associated with the
wedding celebration, including the hijras' performance, may be dis-
pensed with. As people become more educated and sophisticated, the
role of traditional figures like hijras becomes less compelling, and with
this, hijra income from traditional performances declines. Even where
work is found, the payment for these performances must be divided
among a group (usually not fewer than three or four people), as well as
including a portion for the guru. Further, performing does not suit
everyone's temperament, as it requires some talent and can be physically
exhausting. In addition, performing means exposure to possible public
ridicule and even abusive rejection.

A second traditional occupation of hijras is publicly asking for alms,
either from people on the streets, or, more commonly, from shopkeepers.
In every city specific groups of hijras establish their exclusive territories
for this activity, and each territory is under the control of a local guru.
Earning a living in this manner is considered unpleasant work; it requires
working almost all day, every day, and becoming vulnerable to ridicule
and sometimes even physical abuse. Such a practice is a steady source
of income, however, and is also consistent with the equation of hijras
with religious ascetics.

Prostitution is a third source of earnings for many hijras, although
it is looked down upon within the hijra community. Prostitution
contradicts the ideal hijra self-conception as *sanyasi*, ascetics who
have tamed their sexual passion, and sexual relations are considered
offensive to the hijra goddess. In cities with strong hijra culture,
prostitutes are not allowed to live in the respectable houses where
hijras earn their living by performing in their traditional ritual

capacities. In large cities, such as Bombay, for example, hijra prostitutes live in their own areas and flats, often in the red-light district. Because excluding prostitutes from the community altogether would result in a significant loss of income, a compromise is reached: Although they cannot live with respectable hijras, hijra prostitutes are otherwise considered full members of the community, invited to social functions, maintain relations with their gurus, and participate in fictive kinship networks. In other cities the rules are less strict; hijra prostitutes and performers reside together, and one individual may both perform in traditional roles and also engage in prostitution. In different parts of India, hijras engage in other kinds of work that are not specifically related to being a hijra. To find them as cooks, household servants, or construction workers is not uncommon.

The hijra world is a deviant world but one that is not outside, but incorporated into, Indian society. Although becoming a hijra means making a commitment to a deviant and stigmatized social role, it is a role that is nonetheless given religious meaning and social support. Hijras view their lives as "an unhappy fate God has chosen for us" and "one we wouldn't wish on our worst enemies." It is a fate, however, that includes a dimension of power—and provides a cultural and social niche that gives shape and meaning to sexual ambiguity, linking persons with variant gender identities to a larger world, rather than isolating them.

Equally important, the cultural definition of the hijra role ensures individuals of an economic niche, and even monopoly, in society. Indeed, their very deviance ensures their livelihood. The attitude of Indian society toward the hijras is ambivalence, and the hijras exploit this ambivalence to their own advantage. While Indian culture is much more accommodating than Western culture toward variation in sexuality and sexual identity (Bullough 1976), the anomalous sexual attributes of the hijras are both feared and mocked. Overt homosexuality is stigmatized (though less so than in much of the West), and the hijras' effeminacy and transvestism are often the object of ridicule and abuse. For a society like India, where reproduction is so highly valued for both men and women, the hijras' impotence stigmatizes them as useless, a stigma that is keenly felt. Their birth is a source of sorrow for their parents, and their presence at home is generally considered a burden by their families. Their presence becomes particularly problematic when their siblings are ready to be married, because in India the stigma of the individual falls heavily on the family. The reason many hijras give for leaving home is that they wish to relieve their families of the embarrassment of their presence (Pimpley and Sharma 1985: 42).

Hijras may also be feared. While as sexually anomalous persons they can become vehicles of the power to give blessings of fertility, these powers can also be turned against those who do not give in to their demands. Thus hijras are often viewed as extortionate by those from whom they seek alms or payments. The curse and shame of a hijra lifting her skirts and exposing her mutilated genitals is usually enough to make most people give them something, if only to get rid of them. As Carstairs (1967: 64) shows, in the village in Rajastan in which he worked, hijras are adept at coercing their social superiors. Indeed, this ability to coerce is an important source of hijra income, and it is certainly this economic viability of the role that at least partly accounts for its continuity.

DEVIANT CAREERS

A deviant career is an individual's movement through the deviant experience. In this section I describe some hijra careers in detail and explore the social structure of the community as it relates to possibilities for social mobility and career choices.

Because of the variations characteristic of deviant careers, I hesitate to call the cases presented below typical. They are actual, however. Based on my fieldwork and interviews among a variety of hijra groups, these careers appear to contain elements that are found among many hijras, though perhaps not combined in exactly the same way. The career paths I describe are those of a prostitute on her way up, a performer on her way down, a guru, and a wife.

Mira: Becoming a Guru

Mira, at forty-two years old, is a successful guru. She started her formal hijra career in her mid-thirties after having been married and the father of nine children. She had an effeminate homosexual orientation since her early teens, having been "spoiled," as she describes her first sexual experience, by a neighbor's son. Her marriage was arranged. However, after being married for some fifteen years, she simply left her family and came to Bombay, where she was formally initiated into the hijra community. Because of her maturity she was immediately put to work supervising a hijra brothel in Bombay. She found the work very hard, however, as it required her to stay up until the last customer had gone, often until two in the morning. She also did not feel she lived very comfortably, and she found the people in Bombay "too greedy, all they thought about was money." So Mira returned to south India (her native place was in Tamil Nadu) and organized a hijra brothel in connection with a hijra-run bathhouse in Madras. This business did well. As Mira says, "We had plenty of customers. They come to us in the same way that they come to a woman. This is God's way, he made those people so that we, too, could earn a living."

After a year or so, Mira had the emasculation operation. Not long after that she had a dream of the hijra goddess, which she interpreted to mean that she should perform the operation on others. Within a few years she had successfully performed eighteen operations. This brought her prestige, as well as considerable earnings (an operation costs several thousand rupees). Mira then began to establish herself as a guru, taking on chelas by paying their initiation fees in Bombay and setting them up in prostitution. Within several years, Mira became a leader in the local hijra community. She used her money to sponsor rituals of fictive kinship, taking on daughters, chelas, and sisters. She has tried to increase her respect in the community by assiduously learning hijra myth, culture, and ritual from the Bombay elders and by trying to reproduce these among the Madras hijras. She acts as hostess for any important visitors who come from Bombay and visits there often. Last year she ceased performing operations after having had a dream in which the goddess appeared and told her to stop. More than likely, she now earns enough from her chelas' prostitution so that she does not need this illegal and very risky source of income. (Although prostitution is illegal, hijra prostitutes are rarely arrested because they pay off the police. Further, the criminal sanctions for performing the emasculation operation are far greater than those for prostitution.) Although Mira is admired for her skill as a *dai ma* (literally "midwife," the one who performs the operation), she is also criticized behind her back for "taking on cheap chelas, just for prostitution."

Mira has also taken a husband, a much younger man from her neighborhood, with whom she lives in a house separate from that where her chelas engage in prostitution. She divides her time equally between being a wife and a guru. The two roles are not incompatible; in fact, the money that comes to her as a guru has allowed her to provide a comfortable setting for her marital relationship. Although this relationship causes some gossip, and Mira's extreme attachment to her husband is considered unbecoming for a guru, Mira is given all the outward respect due an important elder in the hijra community. The role of guru is the major one around which she organizes her life and her self-image.

Kamaladevi: A Prostitute on Her Way Up

Kamaladevi is a young hijra who can, as she says, "earn a living with my feet." She joined the hijra community in Bastipore in her late teens and has been a hijra for about five years. She had the emasculation operation six months after joining the group. She began by earning her living as a prostitute but always wanted to dance. Although she made the most of the very limited opportunities to perform traditional hijra rituals in Bastipore, she was more likely to be asked to dance at college functions and stag parties than on ritual occasions. Kamaladevi had a steady customer whom she liked to call her husband, but he was the son of a local politician and she knew there was no real future in that relationship. She continued in prostitution but went back and forth to Bombay to visit her guru and take advantage of the more numerous performing opportunities there. Last year one of her Bastipore customers became jealous and threatened her life. Kamaladevi decided to move to Bombay, more permanently this time, thus solving two problems at once: escaping the threat and inceasing both her knowledge of hijra culture and performances, and finding opportunities to dance and get out of prostitution. Because she is young, beautiful, and a good dancer, Kamaladevi was eagerly claimed by the most prestigious hijra household in Bombay. They send her on choice assignments, she has beautiful clothes, and she comes and goes by taxi, avoiding all the potential humiliation hijras are subject to when they travel in public. Since the hijra house in which she now lives is such a respectable one, however, she is closely watched to make sure that she has no relations with men, that she behaves in a respectable manner, and that she works hard. "These Bombay gurus are very strict," Kamaladevi told me. "If you don't cover your head with your sari, if you don't eat your food in a proper manner, if all the dishes are not served properly, and if the house is not kept perfectly clean, you can't imagine how they scold you." But for now, Kamaladevi is satisfied. As a beautiful, talented dancer, she was able to move out of prostitution by moving into the most prestigious aspect of the hijra role. This has confirmed, for her, the rightness of her decision to become a hijra.

Salima: A Performer on Her Way Down

Salima, a Muslim, born in Bombay, is a "real" hijra: she was born intersexed. Her family noticed from a very early age that her male genitals were very small, but, as she says, "my mother thought they would grow as I grew." When this did not happen, her mother took her to several doctors, to no avail. She recalls dressing in girl's clothes from a young age. Finally, accepting that Salima was "neither one thing nor the other," her mother brought her, when she was about ten years old, to a community of hijras who lived nearby.

Salima's early years with the hijras were good for her. In fact, she said, the hijras treated her better than her mother, who often beat her. The hijras, and particularly her guru, were very kind to her, and insisted she work only inside the house until she got older. Because she was born intersexed, Salima did not undergo the emasculation operation. Instead, she had a very elaborate nose-and-ear-piercing ceremony (which is also part of the traditional hijra initiation). She was given gold earrings at a big party, to which all the important Bombay hijras were invited.

In her early teens Salima, along with a group of her sister hijras, began to be sent out to both beg and perform. She played the *dholak* (the special drum that accompanies all hijra performances), a prestigious function in the group. All day, every day, Salima and her group would go either to the big Bombay vegetable market to beg cash and kind from the stall keepers, or go around to their exclusive territories in Bombay, seeking out families where a wedding was taking place or where a child had been born. Salima was the leader of this group of chelas; she had not only been a hijra longer than most of them, but also was a real hijra and the favorite of her guru since she had been with her as a child.

Salima did this for about fifteen years. During those years she had found herself a husband, a man who was Muslim like herself. She lived with him for about six years, until his parents took him to Bastipore, in the south, partly to get him away from Salima. Although at first Salima used to secretly see this man—spending time with him at the market during the day when she was supposed to be begging, while her colleagues covered for her with her guru—one day the news got back to her guru. After a period of time during which Salima convinced her guru that this attachment would in no way undercut her own loyalty and economic contribution to the group, Salima's guru arranged a marriage ceremony for them and gave her blessings for Salima to live with this man. The couple lived in a separate house from the hijras, but Salima continued to work with and earn for them.

After this man moved away from Bombay, Salima moved back in with her guru, who by this time was living with a husband of her own. Salima was the most senior chela and claims she was respected by all the other chelas. She believes that she was clearly slated to take over her guru's position when the latter died. At this point her guru fell ill and returned, as some hijras do, to her native place to visit her relatives and recuperate.

During this time Salima remained in the guru's house along with the guru's husband.

According to Salima, this man made sexual advances to her that she repulsed. In an attempt both to get back at her for this rejection as well as to undermine Salima's credibility and presumably inherit the guru's considerable material assets for himself, this man forced Salima to have sex with him. He then made this public knowledge and turned the Bombay guru elders against her. Apparently with the consent (even connivance) of the elders, Salima was thrown out of her guru's house. When her guru returned, Salima attempted to tell her side of the story but was rebuffed. In anger, she hit her guru, an unforgivable act among the hijras, and was thrown out of the community.

Formal ostracism from the hijra community is a very serious matter; those hijras who would work with Salima, talk to her, or even so much as give her a drink of water would be cast out of the community themselves. In order to gain reentry, Salima would have to pay a 500 rupee fine. Unable to earn, much less save, this amount of money, Salima has lived on the streets of Bombay for the last seven years. Sometimes, with other hijra outcasts, she begs in Victoria railway station, but if they are seen by other hijras they are chased away. Sometimes Salima joins up with a group of *jankas* (non-hijra female impersonators) and they attempt to perform at weddings or childbirths. Because they are so shabby looking, it is hard for them to find performance opportunities. Further, as hijra performers are often challenged by an audience as to whether they are men or hijras, they become vulnerable when they perform with jankas. If someone lifts their skirts and finds out they are not hijras but men, they will be abused and driven away without payment.

At present, Salima lives under a makeshift tent on a street corner in the neighborhood where she grew up. She occasionally takes care of some of the neighborhood children to earn a few rupees, and is given some food by her neighbors. When the monsoon rains come, she sleeps under a bus or truck. She sometimes borrows money from her parents, but more often she has to lend them money that she receives from pawning some article of clothing. She is also subject to harassment from the local rowdies who hang out in the neighborhood. Salima would consider doing prostitution, but as she so pathetically says, "No customers are coming to me." When one sees her in her present state of dishevelment, with three days growth of beard, and her dirty hands and feet and clothes, it is perhaps not hard to understand her lack of clientele. Salima hopes some day to be able to raise the 500 rupees she needs to pay her way back into the hijra community, where she would again have a roof over her head, a role to perform as *dholakwallah* (drummer), and the congenial company of the hijras. In the near future this looks unlikely. I was willing to offer her the money myself, but my hijra friends advised me not to interfere.

Having a Husband: Sushila

Sushila is a person who would be described in Western terms as an effeminate transvestite homosexual, or drag queen. She has not yet had the emasculation operation, though she has been a hijra for almost twenty years. Sushila used to be a prostitute. She started her deviant career in her early teens while living in Madras. Her first stable relationship was with a fisherman who sold fish in the market in Madras; after that episode she went back to live with her family. At that time she used to have sexual relations with men in return for money. One night her brothers found some money and accused her of stealing it from them; in the shouting match that followed they abused her verbally about her homosexual activity, and she left the house. After wandering around Madras for a few days, she was so "bored and lonely" that she joined up with a hijra who took her to Hyderabad and eventually to Bombay. After her initiation, she remained in Bombay a few months, asking for alms from the shops in the areas controlled by her guru's guru. She soon got "disgusted with that life," however; she found it a "hard way to make a living," and she resented the constant restraints placed on her by the elders. So she returned to Hyderabad.

While in Hyderabad she worked out of a hijra house of prostitution managed by her guru. In the evenings she plied her trade from a bar as well as a local park. Her guru demanded every cent she earned and "would hardly give [her] a cent for a cup of coffee." On the other hand, her guru once bought her beautiful jewelry, and when she went back to visit her family several years after joining the hijras, her guru insisted she wear the jewelry and gave her some additional cash to buy gifts.

Still, Sushila was unhappy here. She felt that she was contributing more than her share to the work and income of the house and had no money to call her own. Once she fought with her guru over these matters, and her guru hit her in public. Although she "could not hit [her] guru, back, after all she was [her] guru," she decided to leave that very night. She piled up her belongings—by this time her guru had taken back and pawned all the jewelry—and moved into another part of Hyderabad, where she joined a hijra brothel. Around this time she met her first husband—she has had three, including the present one—and this relationship lasted six years. Then she met her second husband, a Brahmin, who had a good job as a chauffeur for a big corporation.

Sushila moved into a separate house with this man. She continued to practice prostitution, even though her husband asked her to stop. For a while she talked about buying a part interest in a bathhouse and managing it herself, but made no practical steps in this direction. When I saw her again in 1985, her life had taken a different turn altogether.

Sushila had deep feelings of sexual and emotional attachment to her husband, the Brahmin chauffeur, but was saddened by the fact that she could never give him children and therefore that he would never have a real family. So Sushila decided to adopt her husband as her son. This adoption involves a small ritual, and the parties then take on the reciprocal obligations characteristic of a mother and son in a normal family. Following Sushila's adoption of her husband as her son, she decided to arrange a marriage for him. His Brahmin status was a distinct advantage, as was his high-paying and secure job, and so Sushila was able to arrange his marriage with a poor but attractive girl in the neighborhood, an orphan living with her married sister. Sushila's son and his wife now have a son. Sushila has gained tremendous status, first by being a wife, and now even more so by becoming a mother-in-law and grandmother of a male child. She has given up prostitution and has taken another husband, who does not, however, live with her. "I no longer have any need to earn," she says. "My husband and son take care of me, and my daughter-in-law does all the work in the house. Now I have full respect."

Sushila's view of her life is that of many, if not most Indian women. Being a wife, mother, grandmother, is the epitome of self-esteem and prestige. Sushila has managed to achieve this even though she was born a male. This is no mean achievement!

SOCIAL STRUCTURE, SOCIAL MOBILITY AND HIJRA CAREERS

There is a widespread belief in Indian society that hijras recruit their membership by kidnapping infants and small children whom they have observed to be intersexed. This belief is sometimes given as the explanation as to why the hijras closely inspect the genitals of a male infant when they perform the blessing ritual. As part of the myth that hijras are taken away from their families, it is also believed that they have no contact with their kin and have lost all memory of them. Some hijras perpetuate this view when talking about themselves in order to win sympathy from the public (as well as from anthropologists). Empirical data on the hijras

(Nanda 1990; Ranade 1983) contradict this myth, suggesting that the vast majority of hijras join the community in their youth, either out of a desire to express their feminine gender identity more fully, or under pressure of poverty, or for a combination of reasons and various pressures.

All my informants reported having the desire to dress and act effeminately from early childhood. In all cases their parents actively discouraged their cross-dressing by scolding and beating them. All who admitted that they are currently having sexual relations further indicated that they had engaged in sexual activities with males during their early teens, and that this spoiled them for normal, heterosexual relations later on. They sometimes explained why they feel spoiled by saying that after a man has had homosexual relations in the receiver role, "the nerve in the male organ breaks and is no longer good for sex with women."

Typically, hijras voluntarily join the hijra community in their teenage years, though some, apparently from the poorest families, join as early as ten or twelve (Ranade 1983). After noticing and perhaps talking with hijras whom they observe in the areas where they live, and usually after some quarrel with their family members over their increasingly frequent and public effeminacy, the individuals leave home to join the hijra commune in their own city, or in one nearby. Within a few days or weeks at the most, if the individual remains in the hijra house, his ears and nose will be pierced. This strengthens the commitment on both sides; it is particularly binding upon the new recruit, who now has the external stigmata of the female role that makes it more difficult for him to return to his parents' home.

If a new recruit proves honest and willing to work, he is urged to make the further commitment of formally being initiated by the senior gurus. For individuals who come from places other than the major centers of hijra culture, this means going to Bombay, Delhi, or Ahmedabad. Most hijras do not remain permanently at this original point of entry into the community. After a few weeks or months, they either get homesick, feel they are working too hard, experience mistreatment at the hands of their guru, or dislike being under the control of another person. They may then return to their family's place, or to a smaller city. They find returning to their parents' home is no longer a satisfactory alternative. Even when their parents welcome them home, they find their own commitment to the female role too strong to allow them to live in peace with their families. Thus they return to the hijra community.

Once they rejoin the community, there are a number of choices open to them. An individual's choice is partly determined by his own talents and temperaments, and partly by the social organization and norms of the hijra community within which career options and advancement must be structured. The occupational and hierarchical nature of the deviant world of the hijras allows some social mobility, and the desire for moving up is an important factor in many, though not all, hijra careers.

A basic dimension of social hierarchy in the hijra world is the relation between gurus and chelas. The advantages of seniority—becoming a guru—involve both prestige, inherent in seniority, as well as material and psychological advantages such as increased control over material resources, other people, consumer goods, conditions and type of work, personal autonomy in one's movements and the use of one's time.

The prestige attached to the position of guru is expressed in the deferential behavior of junior members of the community, especially one's own chelas, who treat the guru alternately as father, husband, teacher, mother, and mother-in-law. These relationships are expressed in the use of honorific word endings, such as *ji*, by the use of the respect form of verbs: by such gestures as touching the guru's feet when one enters the house and not using vulgar language in the guru's presence; and by breaking one's bangles when one's guru dies, as a woman does for a husband. Further, the obedience due a guru is unquestioned: the sanctions for physical or even verbal aggression against one's guru are severe and may, as in Salima's case, result in being cast out of the hijra community. Gurus have responsibilities, however; they must successfully manage and protect their economic enterprises and territories and must also manage the social relations between their chelas so that they live in harmony. A successful guru is one with the wisdom that comes from experience, and thus gurus are middle-aged or older. The responsibilities and burdens of the guru role are most keenly expressed by gurus themselves, but also freely acknowledged by chelas.

In spite of the importance of the guru role, and its many advantages, the number of gurus in the community is theoretically unlimited, since any individual may become a guru merely by taking on chelas. Further, by using one's material resources wisely to build social networks of both chelas and fictive kin, anyone with ambition can attempt to build a reputation as an important guru in her local community. Even if one does not become an important guru, one can establish a position of superiority at least with regard to one's own chelas. Social mobility through becoming a guru is thus at least theoretically open and under the control of the individual.

A second dimension of social hierarchy among hijras is the degree to which an individual comes closest to the cultural ideal of the hijra as an intersexed person. Position in this hierarchy is based on both ascribed and achieved characteristics. The hijras who are born intersexed have the highest status. As real hijras, these people do not pay an initiation fee into the community; rather they are feted when they join and given clothes and jewelry of real value, as well as a major feast. Given that sex research indicates that hermaphroditism is a very rare condition in the human species, the number of real hijras must be very small. Among thirty of my informants, only one appeared to have been born intersexed. She described herself as a "true hijra," in contrast to "those converts, who are men and can have children, so that they need to have the operation." A study of 100 hijras in Delhi (Ranade 1983) indicated that about 10 percent had some physical condition that might encompass the term real hijra.

Below the real hijra in prestige are those who have undergone the emasculation operation or become nirvan. The hijra who has been reborn through the operation is now a vehicle of their goddess's power. Only through this power do the curses and blessings of the hijras have any efficacy. The importance attached to the status of nirvan is symbolized by an extended period of preparation for the operation, the expense and ritual context of the operation itself, the intensive postoperative recovery period (Nanda 1984: 74), and the joyous ceremony that attends the end of the forty-day postoperation isolation period. The ritual elements of this *rite de passage* are similar to those for a bride and a new mother in India, both of whom are moving into new statuses connected with fertility.

Like the status of guru, the prestige attached to the status of nirvan is independent of any economic benefits that pertain to the status. However, such benefits may be considerable. Since hijras who have not had the operation have no right to perform at weddings and childbirths, and since emasculated prostitutes are more in demand than nonemasculated ones, an emasculated hijra earns more and is a better source of income for her guru. Further, an emasculated hijra obviously has made a stronger, one may say almost irrevocable, commitment to the community. Her guru can only gain economically from this. Hence the pressure within the community for individuals to undergo the emasculation operation.

In fact, however, many hijra do not undergo this operation; sometimes it is a question of money, sometimes a question of fear, sometimes a question of being reluctant to make the commitment to this deviant identity irrevocable. While for some hijras the operation appears to bring them closer to their desire to be like a woman, others, perhaps those whose feminine gender identity is not as strong, have an understandable reluctance to take this irrevocable step. In Ranade's (1983) study of Delhi,

70 percent of the nonintersexed hijra had had the operation; among my thirty informants, ten said they had undergone the operation.

Below the status of the nirvan is the *janka*. Jankas are physically normal men who dress like women and who earn a living as masseuses, prostitutes, or performers. Some jankas are effeminate homosexuals, an orientation that they express in their transvestism. Others are men, some of whom have wives and children, who join the hijra community simply for economic reasons. Among my informants there were no jankas of this latter type. If jankas are found to be among a group of hijra ritual performers, the entire group will be sent away. Thus, while jankas are acceptable as prostitutes, they are not acceptable as performers, thereby lessening their value to the community. For this reason when jankas join the hijra community they pay a fee, while for real hijras there is no initiation fee. This economic motive may also be at work when pressure is applied to jankas to undergo the emasculation operation.

A third dimension of the hijra social hierarchy is based on what one actually does to earn a living. The criteria by which hijra occupations are ranked include prestige, amount and regularity of income, physical energy expended, vulnerability to ridicule or abuse by the public and state authorities, the amount of control over one's time and one's body, and the social level of one's audience, customers, or clients.

Regardless of the amount of income earned, ritual performances have the highest status both within the hijra community and outside it. This occupation is the respectable link between hijras and non-hijras, as well as the work that attaches religious meaning to being a hijra. Whereas a very talented performer can earn a handsome income (several thousand rupees a month), hijras who limit themselves to earning through ritual performances, except for the very exceptional performers, probably earn less than those who run houses of prostitution.

Prostitution, however, has very low status within the hijra community, in spite of its high earning potential. An individual prostitute has almost no control over her working conditions. She always works under the control of a hijra elder and must take on all kinds of customers, "whether it's a policeman or a businessman." The work is also physically demanding and, despite potentially providing a more than adequate living, does not provide many prostitutes, in fact, with easy living. The prostitutes are often exploited by their gurus, who are entitled to a fixed portion of their income, which ranges from 50 to 100 percent. While some gurus return a fair amount in living and working space, clothes, food, and jewelry, and even money for special occasions, there is little recourse against a guru who is not generous. The working prostitutes are often carefully supervised to see that they do not goldbrick or run away with a customer, and they may be expected to do domestic chores as well. In spite of these difficulties, however, few hijra prostitutes work on their own. The community provides at least some sort of social life, a minimum assurance of physical security in case customers get rowdy, and someone to pay off the police.

Begging alms from shopkeepers is also hard work but involves less continual surveillance by the house elders than prostitution. While begging for alms does not carry any inherent prestige, neither does it, like prostitution, diminish prestige, nor is it stigmatized within the community. It appears to be a common practice for shopkeepers to negotiate an agreement with hijras that in return for a fixed sum of money every month, or perhaps on special days (such as New Year's), the hijras will act respectably and not make a display and a nuisance of themselves by demanding money every week or every day.

Being a wife, while theoretically outside the hijra occupational hierarchy, is equivalent in some sense to other occupational statuses within the social structure. The more the hijra wife emulates the role of a normal wife, that is, staying at home and taking care of the house while her husband goes out and works for her, the higher her status. And as with any wife, this status depends partly on the status of her husband. Being a hijra wife is in some respects, occupationally, like being a guru—someone earns for you, and you need not engage in any demeaning, difficult, or wearisome work yourself.

One dimension of social hierarchy that is absent among hijras is that of caste. Although in some parts of India Hindu and Muslim hijras live separately, no distinction is generally made regarding the religious or caste background of their membership. The Delhi study (Ranade 1983) found members from all castes, including scheduled castes, represented in their sample. In my research, no informant admitted to being from a scheduled caste, but all were vehement in stating that it would not be relevant in any case. No pollution rules hold within the community, and in most places Hindus, Muslims, and Christians easily live together. The most important leaders of the nationwide hijra community seem to be Muslim, and Islam seems to have a somewhat higher status than Hinduism in spite of the fact that the hijra goddess is a Hindu goddess. Many of my Hindu informants talked of "becoming Muslim" or participated in Muslim rituals, such as Muhurram or Ramadan; there was no evidence of a parallel phenomenon where Muslims thought of becoming Hindu. I am not sure why this slight bias exists; perhaps it is related to the important role that eunuchs had in the Moghul empire.

Hijra social structure allows for both career stability and upward mobility. But upward mobility does not depend only on the objective facts of social structure. As the portraits above suggest, upward mobility also depends on the motivations and resources of individuals, who are not equally endowed to exploit the opportunities that structure offers. For example, in spite of the benefits and lack of structural barriers to becoming a guru, many middle-aged hijras I met do not have any chelas, and did not anticipate taking any. Becoming a guru requires initiative, assertiveness, and husbanding one's financial resources. It also calls for ambition and a willingness to undertake responsibility—a certain managerial temperament. Mira, for example, clearly has what it takes to be a guru: initiative, wisdom; an interest in and intellectual capacity for learning the hijra culture and ritual; a sense of responsibility; a desire to live in comfort and be considered respectable; and some special skills. Being a *dai ma* was an avenue for her to amass the material resources upon which she built her career as a guru.

Sushila, on the other hand, is also very intelligent and probably could have moved up in this manner as well. She had thought about it, but then decided that being a wife was better. She has the same advantages as a guru—others are now working for her, and she enjoys the prestige, too, of being a grandmother, as well as a wife and mother. Sushila's decision may be partly based on her reluctance to undergo the operation. In addition, being a wife gives her a degree of personal freedom that even a guru, who must manage a hijra commune, does not have. At one point Sushila thought she would move up by saving her money and buying into a bathhouse. She would then run it, using chelas as workers, but she never really got started on this project. While she has some of the qualities of a good guru (as she is fond of pointing out), especially her fairness and an interest in helping others, she is too irresponsible—often heavily drinking—to want to be tied down to an establishment: this precludes running a bathhouse, which demands constant attention, or taking on the daily management of a houseful of chelas.

Another career option is to become a dancer. For this one needs talent, energy, and a willingness to risk exposure to public hostility and abuse. Kamaladevi, for example, while preferring to perform in the traditional way, dances wherever she can—at stag parties or college functions. In many of these situations, where many of the men are drinking, one is required to keep a cool head, not just to protect oneself when the enthusiasm gets out of hand, but also to know how to wheedle extra money from the audience. Kamaladevi has learned these skills well. While she prefers dancing, she is not above practicing prostitution to supplement her performance income. On no account will she roam the streets asking for alms—it's too hard, there's not enough money, and there's no fun or glamour.

While the concept of career is usually discussed in terms of upward mobility, not all hijras have the desire or temperament to pursue career advancement. Some seem to be satisfied with a good reputation, which rests on many of the same traits valued in the larger Indian community—cleanliness, modesty, obedience, generosity, an ability to get along with others, contributing to one's share of the household work, and the absence of such vices as drinking, gossiping, or making trouble within a household.

Further, if a deviant career is defined as movement through the deviant experience, downward social mobility as well as upward social mobility should be taken into account. Hijras' careers do often contain periods of downward mobility; most often it is a result of conflict with their guru, as in the case of Salima. Trying to earn on their own leads to a fast downhill slide; their earnings decline, their appearance declines, thus further affecting their ability to earn; their isolation may lead to drinking or other habits that negatively affect their health. Hijras who separate from the community often must live on the street, and this, too, has negative physical effects, not to speak of demoralizing psychological ones.

The deviant world of the hijra is in many ways different from the larger society, and yet it mirrors that society also—in its emphasis on hierarchy; in its social connections through reciprocity; in its criteria of personal worth; and in the significance of the group and the power of the group over the individual. Because it is a deviant world, it offers some avenues of mobility not offered by the larger society. If we view the hijras as women—which is what many claim to be—the hijra world offers them opportunities for earning, ritual power, individual autonomy, and geographical and social mobility at least as great as those available in the outside world. That some individuals exploit these opportunities more than others is another way in which the hijra world reflects the larger society.

CROSS-CULTURAL PERSPECTIVE ON DEVIANT CAREERS

The deviant career is in some ways analogous to the respectable career, that is, it includes a sequence of regularized steps leading to more rewarding and higher-status positions. But there are also important differences (Luckenbill and Best 1981). For example, while the entry into the deviant career may be similar to the respectable career in the necessity to acquire relevant knowledge and skills to perform central roles and make contact with useful others, a major difference occurs in the intermediate stages. Deviant careers, unlike respectable careers, take place without institutional supports and are thus more precarious, and more variable, than respectable careers. While respectable careers are characterized by regulated, established pathways that go in, up, or out, deviant careers are characterized by multiple pathways at all of these stages. Because of this lack of institutionalization, deviant careers are more affected by individual career contingencies, including an individual's objectives, resources, and opportunities, all of which have more of a shaping influence on the nature and timing of the deviant's experiences than is true in respectable careers.

Luckenbill and Best (1981) characterize deviant careers as having the following qualities: They develop within ambiguous and unstable structural contexts; the individual does not move through an established sequence of well-defined positions; career progress does not always bring increased rewards and security; and there is more likely to be multiple short term involvements in the career than continued involvement over a lifetime. Another characteristic is that "except in deviant formal organizations which supply illegal goods and services, deviants rarely occupy formal positions of authority over one another"; authority (as in the juvenile gang) resides in the person, not in the role.

This conception of the deviant career, while very useful for studies of deviance in the United States, does not sufficiently take into account the diverse cultural contexts in which deviant careers exist. Deviant careers, like respectable careers, are influenced by the cultural values and forms of social organization that are part of the larger context within which they are enmeshed. Luckenbill (1986), for example, describes the American male "hustlers" he studied as "fiercely independent; they do not have pimps and they do not take orders, even from their lovers." Such independence helps explain why so few hustlers turn to escort prostitution even though they are aware of such agencies, and why most quit in a relatively short time even if they join. Their independence also explains why hustlers exhibit greater geographic mobility than female prostitutes (who are tied to their pimps). This independence and individual geographical mobility also seems characteristic of the careers of American "street fairies" and female impersonators (Newton 1972).

The deviant career of a hijra (and specifically a hijra prostitute) shows a different pattern. The structuring of the hijra career within an organized and hierarchical community is very consistent with Indian values and provides a contrast to American male hustling at almost every turn. Even the geographical mobility of American male hustlers, which is also found among hijras, can be explained by two different and opposing cultural contexts. In the United States, the male hustler moves because he is on his own; in India the hijra moves because she has a social network derived from group membership that assures her of a welcome and a social community wherever she goes.

The independence of Luckenbill's male hustlers is entirely consistent with the values surrounding male behavior in our society. The hijras' dependence on their community, and specifically the hijra prostitutes, is consistent with the values that are important in Indian society: a group orientation, a willingness to submit to hierarchy, a combining of resources and expenditures as in a joint family, and a clear feeling that there is no security without a group. In India, these values hold for men as well as women, so that most hijras, regardless of the depth of their female identification, find them congenial and appropriate in cultural terms. Even the guru role, which requires assertiveness, responsibility, and dominance, is easily incorporated into a female role—that of the mother-in-law—as well as into the male roles of husband and father.

Not only are hijra roles enmeshed to a far greater degree in an organized group than is true in the West, but they differ in four other important ways as well. First, there are some regular, if not absolutely fixed, sequences for career mobility. One must always be a chela before being a guru. Second, while for some hijras their connection with the community may consist of multiple, short-term involvements, for most hijras it is close to a lifetime commitment.

The third and fourth ways that hijra careers are different from those described for Western deviants concern the religious contexts in which the hijra role is embedded. In the Hindu philosophical and religious tradition, one of the most important concepts is that of dharma, meaning moral duty or right action. This right action is different for each individual, depending on the historical era and group into which one is born, the particular life stage one is in, and the innate traits carried over from one's previous lives. Thus any activity or occupation is equally good if it is part of the individual's life task and accepted as such (Kakar 1981). For the hijras, whether prostitutes or performers, their careers are part of their dharma. Emasculation, in this light, is seen as a religious obligation, and it is said in parts of India that any hijra who resists the call to be operated will be reborn impotent for seven future births. Such is the price one pays for not following one's life plan.

This concept of dharma leads to a Hindu tolerance of a wide diversity of life styles including those that many in the West would label pathological and seek to punish or cure. But this tolerance is only extended when the deviance is fully legitimated as the working out of a life path, that is, when it is sanctified by tradition, formalized in recognized ritual, and, usually, part of a group phenomenon—precisely the situation of the hijras. Through their group life the hijras not only find personal, economic, and social security, but, like other such groups—whether faith healers or professional beggars—find a religious meaning in their deviance. Further, while the hijra are labeled, their deviance is soft, their actions staged, and their smart conduct a means to such proper goals as getting married and fulfilling one's dharma.

In this context it is important to note that this conception and tolerance of the hijra as legitimated deviants is not endorsed by the Indian state, particularly regarding emasculation, which is illegal under the modern Indian legal code. But while criminalization has made the hijras more careful about where and under what circumstances they carry out emasculation, not one hijra I spoke with considered criminalization as a factor in their decision to undergo the operation. Thus the criminalization of hijra practices in modern times, and under the influence of British law, has not been able to destroy the more ancient customary law under which hijras had an institutionalized place in society. This institutionalization of the hijra role in India provides many deviant individuals with a chance for self-esteem and self-realization that would not otherwise be open to them and thus stands in marked contrast to the position of such people in the West.

The deviant career of the hijra in India, then, not only differs from the model of deviant careers applicable to the United States, but it is different in ways consistent with the cultural patterns of the two societies. Indeed, while the cultural patterns and social structures of India shape and constrain the deviant career of the hijras, at the same time they provide the opportunity for it to exist. The literature in the United States on deviant male sexual careers suggests a culture and, more recently, a social organization, but certainly nothing as structured as the hijra community. Loosely organized groups may be interpreted by us as independence and, in a positive sense, as freedom. But for the hijra, this is not freedom, but social suicide. In India, in deviant as well as normal society, the values of hierarchy and the importance of the group remain paramount. Group cohesion, not individualism, is adaptive. These are the cultural and structural factors that shape both nondeviant and deviant careers in India.

NOTES

I most gratefully acknowledge the PSC-CUNY Research Foundation, City University of New York for two grants, in 1985 and 1986, which provided me the opportunity to do part of the fieldwork upon which this paper is based. I also want to thank Joel Best and especially David Luckenbill, who were so kind to share their insights on deviant careers with me. My thanks also go to the editors of this volume for their very helpful comments.

1. There are many physical conditions, present at birth, that create gender anomalies. Sometimes these are lumped together as "pseudo-hermaphroditism." In the absence of any medical evidence on hijras, it becomes difficult to confirm whether the frequent statement "I was born this way" refers to an organic condition, a merging of psychological and organic etiology, or a more conscious attempt to approximate the ideal cultural concept of the hijra.

8 TAIWAN: GANGSTERS OR GOOD GUYS?

Thomas A. Shaw

In describing the world view of gangsters in Taipei, the capital city of Taiwan, I will show how gangsters construct a moral reality in which they cast themselves as heroes rather than hooligans, good guys rather than all gangsters. *Liumang* (pronounced lee 'ooh mong, and most often translated into English as "hooligans") are depicted in the media in Taipei as destroyers of common social and moral values, as enemies of the people and of public morality. Gangsters, on the other hand, in discussing their goals and activities among themselves and with the ethnographer, emphasize the peace-keeping, justice-serving, and generally positive role they play in their communities.[1]

I will focus mostly on how gangsters interpret and understand the world around them, rather than on their specific activities within gangs. From this perspective, the deviance attributed to hoodlums in Taiwan can be seen to partly reflect the values that they espouse. Confucian morality emphasizes family as the most salient model of social solidarity; acceptance of obligation and subordination according to one's social position; compliance with authority; and a graded sense of duty and responsibility in different types of relationships, with kin relations representing the highest form of responsibility (Wilson 1970; Solomon 1971; Baker 1979; Pye 1968).

In contrast, gangster morality emphasizes community (as the primary basis for social solidarity), personal freedom, autonomy, equality, and universal responsibility rather than a graded sense of duty. The boundaries of this deviant subculture are reflected in the term used by both government authorities and gangsters to refer to it: the black society (*hei she hui*), or underworld.

In contrast to theories that attribute dysfunction, alienation, or apathy to deviants' cognitive worlds, my approach is to penetrate the symbols and interpretations that infuse liumang's culture or subculture with moral and social value; in other words, to engage in "thick description" (Geertz 1973) of their own evaluations of self and environment. This approach highlights the view that deviance is a social fact, an artifact of the clash of perspectives in a complex society. Many so-called crimes of my informants, in other words, were "wrong" only when viewed from the perspective of the state's interest in social control. That is, while government authorities and their newspapers generally succeeded at stigmatizing liumang as bad guys through and through, members of local communities often supported and patronized their underground businesses, including gambling halls, teahouses, and occult healing centers. Local residents, who were also the parents of liumang, their relatives, and neighbors, often perceived members of local streetcorner gangs to have a less than threatening presence in the neighborhood.

Except for occasional acts of violence that receive more than their share of media attention, most of the unlawful and deviant activities of gangsters in Taipei are of the "soft" variety (see Introduction and Raybeck, Chapter 2), meaning that they have mild consequences with respect to the local population. For many young males, joining a gang means finding freedom from family authority, learning to rely on friends as equals, and using one's own judgment and intelligence as guides to action. In a culture that prescribes obedience, conformity, and a strictly kinship-based code of ethics, only deviants, ironically, have access to such experiences, at least in preadulthood. Bloch and Niederhoffer noted similar functions of gang participation thirty years ago, although they were mainly interested in likening membership in a gang to initiation into the ways and means of adult society:

When a society does not make adequate preparation, formal or otherwise, for the induction of its adolescents to the adult status, equivalent forms of behavior arise spontaneously among adolescents, reinforced by their own group structure, which seemingly provides the same psychological content and function as the more formalized rituals found in other societies. (1958: 7)

A TRADITION OF DEVIANCE

A cultural tradition is not a static set of meanings. Instead its symbols, ideals, and sentiments are arranged to communicate "an argument about the meaning of the destiny its members share" (Bellah et al. 1985: 27). Individuals in Taipei who identified with the status of liumang indeed had a sense of shared destiny and invoked a distinct set of meanings and symbols to communicate this sense. As Geertz (1973) maintains, cultural symbols are manipulated by people to "say something of something," and it is the job of the ethnographer to interpret what is being said.

My informants in this study were males, mostly ethnic Taiwanese, young adults, in addition to being gangsters.[2] To imply that their cognitive worlds are ordered by a single complex of symbols would, therefore, be inaccurate. In fact it is much more realistic to assume that "a plurality of limited systems of meaning" make up their cognitive worlds (Moore 1987a: 730).[3] However, this chapter is not so much about individuals as about the cultural tradition they share.

Also, I should point out that the symbols and meanings that gangsters use to represent their lives to themselves and to others should not be interpreted as somehow inducing them to become, or to remain, gangsters. Nor do their interpretations of their own existence handicap them in ways that limit their access to or understanding of other social realities and opportunities, as the much battered notion of the "culture of poverty" alleges. A much better explanation of the causes of criminal behavior and the existence of gangs in Taiwan would link gangsterism to exogenous political and economic realities, but such an explanation is beyond the scope and purpose of this chapter.

As with culture in general, the subculture of the underworld in Taiwan, when understood as a process rather than as a fixed set of meanings, involves continuous reinvention of the past (Hobsbawm and Ranger 1983). However, unlike some scholars who claim that deviant subcultures are reinventions or revitalizations of core cultural traditions (Wallace 1961; Keniston 1970; Matza and Sykes 1961; Goffman 1967), I do not believe that underworld subculture in Taipei serves to revitalize that society's core values.

Although deviance, far from representing psychosocial alienation or normlessness, is articulated through a coherent and systematic body of symbols and meanings, gangsters' values do not overlap so much as they diverge from and contrast with orthodox values in the larger culture. This divergence permits us to speak of a deviant subculture, even though, as I point out, gangsters borrow a system of meanings already extant in Chinese popular culture.

This system of meanings is part of a long, illustrious tradition of chivalry in Chinese culture. Emerging in history with the appearance of knight-errantry (*you-hsia*) in the Warring States Period (403-221 B.C.), this chivalrous tradition coincides with the decline of the aristocracy and with the ensuing conflicts between the former vassals of the state of Chou. As a result of these conflicts, hereditary warriors lost their positions and titles and were discharged from their posts and regions. As knights-errant they roamed from one state to another offering their services as professional soldiers (Liu 1967; Fung 1948). While Confucians, Taoists, Mohists, and Legalists tried to bring unity to the empire by converting the feudal rulers to their way of thinking, the knights-errant were known for having simply taken justice into their own hands.

Knights-errant are said to have espoused a code of ethics that emphasized personal loyalty, universal altruism and justice, absolute truthfulness, courage, honor, and generosity (Liu 1967). Fung, in fact, argues that these ethics were systematized into a coherent philosophy by the Mohists, who are best known for their advocacy of an all-embracing, universal love. The grand historian of China, Ssu-ma Ch'ien (145-86 B.C.), describes knights-errant in his *Historical Records* as persons whose ". . . words were always sincere and trustworthy, and their actions always quick and decisive. They were always true to what they promised, and without regard to their own persons, they would rush into dangers threatening others," (quoted in Fung 1948: 50).

While I am not claiming that the liumang I knew in Taipei viewed the circumstances of their lives in the same way that Han Dynasty knights-errant viewed theirs, gangsters do articulate similar values and manipulate many of the same ideological and quasireligious symbols to demarcate their social and cultural world from the larger society and culture. Expressed in the terms of Freilich's model, "smart" implies that actions are taken in concert with proper meanings and goals.

How do young men in the modern urban metropolis become aware of these centuries-old symbols and meanings? In Taiwan today, young and old alike follow serial episodes of noontime and evening television sagas centering on bands of chivalrous swordsmen with supernatural skills and abilities in the arts of fighting. Young boys learn the vocabulary of chivalry from these popular TV programs (as well as movies) and also from novels featuring the military adventures of wandering bandit chieftains and their followers.

ENTREE INTO THE BLACK SOCIETY

The data on liumang were gathered as part of a larger study of youth subculture, social identity, and social mobility in Taipei, Taiwan (Shaw 1988). Gangsters were one focus of the study, which also included an ethnography of a junior middle school and participant observation among a disco-dancing, Western culture-oriented youth crowd.

My entree into the black society in Taipei was neither difficult nor prolonged. One day while I was shopping for secondhand furniture I met Ah Ji, a twenty-one-year-old proprietor of a secondhand furniture shop. For some reason, in talking with him I chose to stress my interest in the life styles of local hoodlums. It drew a spark from Ah Ji, who was delighted to draw pictures in my notebook of weapons (swords, knives, spiked iron balls) found in Taiwan's underworld. Drawing on a distinct vocabulary and register of phrases, Ah Ji imitated the way gangsters talk and displayed the pride in their walk. He employed all graphic means at his disposal to express the stylistic behaviors and language of participants in the Taiwanese underworld. Ah Ji was himself a "younger brother" in a small local gang in San Ch'ong, a suburb just to the west of Taipei.

Ah Ji had been associated with three other gangs prior to his present involvement, and quickly became a key informant in the anthropological sense. Through his introductions I met other members of his gang, including the gang "boss" (*lao da*), as well as members of other gangs in Taipei and adjacent suburbs. Ah Ji, like anyone who warrants the term "key informant" in anthropological research, knew exactly what kind of information I was looking for. He knew he had to renew some ties with former gang brothers to satisfy my requests for contacts with members of a variety of gangs around town. Many meetings took place in my apartment. I served beer or coffee to Ah Ji and the other young gangsters while we talked about the rituals, income, turf, authority, and recruitment practices of the different gangs.

Descriptions of authority structures, income-generating activities, leisure activities, recruitment patterns, valued competencies, common phrases, sentiments, and ideologies in the different gangs overlapped tremendously. The most salient differences between gangs were consistently those between the ethnic Taiwanese streetcorner gangs (so called because the term for "gang" in the Taiwanese dialect translates in English as "street corner," whereas the Mandarin term for "gang" does not) and the larger Mainlander gangs.

I also met regularly with members of a Taiwanese streetcorner gang whose primary hangout was a teahouse on a small alley off a main road in my neighborhood. As we drank tea and talked about the liumang life style, other local hoodlums from several neighboring streetcorner gangs dropped by and I was introduced to them. I also met young members of gangs at a local rollerskating rink in a nearby entertainment district, and I approached hoodlums in temples, night markets, recreation centers, and in front of barber shops, which are usually fronts for prostitution.

Openness with me, even though I am a foreigner (or perhaps even because of it), was rarely considered risky or dangerous. My liumang informants even seemed to enjoy becoming the object of a foreigner's attention, which probably earned them status among their peers. Besides, being extremely rooted in and familiar with their local communities, members of Taiwanese streetcorner gangs know who their true enemies are all too well. Even brief encounters with young hoodlums yielded information that confirmed and added to data already gathered with Ah Ji and his friends, and I found that the more I revealed I already knew about the gangsters' life styles, the quicker and easier it was to learn more.

THE IDIOM OF COMMUNITY

Hoodlums in Taipei tend to identify strongly with a local, spatially defined community. The term for "turf" in Taiwanese, *kak-thau*, also means "gang," but literally translates as "street corner," or simply "location." Taiwanese gangs consist of around ten to twenty core members, the majority of whom live within the gang's turf, which is usually no greater than one or two city blocks. When one hoodlum asks another hoodlum, "Where do you operate?" (meaning "Where is your gang located?"), it is the same as asking, "What is the name of your gang?" This is because gangs take their name from some landmark in the gang's turf. For example, gang names may come from the former Japanese name for a section of the city, the name of a street or alleyway traversing the gang's territory, the name of a temple in that territory, or an informal designation of the general area. Belonging to a gang thus entails identification with a spatially defined territory. When introducing themselves to strangers who are members of other gangs, liumang actually say, "I am [gang's name/gang's turf]."

Common residence in a particular neighborhood, while neither a necessary nor a sufficient condition for recruitment to a streetcorner gang, is nonetheless significantly valued. The value of common residence is clearly due to the opportunities for frequent interaction that are thus made possible. The importance of growing up together was affirmed by several of my informants when they discussed how one joins, or is recruited to, a gang. One member commented: If you've grown up in the neighborhood and had contact with the local gangsters all your life, then there's no problem [joining a gang], but if you come from outside the neighborhood, unless you are strongly recommended by a brother, you usually have to fight with gang members."

Within their turf, gangsters see themselves as a kind of self-appointed council of overlords.[4] They are not particularly opposed to government authority as government officials often insist, but they do feel competition with authorities over the control of the area within their turf. Thus the leader, or lao da, of Ah Ji's gang spoke of the important peace-keeping role that the gang played in its community by helping to settle local disputes. "We relieve the government of some of its responsibilities," he asserted.

In fact gang action is taken most often to exploit hostilities that are, for the most part, not initially caused by the gang itself—hostilities arising from overdue debts, local business disputes, political factionalism, and economic competition.[5] Gangsters are also known to provide divine mediation through the occult arts, or *fa li*, and they accept clients whose troubles are believed susceptible to Taoist charms and spells. Gangsters thus see themselves as mediators, rather than as instigators, of conflict in their communities.

Collection of protection fees from local merchants, for the service of protection against other gangs, is frequently timed to coincide with local community festivals in order to accentuate the link between the gang's and the community's welfare (see Lin 1958; Fried and Fried 1980: 84). The similarity to governments of nation-states who collect taxes to protect people from encroachment by other governments is not accidental. As Eberhard (1965) points out, one way that peasant rebellions were initiated in China was through the self-protection activities of a village, or group of villages. Starting as a band of local juveniles organized to protect a particular community, peasant rebellions have in the past culminated in the founding of new dynasties (Wolf 1969: 115; Eberhard 1965).

The subculture of the black society thrives on the shared idea of community. The idea of community has no clear social boundaries and does not require any (Anthony Cohen 1985). Like the "Communist rebel," a type of community leader in China described by Madsen (1984), the hoodlum in Taipei arouses neighborhood residents' community/chauvinistic spirit. And like the Communist rebel, local hoodlums appeal to residents' notions of the cultural homogeneity of their communities and garner support by claiming to treat everyone in the community the same, regardless of wealth or family background. The fact that the ideal of such leadership often diverges from actual behavior does not lessen people's support for people who are so ideologically disposed.

For example, one of my informants, who was well educated and upwardly mobile, described the hoodlums whose headquarters happened to be across the street from his home. When thinking locally, in terms of his family and the community, he pointed out that he was on friendly terms with all the gangsters and that "they have never done anything to hurt my family or cause us any harm." "Actually," he continued, "I admire the way they get together as a group, cooperate, and keep other gangs out of the neighborhood." However, at other times he took the perspective of the larger society and articulated the official view of their deviance: "Liumang hurt people and use violence."[6]

Another informant, an unemployed middle-aged male who lived in my neighborhood, once explained that because he and several other friends often met in the afternoons at a local teahouse and appeared to have "idle hands," they were given a name and henceforth considered a gang by local residents, even though, he claimed, they did not run gambling operations or collect protection money in the area. Also, a young boy who frequently met with his friends at a particular noodle stand in another neighborhood told me that residents there considered him and his friends, all recently graduated from the local junior middle school, to be protectors of the neighborhood. They even gave them a gang name, using a local term that referred to the neighborhood.

Gangs thus serve to externalize residents' feelings of attachment and belonging to their urban neighborhoods in spite of the fact that the neighborhood is in no way culturally or structurally discrete, possessing its own regional culture, as was the case in the past in towns and villages in China (Huang 1985). For example, in parts of Taiwan and in southeastern China especially, the local tough or strong man as a social type is said to have been his "kinsmen's champion," and his territory the "surname turf" (Meskill 1979: 88-89; Hsiao 1960: 465).

The cultural construction of community in the urban context may instead be an expression of residents' awareness of and embeddedness in a class-stratified social system. Class, at a structural level, translates into images of place at a symbolic level. People move between places as they move between classes, and as Strathern (1982) notes, moving out is often seen as moving up (and vice versa). Also, particularly for those who are not upwardly mobile, images of community may be exaggerated in response to circumstances that threaten or weaken the boundaries of a local urban neighborhood, such as shopping malls and other centralizing forces (Cohen 1985). People create history in order to secure a place for themselves in the present.

Personal Freedom

While liumang speak very positively of the camaraderie, intimacy, and support offered by brothers in their gangs, they tend to interpret gang membership as something not so formal as to entail stiff role definitions and social obligations that limit their freedom. For one thing, commitments to streetcorner gangs are not enforced ritually or codified in any formal initiation ceremony. Members of Taiwanese streetcorner gangs rarely swear oaths of brotherhood (*jiebar xiongdi*). This ritual acknowledgment of alleged lifelong support and intimacy, commonly involving the drinking of wine mixed with blood from the pin-pricked fingers of chosen partners, is practiced widely in Taiwanese society and cross-cuts age, class, and gender boundaries (Gallin and Gallin 1977; Jordan 1985; Shaw 1988). However, the common sentiment among my liumang informants was that swearing brotherhood was unnecessary and sometimes a nuisance. The reason given by one informant was echoed by many others: "It is enough that we are brothers in the same gang. We always treat each other well." Since commitments in a gang are not sanctioned by external ritual, they must be regularly reaffirmed through demonstrations of loyalty and devotion to gang brothers.

The fact that commitments within streetcorner gangs are not externalized ritually implies that displays of loyalty to gang brothers are in a sense voluntary: the gangster's self is emphasized as the "agent" of those commitments. It is important to recognize that loyalty and support for one's brothers are seen to be produced by an act of volition, rather than by any binding external rule. Gangsters do not say about loyalty: "That's just how you treat brothers," as is otherwise heard in the context of relations between *blood* brothers. Instead, they are inclined to emphasize their own self-determination and effort: "I help my brothers whenever I feel I am needed, and they do the same for me." It is not the relationship of "brotherhood" that is institutionalized in the underworld subculture, but the autonomy of the self. The locus of the commitment is the individual, not the relationship, and agency is attributed to the self, rather than to the relationship norm. Gangsters' self-willed cooperation is frequently contrasted with the external structures of authority that are believed to be necessary to induce members of Mainlander gangs to *jiang i qi*, or "talk loyalty."

Also, as my informants pointed out, the utility of swearing oaths of brotherhood is limited by the tendency for alliances to shift and leadership to change hands. Violent power struggles are common in Taiwanese gangs. In fact, gang members unabashedly adopted a Machiavellian attitude toward opportunity in the gang, and I was often told that "to move up in a Taiwanese gang you have to kill the leader." Not surprisingly given these circumstances, alliances *between* members of different streetcorner gangs were more likely to be sealed through the ritual swearing of brotherhood than were alliances *within* any one gang.

Although to accept the label of *gang* is to admit to criminal behavior according to Taiwanese law, I believe another reason that many of my informants resisted the classification of their brotherhoods as gangs was because the latter implies an imposed structure that constrains one's personal freedom. My informants, including several ethnic Mainlanders who belonged to Taiwanese streetcorner gangs, communicated that they had no interest in living the disciplined, yet more lucrative life style associated with membership in the more tightly organized Mainlander gangs and preferred, as knights-errant are also said to have preferred, the freedom of being "loosely associated on a voluntary basis" (Liu 1967: 12). As a veteran student of crime and deliquency in Taiwan once commented:

The organizations of delinquent youth are structured around the individual activities of a few young people. These activities are often not connected to the group, and only become related when the individual assumes some role within the organization. The reason such a role is assumed is usually to fulfill certain individual aspirations and desires. Conditions of group allegiance are not established that might restrict the individual. Instead a spirit of mutual involvement is the only form of governance. (Chen 1967: 14)

Just as knights-errant are said to have enjoyed much personal freedom, often at the expense of family solidarity and subjugation to family authority (Liu 1967: 11), my liumang informants' high regard for their freedom (*ziyou*) was often expressed in comments that indicated a desire to avoid obligations to kin:

Researcher: Why don't you work with your father in his business?

Informant #1: I don't like to be disciplined by other people. Anyway, I'd rather change jobs often. I would rather be free.

Researcher: Why don't you live at home with your parents?

Informant #2: Because at home, I'm forced to be under the control of my parents. Not enough freedom. I'd rather depend on friends for support.

Researcher: Do you contact relatives in Taipei to ask them for any kind of assistance? (Asked of gang member who moved from his home in central Taiwan.)

Informant #3: No, because I would lose face.

Researcher: How is that?

Informant #3: Because if I accepted help from them I would then be obligated to do whatever they told me to do. This is an obligation I could not fulfill.

"More freedom" was regularly asserted as an important reason for choosing the life of the liumang. In fact, several informants framed their decision to become liumang, and thus explained this decision to themselves and to others, as *qu lai* (coming out) of the family, implying separation from the moral obligation to obey parents and other relatives.

Universal Morality

In a cultural environment that places a high value on autonomy and personal freedom, social responsibility tends to be defined according to the vagaries of individual will or emotion, as Bellah et al. (1985) argue to be the case for Americans in general. This kind of ethical code is very different from the traditional Chinese Confucial moral order, which demands selective sacrifices in the context of one's "natural" sympathies, as these are predefined by existing family and patron-client arrangements (Madsen 1981).

Liumang, on the other hand, reject predefined social commitments. Domains in which they feel committed to acting fairly and justly extend beyond the natural boundaries of kinship and friendship. But in fact what is right and just are completely open to interpretation and personal discretion, in effect giving gangsters carte blanche to police all social settings for any perceived injustice. Their deviance is thus widely and often publicly "staged" (Savishinsky, Chapter 3), and they use this visibility as a way to enforce their power and to attest the legitimacy of their collective existence. Whatever their personal motives might be, these are easily sanctioned by invoking the traditional notion of acting in the spirit of *i qi*, or righteousness.

Indeed the concept of righteousness in the underworld is practically content-free. The only proscribed activity I was aware of was that involving hurting women and other "weak" persons. Because the concept of "righteousness" does not delineate particular values that may serve as yardsticks for distinguishing right from wrong, liumang are free to justify gang activity and intervention on just about any grounds, and in a very broad range of contexts. Judgments about whether a particular action is warranted or not tend either to mirror popular moral sentiments common throughout Taiwanese society, or to express very idiosyncratic, personal emotions and beliefs.

For example, Ah Ji stopped a foreigner (non-Chinese) on the street one day because he felt the young man was mistreating his Chinese companion, judging from the tears he saw on the girl's face. He went to get the lock and chain from his motorcycle and was "ready to teach the guy a lesson" when the girl talked her companion out of fighting. Although Ah Ji never admitted as much, this incident might be interpreted as an instance of antiforeign sentiment: the foreigner had no right to mistreat a Chinese. However, cases involving conjugal squabbling between Chinese are overlooked by gangsters all the time.

There is no (typically Confucian) rule in the underworld against intervention in the family affairs of persons with whom one is not related. For example, Ah Ji's gang was once contemplating possible action against a young man after it was learned he had borrowed money from his older brother and returned only a tiny fraction of it when their mother was sick—not enough even to dent her substantial medical bill. Ah Ji and the other gang members, angered by the young man's unfilial behavior, discussed various ways to make him pay for his depravity.

While a hodgepodge of family values and other extant moral values fill in as content for the liumang's code of ethics, it is the universal quality of this code that generates feelings of obligation to kin and strangers alike. As James Liu (1967) points out, this is foreign to Confucian morality because "if one died for a stranger, what should one do for one's parents?" Although the immensely popular idea of righteousness in the underworld is virtually devoid of content, its very universality becomes its message. In contrast to Confucian ethics, which stipulate correct behavior and proper values within narrowly defined social domains, righteousness is meaningful precisely to the extent that its applicability is not so limited. For example, this universality is evident in gangsters' seemingly irrational readiness to fight at the drop of a hat.

One of the most perplexing and yet frequently cited reasons for engaging someone in a fight is quite simply *Kan bu xun yan,* or "what I saw did not please me." Although I searched for hidden, unspoken sources of conflict in circumstances that were explained as leading up to fights, many fights appeared to begin simply when someone looked at a gangster in a less than amiable manner. For example, one day I was walking with a young boy, a member of a local gang in my neighborhood, in a crowded district of the city; suddenly he called out angrily in a loud voice to someone passing on the street: "What do you want? Get lost!" When I asked him what had caused his reaction, he simply said, "What I saw did not please me." As with the knights-errant, a heightened willingness and readiness to respond in all situations where some vaguely defined injustice is perceived is itself part of the moral code of the liumang. As Yang notes, the knight-errant "is determined to repay every meal served with kindness and return every angry glance from the eyes of another person, irrespective of whether the latter is a gentleman or a small man, a relative or a stranger" (Yang 1957: 306). Yang contrasts this with the Confucian gentleman, who "refuses to fight against an unreasonable person, whom he compares with a mere brute."

Liumang indeed think of themselves as persons who invoke standards of fairness and justice in a wide range of situations, even though these standards are not easily articulated or defined. Several liumang who were active in debt settlement for their gangs explained, for example, that this activity made them feel *zhengdang* (legitimate); when the gang's settlement terms are agreed to (the gang's terms are often more attractive than those of the courts, since the latter might force the sale of family possessions or land), it implied that the exercise of gang authority was deemed fair and just by normal citizens. According to my informants, gang intervention takes place only after the parties to a debt, or a dispute, have been thoroughly investigated and their claims determined to be true and fair.

Equality

In answer to my question concerning who may be recruited to streetcorner gangs, one of my informants responded, "It doesn't matter what you are, as long as you are human." Although distinctions between Taiwanese and Mainlander gangs continue to be drawn, my liumang informants insisted that "ethnicity doesn't matter much anymore." Such statements, in contrast to apparent facts, are in keeping with a popular saying among gangsters that "In the underworld, all men are brothers." Historically, within enclaves of secret-society activity in China as well as overseas, there was often a self-conscious openness to all persons regardless of surname, dialect, or region (Perry 1980; Woon 1984; Chiang 1954; Fei-ling Davis 1971; Mak 1981).

Regardless of differences in family, ethnic, or economic background, mutual assistance and loyalty are expected from all gang members. When gang members marry, their brothers in the gang are among the guests bearing "red envelopes" (filled with money). More than thirty envelope-bearing brothers showed up at the wedding of one gang member I spoke with. "Would gang brothers help out if someone in your family were ill?" I asked. "They certainly would give money if they had it to give." Liumang consciously single out the warrior god, *Guan Gung*, for worship in local temples because of this god's reputed personal integrity, loyalty, and devotion to comrades-in-arms.[7]

Most of the gang members I knew did not have any regular or reliable means of support, and they were usually not sure where their next Taiwan dollar would come from. Still, most were like Ah Ji, who was more than content to sacrifice economic security to be able to spend afternoons with gang brothers simply talking, chewing betel nuts, and drinking tea. Membership in a gang may provide basic sustenance for a few core members, but none of my informants claimed to have been attracted to the gangster life style by the promise of wealth or riches. "We get money from the leader, but you can't get rich from this. To get rich you have to become the leader," I was told. The leader of the gang may operate a small gambling hall, or perhaps a teahouse or small restaurant, but usually only *he* profits from this. Protection fees collected from merchants in the gang's turf are redistributed to gang members, but the amount that any one individual receives is not nearly enough to live on. The gang may also be involved in settling local disputes and collecting debts in the community. Depending on the sum owed, debt collection can be one of the more lucrative forms of gang activity.

The expectation in the underworld is that when someone brings in money—"black money," as it is called in the "black society"—he should treat everyone in the gang to his good fortune. Large profits, sometimes resulting from an occasional gambling boon or debt settlement, were thus often just as quickly spent on feasting or reveling. My informants described many such occasions when a leader's, or elder brother's, largess was enjoyed by all members of the gang. Such events served to redistribute surpluses, while elevating the status of the leader.

Status differences in Taiwanese streetcorner gangs reflect differences in age, wealth, and seniority in the gang, but these differences are simultaneously played down by gangsters. "There is the leader, and then there is everyone else," I was frequently told. Although the lao da is the final authority in the gang, he is really just more equal than the rest. Unlike the head of a household, with whom members of the younger generation rarely interact in a spirit of mutuality, a gangster explained that "you can talk things over with the leader [of a gang], and he will listen to you."

A gang leader may assign different duties and responsibilities to gang members, and these assignments often reflect subtle status differences in the gang. However, a spirit of equality usually overshadows any consciousness of a status gradient. For example, one afternoon I questioned two boys who were members of a gang in the Taipei suburbs, with these results:

Researcher: Are there any ranks or levels of authority in your gang?

Boys: No, there is just the boss, and everyone else is the same. The boss tells us what to do. He may ask certain brothers to go and collect protection money, and others to be in charge of settling debts. We are in charge of settling debts.

Researcher: Why did he pick you and not someone else?

Boys: I don't know.

Researcher: Are there brothers in the gang whom you could ask to go and do a certain task?

Boys: Yes, we could do that.

Researcher: Could these same brothers ask you to go and do something?

Boys: They could but we wouldn't do it.

Researcher: This is because your authority is higher than theirs?

Boys: No, not really. We all get along together extremely well.

At the same time my informants often complained about the increasing selfishness of some liumang, as if to point out that the nonmaterialistic or spiritual life of the underworld subculture is slowly disappearing. What gangsters in particular feel is being eroded is a willingness to place loyalty to brothers before all else, as well as the alleged egalitarianism in the gang. Thus I frequently heard complaints from gangsters in Taipei to the effect that too many of today's liumang worship name-brand goods, ranging from cigarette lighters to knit shirts to imported brandy. Unlike "the old-style liumang," who are said to have valued the intrinsic, spiritual rewards of gang life, liumang today are said to want external, material rewards, that is, symbols that differentiate the status of persons in the larger, stratified society. Increasingly, the outside world is felt to impinge on the socially constructed cultural purity of the gang.

CONCLUSIONS

Concern over the changing character of liumang, reflected especially in comments about their increasing desire for name-brand goods and wealth, suggests that the boundaries of gangsters' moral community are slowly changing. Identification with a neighborhood-based brotherhood as the locus of the streetcorner gangster's commitments is slowly being undermined by the tendency to base one's identity on common class interests, which shape one's life style in accordance with others of the same or higher socioeconomic status.

The evident tension between an identity based on symbolic constructions of community and an identity emerging from class interests (and cross-cutting local neighborhoods) seems to be increasing with the rising standard of living in Taiwan; in particular, this is the result of increasing opportunities for more and more gangsters, vis-à-vis their leaders' entrepreneurial savvy, to prosper economically. The measure of the man in the "closed" symbolic community is the solidarity of the group to which he belongs, including the trust and loyalty shown to him, and which he in turn shows others. But nowadays, as I was frequently reminded, "Whether or not you can 'talk loyalty' [*jiang i qi*] is not as important as whether you possess riches and wealth." The image of the hero as the loyal and righteous comrade-in-arms is gradually being replaced in the black society with the image of the hero as successful entrepreneur.

As class replaces community as a stronger and more meaningful basis for action and loyalty, streetcorner gangs will probably abandon their street corners and consolidate. Like Mainlander gangs, they will begin to act like small hierarchically organized corporations that operate for profit and trade in illegal products such as guns and drugs. While the different niches that Mainlander and Taiwanese gangs presently occupy in Taiwan's political economy are associated with different meanings and life courses, an increasing overlap of niches is likely to render Taiwanese and Mainlander gangs more and more indistinguishable. Moreover, the need to use ethnic symbols to differentiate them will probably disappear.

At the same time, certain benign, if not actually positive functions of streetcorner gangs, such as providing knowledge, mutual assistance, intimacy, and solidarity to young teenage boys who are unwilling or unable to ascend the educational ladder, will be subordinated to the more long-term and far less benign function of generating lifelong criminal careers. As a member of the younger generation, Ah Ji felt that it was incumbent upon him to learn from his older gang brothers. By his own admission, he had learned a great deal about society, morality, and people in general from them. He was advised by his brothers to be a *shenshi* liumang ("gentleman liumang"), in contrast to one who is rude, and "has no class." He was even advised not to become involved in illegal, underworld activities. "Earn money in some legitimate business," he was told. "The gangster life has no future."

NOTES

1. It is undeniable that the government manipulates the meaning of the term liumang, to curtail the activities of persons suspected of opposing the current political regime (Peng 1971). In 1985, legislators were unsuccessful in making the official definition of liumang specific enough to prevent misuse and misunderstanding by government agencies, and after much heated debate, a liumang remained, among other things, someone "who is by nature evil or a vagrant with no visible means of support."

2. I use the term gangsters to refer to males, mostly in their early twenties or younger, who are members of small, loosely organized streetcorner gangs located in the greater Taipei metropolitan area. In Taiwan there are two types of criminal gangs. Mainlander gangs (headed by men who left mainland China in the late 1930s or after, or their sons) are larger than Taiwanese gangs, operate nationally or even internationally, and are highly structured with centralized authority. Taiwanese gangs (headed by men whose ancestors, going back at least two generations, were born on Taiwan) are small and take their names from places or landmarks in the local community. Usually their turf extends no more than a few city blocks. References to liumang in this chapter refer only to the Taiwanese streetcorner gangster whose turf is confined to a particular neighborhood in the urban setting, and not to the Mainlander type gangster, who is more likely to blend into the larger society and culture in terms of both behavior and ideology. Subethnic differences in Taiwan between Mainlanders and Taiwanese are reflected in many different spheres and are especially salient in the political arena. (For a discussion of the role of ethnicity in politics, see Winckler 1981.)

3. Psychocultural analyses of China's political culture too often take for granted that a Confucian moral order has an exclusive influence on China's (or Taiwan's) vast and varied population (Pye 1968; Solomon 1971; Richard Wilson 1970). As Dittmer (1983) points out, these analyses fail to take account of the non-Confucian aspects of China's tradition, including the tradition associated with knight-errantry. As Fried (1951) once remarked, cultural traditions that deviate from Confucian orthodoxy are unduly eclipsed by the assignment of China's "Great Tradition" to Confucianism.

4. Governance in late imperial China, particularly at the lowest levels of the bureaucracy, often entailed squeezing the population mercilessly for profits. Thus according to a nineteenth-century Western observer, the difference between good and bad magistrates was only a matter of degree: "The mandarins take advantage of a system thus endured as a necessary evil, to enforce arbitrary extortions, and oblige people to offer bribes. Hence in the whole country corruption and injustice abound. I believe, in fact, that all mandarins take money exclusive of their salary and that the grand difference between what the Chinese call the 'good' and the 'bad' mandarin is that while the former makes people pay for justice, the latter sells injustice to the highest bidder" (quoted in Hsiao 1960: 438-439).

5. See Chiang (1954: 17) for a description of how Nien rebels exploited local feuds for their own purposes.

6. This double standard is reminiscent of past attitudes toward bandits in rural settings in China, which may have induced one researcher to claim that "The common people consider that the bandits of their own side [of the river] are a nuisance, but part of the natural social order and usually amenable to diplomacy and reasonable arrangement, while the bandits from the other side of the river they loathe and dread" (Lattimore 1962: 323).

7. Although *Guan Gong*, the "god of war," served as a model for antistate secret society activities in imperial China, merchants also regarded him as a god of wealth and fidelity in business. Shansi/Shensi merchants thus installed the image of *Guan Gong* in their guild hall, and this was wholly approved of by the state (see Rawski 1985: 410).

9 FAEROE ISLANDS: CLOWNING, DRAMA, AND DISTORTION

Dennis Gaffin

Social scientists from various disciplines are still struggling to overcome the simplistic dichotomy "deviant versus conformist." Jack Douglas and Frances Waksler conclude their textbook with a plea for a new perspective on deviance, one that overcomes the discontinuity between deviance and nondeviance: "By recognizing the ordinary nature of deviance, we see that in studying deviance we are not studying 'them,' people of a different kind with special characteristics or acted upon by a different kind of fate; we are studying 'us,' for all of us are in some ways deviants" (1982: 393-9).

One way to forge a closer link between deviance and conformity is to treat deviance as a grievance process. A grievance is "a circumstance or condition which one person (or group) perceives to be unjust, and the grounds for resentment or complaint" (Nader and Todd 1978: 14).[1] A grievance, a feeling of being wronged, may be a consequence of an action taken against someone, but may also be any act that offends a person's sense of propriety, regardless of whether the act was done directly to that person. By so extending the concept of grievance, any inappropriate act can become an opportunity to express social values and to impose sanctions.

This approach allows us to regard troublesome behavior as something everyone is capable of committing. Moreover, it reminds us that talk about other people's deviance is itself conformist behavior. The ways people create others' deviant identities and express their grievances are keys to understanding the cultural dynamics of deviance. This chapter explores these processes in the small village of Koppbøur on the Faeroe Islands.

Everyone in Koppbøur is a stigma-maker and is likewise open to stigma from others. Through names, nicknames, social comments, anecdotes, and stories everyone yarns about the deviance of nearly everyone else. Yet people are largely unaware of the labels applied to them. Their talk about each other differs from gossip in that it is not vicious, scandalous, accusatory, nor used as a tool to maintain the exclusiveness of groups (Gluckman 1963). On the contrary, people are generally on good terms with each other in face-to-face encounters. In this egalitarian community where villagers assiduously avoid direct conflict, everyday folklores about everyday persons act as indirect responses to, and sanctions against, nonconformity. Moreover, discourse criticizing others extends to both those who are alive and those who are dead and those who live within and those who live outside the community. Villagers construct living legends about others that are often entertaining and humorous and, more than gossip, part of a cultural complex which has always emphasized satire, legend, narrative ability, and the caricature of characters of the past and present.

If hard deviance is something that only a minority of people can do in any community, then there are virtually no hard deviants in Koppbøur, although almost everyone is a soft deviant (Raybeck, Chapter 2). The mere fact that the community and its small size discourage hard deviance does not mean that by local standards people are not seriously deviant. But, more to the point, the vast majority of people receive reputations for deviance, which register among their most salient social identifiers. People ridicule and joke about the two or three fat people in the same manner they talk and amuse themselves with accounts of the one or two persons who have physically harmed property or people. Just as the social structure and ethos eschew ranking, so do people eschew the ranking of offenses. In this way each person is talked about as more or less deviant. Indeed, deviance—everyone's deviance—is the basis of social order.

As villagers incessantly evaluate each other socially in verbal accounts of various lengths, they revoke and streamline legendary reputations and caricatures. They negatively characterize each other as one thing or another and personify broken norms as putative character traits of particular individuals. Within this egalitarian society these negative characterizations act as leveling techniques to maintain social equality and to avoid social rankings. In terms of Savishinsky's model (Chapter 3), publicly told tales put the deviant actions of others "on stage." Storytelling, in Freilich's scheme (Chapter 1), works as a "smart" technique to put people in their "proper" place. Thus, constant ridicule and critique of others' behavior makes listeners sensitive to community norms and cautious in their own behavior. They epitomize each other as drunks, hotheads, fools and lazy, arrogant, unsociable, quarrelsome, greedy persons—deviants. This epitomization is central to village life and community cohesion.[2] Nearly everyone is a living legend of deviance.

THE SETTING

The Faeroes are an isolated group of small islands about 200 miles north northwest of the Shetland Isles and approximately equidistant from Norway, Iceland, and Scotland. Inhabitants live on eighteen of the islands and speak their own Norse tongue-Faeroese, one of the five Scandinavian languages. For a thousand years Faeroe Islanders have been leading a precarious existence, wrenching livelihoods from fishing, fowling, raising sheep, and hunting whales. Their lives are directed by the winds and seas. Each year fishermen drown in the stormy North Atlantic or fall off steep mountain cliffs searching for fulmars, puffins, guillemots, and other seabirds.

Although Faeroese is an ancient Scandinavian tongue, it has only had a written form for about one hundred and forty years. Before the Reformation of 1540 Norway owned the islands and Old Norse was spoken. Today the Faeroes are a bilingual country, with Faeroese as the common household language and Danish as the second language. First Norway, and then Denmark, ran the Faeroe Islands as a fiefdom for a total of seven hundred years. In 1948 Denmark granted the Faeroese home rule, and since then the islanders have maintained their own parliament. They are a highly successful fishing nation of over 45,000 inhabitants who, unlike Danes, have chosen not to be part of the European Economic Community (EEC).[3]

Partly because the native language was not standardly written until about a hundred years ago, and partly because of a long history of isolation and self-reliance, the Faeroese oral tradition is strong. Even after the turn of the century, villagers gathered in *kvøldsetir* ("evening sittings") around kitchen hearths to listen to local legends. Stories, legends, and other oral artforms like balladry remain part of everyday life. *Kvaeðir* are Faroese ballads still chanted without accompanying music during medieval ring dances in village dance houses. They speak of the exploits of legendary heroes from the past. Another ballad form, the indigenous satirical ballad (*táttur*, pl. *taettir*), pokes fun at the behavior and character traits of local villagers. Although villagers now rarely compose new taettir, these poems epitomize local social control and the ever-present public ridicule of improper behavior. Villagers talk daily about each other's negative characteristics. "Folk talk"—social talk about other folks—suggests that villagers have a preoccupation with deviance.

The constraints of isolation, tight settlement patterns, and harsh environment, together with the need to work together on small Viking-style rowboats and fowling lines, have necessitated an emphasis on circumspection, self-control, and amiability. In the historical context of lives filled with the uncertainties of sea, weather, and subsistence activities, comment and lore about impropriety give villagers a necessary sense of social and moral assurance.

Koppbøur is a small village of 350 persons located on a large isolated island, Skúgvoy.[4] The high mountain that separates the village from the other villages of the island has helped to maintain the independence of people there, as well as to provide a close, continuing food source from the bounty of seabirds that nest on the sheer mountain cliffs. Most men primarily earn their living from fishing on small boats on the fishing grounds surrounding the islands or on large Faeroese or Norwegian trawlers that work in more distant waters. Yet local fishing, bird fowling, sheep raising and whale hunting are still important economic and cultural activities. The village has several egalitarian features: In addition to a democratic sociopolitical structure, socialized medicine, and the lack of strong extrafamilial alliances, its inhabitants belong to families who generally own the same style houses, own automobiles of comparable value, own relatively equal plots of land, and raise about the same number of sheep. Although they live in a recently modernized community, men still jump out of their cars into the bays to slaughter pilot whales (*Globiocephala melaena*) and leave their cars at the top of mountains to climb down ropes over mountain and cliffs to hunt birds. Their life mixes modern and peasant activities.

In Koppbøur, as elsewhere in the Faeroes, there are no trees, and houses are laid out along the sides of one main street of the village, which is located at the base of sloping hillsides. Therefore almost all activities outside the household are in public view. Villagers are intricately intermarried and connected via kinship ties, including some first-cousin marriages. Seven surnames belong to 157 villagers, and almost all native villagers can trace their ancestry to less than twenty families. The closedness of the community was eventually revealed to me when I discovered that every villager was related by blood or marriage to a native villager (*Koppbingur*, pl. *Koppbingar*), and that my wife and I were the first outsiders (other than spouses marrying into the village) ever to move into the village for more than a month. This intense familiarity with other persons complements the visibility of activity. Crimes common in other parts of the world such as theft, vandalism, and assault are virtually absent in the peaceful village. Local forms of deviance such as adultery, excessive drinking, heterodoxy, emotional dysfunction, physical deficiencies, and quarrelsomeness usually do not directly threaten the physical or economic safety of a household. Villagers leave their houses unlocked and unattended. Moreover, there is a local custom of visiting that permits people to enter houses unannounced without knocking on doors. In this community, group order is maintained by the interconnectedness of kinship and social ties, by the tight settlement pattern, and, most importantly, by public scrutiny and comment.

Daily talk is the primary form of social control. Villagers may appeal to the islands' formal systems of social control, which include village council meetings, sheriffs, courts, and judges. But they rarely use them even in the unusual cases of overt disagreement or dispute. Villagers prefer to handle affairs without public ceremony so as to maintain their own reputations for amiability; to avoid calling upon authorities; and to avoid subjecting themselves to the possibility of official sanctions, which would entail public ridicule for them. Daily oral social control takes the form of ridicule in informative, often amusing place names, nicknames, comments, anecdotes, and stories. These names and accounts are symbolic statements that transform the mundane details of and grievances about others' everyday behavior into parables about proper and improper behavior. These statements create both social caricatures and everyday mythologies, neither of which are usually known to the subjects themselves. Since people do not directly attempt to check on the veracity of these normative statements, the accounts take on a life and truth of their own.

DEVIANCE AND NAMES

The island of Skúgvoy and the local environs of Koppbøur abound with hundreds of place names. Many of these derive from the events and stories of villagers' lives. Villagers can often relate incidents associated with the name: some explain its reputed origin, others an event supposed to have happened there. One place, Marjunigjógv (Marion's Chasm), is named after a woman who is said to have committed suicide by jumping into the sea at that spot. Another place, Hundagjogv (Dog Chasm), is said to be the location where a dog, having been thrown into the sea, escaped drowning through an under island passageway, and Gentuhylur (Girl's Pool) is where a girl is said to have drowned.

Villagers also talk about places where specific events occurred. That is, the place names become known for more than one trait or experience. Such places are double reincarnations of the past. For example, Viðagjógv (Wide Chasm) is where Hjartvar played as a child and was hit by a rock that permanently damaged his hearing. Similarly, Gandasteinur (Black Magic Rock) is both the heavy boulder that the legendary witch Barbara i Geilini moved and also the location where fat Tummas tripped and broke his leg. Local history is a congeries of tales associated with particular places and people.

Although most place names seem ancient, Koppbingar continue to create them. For example, during the summer of 1985 the town council employed local men to repair the village road and side streets. Covering a dirt street with concrete necessitated building an adjacent wall to keep earth from coming down upon the road and construction site. The wall became known as Berlinarmúrin (The Berlin Wall), reportedly because the construction took so long to build. The village wall, like the real Berlin Wall, took on emotional and social significance as the product of a "great," overly lengthy task of local importance. In a village whose people prize being *raskur* (energetic, efficient, hard-working), and who had already saddled the project's supervisor with a reputation for "talking too much" in idle chat, the place name made a mockery of this man's behavior.

Not all place names or personal names mark unusual events or nonconformist behavior, nor, like comments and stories discussed below, do they necessarily note particularly serious transgressions. But they morally mark the countryside and village with long living testimonies to the scrutiny of deviance, regardless of the age or severity of an offense. Personal nicknames (*ekenøvn*), often unknown to their owners, especially demonstrate how villagers make witty, if sometimes nasty comments on others' character traits and flaws.[5] Koppbingar also entertain each other in this way. Anecdotes about the origins of nicknames also point to the close knowledge villagers have of each other and the legendary quality of individuals' social histories and identifiers. Nicknames are of several types: they come in anatomical, behavioral, moral, and locational varieties.

Anatomical nicknames allude to physical characteristics alone or to physical characteristics together with other traits. Stóran (Big One) is actually a short person and Tjúkkan (Pudge) is skinny. Such irony is common. Since villagers also consider Storan to have little mental ability, there is added amusement, irony, and criticism in the name. Feit Frida (Fat Frida) is literal in description but implies, as one man mentioned, that she is too lazy to lose weight. Discussing Feit Frida, a villager compared her to a formerly fat person who had worked to lose weight. Karl í Skalini (Karl in the Bowl) refers to Karl's bowlegs. Í Skalini is a nickname that villagers also attach to Karl's descendants, using it like a patronym. In this way the physical problem of the ancestor remains a source of potential shame for his descendants. Thus nicknames referring to less common physical traits can imply personality characteristics and taint various roles a person may fill.

Villagers comment on behavior by nicknames such as Tubbackmunnur (Tobacco Mouth), Umgongds Maria (Walkabout Maria), Skundari (The Hurrier), and Aftur og Fram (Back and Forth). Such names are not used face-to-face. A young woman discusses Tobacco Mouth:

They used to call him Tobacco Mouth, because his father used to have this chewing tobacco in his mouth. His father used it.
[I ask if it was a bad name.]
No, it was not really bad. But he was not called directly by that name. He would be referred to by that name.

Walkabout Maria is the name of a woman who for some time had no permanent home of her own and lived at different places for short periods of time. The Hurrier is a man who often hastens between a few different houses in a particular part of the village. He usually does not put on outer clothing when going between houses and, according to several informants, often hurries to other houses soliciting drinks to quench his excessive alcoholic thirst. Back and Forth is the man frequently seen aimlessly walking back and forth short distances on the road. Since he is known to be mentally unbalanced, the name literally describes his walking habits and metaphorically refers to a mind "with no direction." Many villagers have such names, but since they rarely hear them, their power as mockery is mostly by example, without outright formal labeling.

Ethically questionable behavior is tagged in names such as Vágskona (Woman of the Bay), Fløskur (Bottles), Presturin (The Priest), and Jørðmeistarin (The Landmaster). The Woman of the Bay is the name of a woman who lives in a house by a bay that everyone must pass by and has a reputation for frequently participating in sexual activities with different men. Villagers think that Bottles drinks too much beer; he has lots of bottles around. The Priest is a tongue-in-cheek name for a man who is very active in the evangelist movement and thinks of himself, according to some, as very religious. Unordained, he is thought to be self-righteous and fanatical. One person said he is "a priest with the devil behind him." The Landmaster refers both to a part of the village, one man's larger-than-usual landholding, and to this man's acting as if he is master over other villagers. Simultaneously, then, the nickname refers to a place name, economic status, and the social delict of arrogance.

Locational nicknames usually attach physical structures, homesteads, or sectors of the village to people's first names. Villagers especially distinguish between people with the same first names by referring to locations where they live: an example is Leif and Frida Posthús (Leif and Frida Post Office), a couple who work in the village's post office and live in the house above it. Such names may have behavioral and normative implications as people's social identities take on some of the characteristics of place. For example, for a man to be a post office worker, and not a fisherman or physical laborer, carries certain (negative) connotations. Also, as certain families descend from certain houses, families and their ancestors (*slektir*) are often noted for characteristics associated with where they were raised. One villager said that a man was violence-prone because he came from a certain place. Reportedly the violent temperament began hundreds of years ago with the family mentioned in a now-written legend of the sixteenth century.[6]

Since each person fears being ridiculed, they listen closely to each other, avoid behavior that incurs the ridicule they hear others lavish upon third parties, and generally adjust their behaviors to conform with public sentiment. Thus in names and, as I shall discuss below, in listening to comments and stories about others, social control is maintained indirectly, symbolically, and parsimoniously. In this way there are no direct, murky, or time-wasting accusations, emotional entanglements, and legal procedures.

EVERYDAY COMMENTS AND DEVIANCE

As Koppbøur is intricately interwoven by names, nicknames, kinship ties, familiarity with people of the past and the present, and people's public visibility, every person literally becomes a tradition of the village. Koppbingar further celebrate the distinctiveness of local life and the characters within it by making comments and telling anecdotes about local personalities. Such accounts usually detail or allude to deficiencies or unfavorable character traits.

One often hears relatively mild though critical remarks such as, "Andreas is always driving up and down the road," "Magnus drinks a lot," or "Birgir never has anything to do." Or one villager may relate short incidents to another: "Eivindur, when he was pitching hay with his hayfork, stabbed his own foot" or "Did you hear about when Arne was in Norway and asked a storekeeper for a bag in Faeroese, and the storekeeper thought that Arne had asked for a whore?!" Villagers like to amuse each other with third-person ridicule. Such remarks, and the grievances that mark more serious social offenses, can be linked to various aspects of culture such as family, economics, politics, and religion. Not only does each realm of culture have its deviant(s), but each villager is deviant with respect to at least one cultural realm. That is, people have something negative to say about virtually everyone.

Some comments refer to sexual, familial, or kinship-related activities. A man named Jens appeared in several comments and anecdotes. I heard, "Jens is a flirt," "Jens is a lady's man," and "They say Jens slept with another woman while his wife was pregnant, about to give birth." Another man revealed to me that Leivur, a married man with three children, was not the legitimate son of his father, Hilmar. He was the product of a union between his mother, Alma, and another villager, Olaf, who was married to Marianna. The man said that he thought that Leivur did not know that Hilmar was not his real father. Further he commented that "Alma was all that Hilmar could get [for a wife]."

One day a neighbor of mine told me about Paulina. He said that she was temperamental and unsocial and that every villager knew it. My neighbor, mentioning that there was a problem between Paulina and her husband, asked, "You know that Paulina had a child by another man, a previous husband?" The interjection of the comment provided more evidence that Paulina was not a respectable person.

Koppbingar practice monogamy and prize female sexual virtue; male-female relations in the village are thus well defined. Men and women (other than an engaged or married couple) generally avoid being in the company of a member of the opposite sex without a third person nearby. It may not be the case that Jens slept with another woman during his wife's pregnancy, but the searing story gives credence to the possibility that men and women are capable of infidelity. That comment, along with others attributing flirtatiousness to Jens, indicate that villagers notice such sexual antics, that minor sexual indiscretions might lead to infidelity, and that such behavior is sanctioned by public scrutiny and comment.

The comment about Leivur's parentage is instructive about sexual norms and the desirability of mates with particular traits. Women with less sexual experience are more desirable mates. Since Hilmar could only "get" a wife who had borne a child by another man, the story infers that he too lacks desirable social/sexual qualities.

The comments about Paulina also point to sexual norms and general social skills. Paulina not only broke traditional norms of monogamy and one-time marriage, but the comments infer that Koppbingar link sexual behavior with other personal characteristics, specifically temperament, sociability, and morality. In this way it is possible for villagers to attach a person's deviance in one realm of culture (sexuality) to another (sociability). In the process of relaying comments and anecdotes, reputations for deviation gain power and momentum.

Some comments discuss economic or workaday skills. Statements I heard include "A sheep died at Poul's, I don't understand Poul, he is lazy"; "Johan couldn't take the life of the sea"; and "Gunnar is a good foreman, but he is too fiery-tempered." A schoolteacher, an overweight person, and a handicapped person are often subjects for derogatory remarks about "not doing anything" or "having nothing to do." Publicly visible physical work—from men's fowling to women's knitting—spares a man or woman from gaining a reputation for laziness. Laziness wastes precious economic time and material. The comment about Johan also points to the local emphasis on hardiness and seaworthiness.

People also like to talk about individuals who are inept in everyday social interaction, especially the shy and those who cannot control their emotions. Being quick to anger is particularly disliked and offensive. "He is so ill-tempered," "He does not know how to take practical jokes," or "He always becomes angry immediately when someone makes jokes with him" are favorite comments about some persons. There is a local type of deviant called the *rukka* (easily angered fool) who is said to exist on nearly every fishing trawler and exists in several stories about local villagers.[7] Control of emotions is necessary for dangerous, confining small-group fishing, fowling, and whaling pursuits. In a land of self-control, emotional display is dangerous. The link between getting angry and being bad for the community is epitomized in the Faeroese word *ondur*, which means both "angry" and "evil."

Other comments tell about the deviance of excessive drinking. It is not uncommon to hear things like "Jón drinks too much"; "There goes Eydtor, stumbling drunk again"; "There goes Johan to buy booze from Tummas"; "Pauli talks filthy when he's drunk"; or "Magnus drinks by himself in the *hjallur*" (the Faeroese wooden drying shed). Villagers know that others might talk about them; even folks who drink little sometimes hide their liquor bottles. Drinking is a tricky affair. Depending on circumstances and personality, it can either increase friendliness or start arguments. In this context grievances about villagers' drinking habits can influence volatile drinkers, acting as a warning that public ridicule will be served up to those who overindulge or behave irascibly when drinking.

Other comments refer to the incompetence of town councillors, the fanaticism of those who belong to religious minorities, and the arrogance of particular individuals. A person's deviance is thus linked with one or more of the working, social, or religious roles he or she occupies. Some accounts are longer than the comments and anecdotes of everyday conversation and take shape in stories.

EVERYDAY STORIES AND DEVIANCE

Stories, like their shorter counterparts, often relate the improprieties of village characters and encode norms that relate to various aspects of community life. One story tells of the time, fifty years ago, when some Koppbingar got a man drunk and put him on a small off-shore island with no transport back. This man had arrogantly walked barefoot in the snow over the mountains to demonstrate his bravado while courting a girl from another village. But most stories are contemporary and recount recent village behavior.[8] One describes the time that Johan believed the story about the submarine that came close to the village to pick up a visitor; another deals with a woman who believed in trolls; and a third ridicules the fisherman whose sweater sleeves were sewn together by shipmates. Such character portrayals are often humorous and skillfully told. In the context of local history, they make people into social caricatures.

In the following story, drinking alcohol becomes the forum through which storytellers portray another form of socially disapproved behavior. One day Sverre joined a friend of his to buy two cases of liquor from Denmark. They divided up the liquor. After a few days Sverre went over to his friend's house to help his friend drink up his share. It seemed that Sverre had already drunk up his own share. When they finished drinking his friend's share, Sverre told his friend that he knew where they could get some more liquor. So Sverre went away and later came back with a bottle. He said that he and his friend had to pay a dear, inflated price because liquor was then scarce. Sverre's friend contributed his share of the price and then together they drank the more expensive liquor. Later villagers discovered that the expensive bottle that Sverre sold his friend was one of the same bottles that he had originally ordered with him. Greedy Sverre is the protagonist of a story that ridicules and castigates those who act against egalitarian and cooperative pursuits.

Villagers also characterize each other in terms of agreeableness, perhaps the most important personal characteristic in the avoidance of direct conflict, so central to village life. One must be careful in talking with someone who is *tvørt* (difficult, stubborn). A difficult person is socially contentious and might bring up age-old disagreements between dead relations or take offense at jokes. Or such a person will not give up old ways or will not admit himself or herself wrong. Leif is allegedly tvørur:

Leif can tell you that his cousin Jacob went to Tórshavn with his own car. And all the people on the bus going to Klaksvík say to Leif, "No, that is not true, Jacob went on the bus to Tórshavn from over there." There are fifteen or twenty persons who have seen his cousin go onto the bus. But Leif, who has not seen his cousin go to Tórshavn with his own car, still says Jacob went with his own car. Leif, he is like that.

In the following case stubbornness appears in the context of conforming to modern times and using modern conveniences.

And Jón is like that. *Ja*, he wants to be old-fashioned. In older days, when he went to Skalavík he did not want a car. He wanted to walk. He wanted to use peat for his oven, even if coal is cheaper. He did not want electricity in his house, and he didn't want a refrigerator. He eventually did get a refrigerator in his house, but he misused it. One time he wanted to make a fool out of his wife with it. In the older days fisherman used to take their fish whole without gutting or cleaning them and drop them in the *hjallur* [the outside drying shed]. But one day recently Jón came back from the harbor with his catch and said to his wife, "Yes, now you have bought a new *hjallur* so I'm going to throw all this fish into it." And he emptied his whole catch into his wife's new refrigerator, because he was stubborn.

Such stories aim to ridicule those who make life difficult and wasteful for others. Such impractical acts and uncooperative temperaments endanger the community's maintenance of peaceful cooperation.

Another amusing story talks about self-righteousness and religious fanaticism. The story focuses on a religious man, Regin, formerly a heavy drinker who now drinks no alcohol at all. This man is quite active in the village's mission house. It is the prayer house and meeting place for *intermissionar*, a fundamentalist subgroup of the dominant Lutheran church who practice temperance and actively preach a conservative morality. There was a problem between another man, Gunnar, and his wife a few years ago. They were having marital difficulties and Gunnar would sometimes come home drunk. One day the religious man, Regin, went over in his good clothes to the house of Gunnar's father to volunteer to visit Gunnar to help him with his martial problems and to talk about the evils of drinking. The conversation took place in the *hjallur*, while the father was slaughtering a sheep. After Regin offered his help, the father grabbed the shoulders of Regin's jacket and said "Out!" In taking hold of the man's shoulders he left bloody handprints on Regin's clean jacket.

The end of the story is told with amusement, with the bloodied jacket standing as a sanction against the social sin of arrogance. The story also implies that interfering in other people's personal and familial problems is wrong. As the storyteller explained, "One must be a good example, if one is to preach to others" and "Such interfering fanatics think they are nearer to God than us." To nominate oneself as a leader and moral exemplar is offensive. Being a good example, or rather not being a bad example, is much closer to the philosophy of normative behavior in this village. Fundamentalists especially are deviant in their self-righteousness, assertiveness, and vocal nature: they challenge local values on reservedness.

Niclas, a Koppbinger who no longer lives in the village, is a special legendary figure in that he offended the community in a number of ways. Niclas was lazy, "crazy" (*svakur*), and contentious.

He was special, all right. He had little schooling also. He was special in that he was almost impossible. You could have him one day for work, and the next day he did not bother to come any longer. Yes, he also sailed as a fisherman up to Iceland with his cousin, but somehow he managed when he was on board ship, but he was a *serlingur* ["eccentric"] in that he didn't bother to work.

A younger villager, Johan, said that one time Niclas burned down part of his family's *hjallur*. Johan continued that when he was a teenager, Niclas came up to him by the village dock one summer day and told Johan that if Johan did not give him the fish he had just caught, he would throw Johan into the sea. Johan was so afraid he gave Niclas the fish.

Niclas is one of only two persons I heard villagers portray as physically aggressive. (The other is a drinker who hurt his wife.) His arson and menacing radically violate village norms. But villagers did not speak of him as a criminal, or in tones any different than other village characters, but simply as a special, crazy person. Their analysis stresses norms on hard work, fair treatment of others, and nonaggressiveness rather than the state's more formal prohibitions of assault, vandalism, and so forth. Moreover, Niclas' legacy reinforces local social control by keeping Niclas as a local legend rather than an incarcerated criminal. Ultimately he remains Koppbøur's "property," an epitome of deviant behavior. One man speculates about Niclas' current whereabouts: "I think he is in a museum somewhere on the island of Eysturoy." Not so. He is in the living museum of Koppbøur's mythmakers.

There are several tales that deal with the same individuals and refer to particular, negative characteristics of those persons: the focus may be an individual's foolhardiness, sloth, irascibility, excessive drinking, quarrelsomeness, adultery, arrogance, or religious identity. Such tales, like nicknames and comments, constitute a form of labeling and reinforce a person's social identity as deviating from norms in certain ways. All these verbal accounts involve the establishment of an agreed-upon social identity that other members of the community participate in promoting. Indeed Koppbingar associate virtually every villager with one form of deviance or another, and those deviations are built into names, descriptions, comments, anecdotes, stories, and general reputations that together comprise a kind of living legend of a social identity. Moreover, it does not matter whether the legend is correct as long as it supports the community's continuing narrative.

EVERYDAY DEVIANCE AS CARICATURE AND LIVING LEGEND

My first inkling that villagers' anecdotes about other villagers were often not wholly accurate came when I began to hear bits of what other villagers said about my wife and myself. Some villagers said I was an ornithologist. Another, perhaps observing me walking near the sea with binoculars and a plain black case (for a portable typewriter), said I was a Russian or American spy. One story concerned my noontime rendez-vous with a Russian submarine off the tip of the island. Reportedly, some people really believed that it was true. Other pieces of information proved to be misreports. A man was surprised to hear that I had not received a present of fish from his brother-in-law, an exchange that had been erroneously reported to him. A woman from a neighboring village had heard that neighbors of ours, to whom she was related, had given me a present of cakes; however, we never received any. Another story circulated about an illness that my wife had; it seemed that the originator of the comments had not seen my wife for a long time. Another villager heard that we had installed a shower stall in our house, but in fact we had no running hot water. Truth seemed elusive.

I began to follow villagers' comments and information about each other systematically, paying special attention to the people frequently mentioned. It became clear that at least some of the stories did not match my experience of the same people. Although my experience was not as representative as the Koppbingars', nevertheless there seemed to be embroidery in many accounts.

After I had lived in the village for only a short time, a nearby neighbor told me about one of my next-door neighbors, who was then away on a fishing trip. She said, with the strong support of her husband, that Eyðtor was a terrible drinker and that he would come over to my house nagging and searching for booze to satisfy his voracious thirst. He was a drunk, they said. I should hide my liquor, if I had any, and if he ever asked me for some, I should say I didn't have any. Otherwise, he would constantly be over at the house intruding and cadging my liquor.

The starkness of their description made me glad that he was away from the village at the time. I had an image of this man as swaggering, frightening, and rude. He came home after a few weeks. He appeared at our doorway sharp and respectful one day with a present of fish for us. He was one of the first villagers to offer us a present. Surprised and relieved that this man appeared more neighborly than most of my neighbors, I later wondered about the gap between our neighbor's description of the man and his actual behavior. Some time afterwards I learned that he did have a reputation for drinking and that the exaggerating neighbors did not like him.

Then there were the often volunteered descriptions of Vagnar í Kálgarði (Vagnar of the Kale Garden) as a *serlingur* (eccentric) who foolishly believed in black magic and had experiences with all kinds of imaginary beings including trolls and *huldufólk* (gray people of the mountainsides who live in boulders). Many villagers said that he was the only man in the village who really believed in such things. Vagnar happened to be one of my primary informants. Even after some intimate conversations, including a discussion of how villagers criticize him, he said he had never seen such beings. He did say he often heard of other people's experiences with them and with black magic, and that he did believe that such beings and other black magic existed. But several other villagers, sometimes privately, sometimes publicly, told me about their own first- and second-hand experiences with supernatural phenomena like *huldufólk*, ghosts, trolls, and black magic.[9] Vagnar's village-wide, infamous reputation seemed a product of exaggeration.

As an outsider, I did not know people well enough to distinguish fact from fiction in stories about them. But I do not think that in most cases anybody knew for sure. Indeed, I seemed to be the only one concerned about the issue. During an interview, in response to my question about what a person does with information he or she finds to be false, and what a person does about the person who gave him or her false information, one man said: "Just forget it. The person won't take it seriously. One is so much used to the fact that maybe a half-part of gossip is true and the other part is not true . . . people just want to have an image of you in their head." This man's understanding of the amount of truth in information was only one of several indications that villagers are not very concerned with the factual basis of information. One man described the way information and stories become "certain":

It [information] becomes more and more true every time it is spread further and further. . . . It is only temporary that they [villagers talking about others] are saying "*Eg haldi tad*" [I think so]. . . . The rumor is spreading for a few days and the rumor is getting more certain. It is just in the first stages where they are using expressions like "*Eg haldi tad*" or "*Eg eri ikki so sikkurt*" [I am not so sure]. . . . I have heard that one person can manage to do all those three things after each other. The first time he tells you one thing and he tells you, "I heard a rumor," "I'm not sure about it," "I don't think it's quite true." And the next day he can tell you the same thing and tell you, "*Eg haldi tad*" and the third day he will tell you, "100 percent certain."

Reputations take shape from ordinary conversation, and with repetition they take on a legendary nature. In the process they gain power and permanence. Information reinforces itself. Especially in a community where accommodation and the avoidance of contention are virtues, accounts about others establish face-to-face bonds of agreement. Character portrayals *are* public agreements.

Villagers generally tended to depict their covillagers as characteristically one thing or another. It did not seem to matter whether accounts were correct as long as they supported the community's caricature of local personalities. People became manifestations of certain traits, either real or imagined. A similar observation has been made of a small Shetland fishing community: "Whatever any person's *actual* attributes and almost regardless of the actual distribution of such qualities among the population, only certain people will be credited with them" (Anthony Cohen 1978: 452).

Cohen, however, refers to the local allocation of respected, positive traits like fishing skills and carpentry. He suggests that for several people to be known for the same trait would provoke competition and "undermine the value of the trait." In his terms, the allocation of negative traits among Faeroese villagers would be a product of the need for someone (rather than many) to represent a negative trait; if too many folks are "it," the trait loses definition. That is, if too many folks become known for deviating from proper behavior in a certain realm, then those deviations might become acceptable. But in Koppbøur many persons have anecdotes and stories attributing to them one or more kinds of deviance such as excessive drinking, arrogance, foolishness, greed, or minority religious group membership. Additionally, although in both places there is the interesting dynamic of talk reducing people to stereotypes—positive in Shetland, negative in Faeroe—Cohen's explanation glosses over the daily process in social talk. The allocation of identity among Faeroese villagers is a product of increasing simplification and epitomization through ongoing talk and legend.

Perhaps the words of Sigga, a seventy-year-old woman who had spent only a few days of her life away from the village, best reveal the legend-making quality of village talk. I had asked her to tell me about conflicts between Koppbingar. Instead, she answered:

Often it happens that a story is false, not quite correct. And that things really happened otherwise. That was so about Barbara í Geilini, that she was full of black magic. But the story remains, not what or how she was as a woman [but as a witch]. She was a farmer's wife—a farm woman.

Ja, so tann er ("Yea, so it is"). Younger days. There have been many stories through the times in Koppbøur and other villages. People take only certain stories away from the lives of man. *And so the story becomes the person.* It can be a story that only one time happened. . . . There is much that is false. (Emphasis added)

Few others made such poignant comments on the nature of social identities. Sigga's analysis reveals how Vagnar í Kalgardi, the living eccentric who believes in trolls and black magic, can also be a subject of legend.

These daily legends forcefully and efficiently, but indirectly through example, define deviant behavior. People behave with the knowledge of the power of narrative: Villagers often hide their drinking and liquor bottles; downplay their beliefs in the supernatural; avoid talk about themselves that might be used later by others for ridicule; avoid male/female contacts that might provoke even ill-founded gossip; and generally adjust what they say and do to try to prevent their fellow villagers from grieving about and ridiculing them in common tales. The fact that popular accounts of others are often exaggerated, distorted, or ill-informed, and yet still work well in maintaining conformity and peace, indicates that their truth value is not that important.

In Koppbøur, as in any community, conflicts arise. The local ethos demands self-control and an even temperament. Villagers must address any grievances, disputes, or conflicts in ways that maintain their own reputations as amiable and composed. To quarrel out loud, to call people names face-to-face, to accuse others of deviance directly, are themselves deviant behaviors in such a context. Indirect methods of maintaining order must dominate. And the use of humor and ridicule makes social control a more palatable and entertaining affair. Moreover, in discussing third parties, Koppbingar need to avoid overt hostility so as not to risk their own social acceptance. In such a context, symbolic and allegorical methods of emotional expression and social judgment become important.

Each person may become a caricature of a certain trait and each person has, or is capable of having, deviant characteristics. Each person, each talker, not particularly "bad guys" or "good guys," are narrators and proponents of the law as well as butts of the law through the misbehavior others attribute to them. In Koppbøur no one can be expert, proper, or law-abiding in every way and people like to point to, name, and magnify deviations.

But we must be careful not to judge this naming and storytelling phenomenon, these grievances, as labeling in the traditional sociological sense. Most often the subject does not hear his nickname, the comment, or the story and may be unaware of the nature of his own living legend. But he is aware of the fact that people, like himself, constantly talk and tell tales about others' behavior. In such a closed, small-scale community each person knows that the person discussed fills many roles. As Raybeck suggests in Chapter 2, this helps to minimize the impact of labeling and keep the reputation of deviants soft. Although a person's social identity revolves around his or her deviance, he or she can also maintain other nondeviant social roles. A man can be a fisherman, fowler, husband, *and* a "drunk." Indeed in this community all the "drunks" maintain steady employment.[10] The ability to integrate deviants into the community arises not simply because everyone can be or is a deviant but because villagers maintain coexistent, syncretistic perspectives about myth and quotidian life. People can be caricatures and full personalities, deviants and conformists. Social caricaturing is itself conformist behavior and ex-presses one's familiarity with other villagers. Storytelling, in Savishinsky's model (Chapter 3), becomes a forum for staging other people's deviance. By directing attention to others' inabilities to live up to expectations, folks' grievances give the impression that they them-selves know and follow the right paths. The practice of folk talk and legend making and the norms implicit in its various forms are more important than the actual behavior of the characters discussed.

CONCLUSION

Wishing to avoid formal laws, villagers and officials are eager to maintain self-control and equality. Koppbingar are loath to invoke ranking of offenses and deviants. In culturally prescribed entertaining, names, and narratives, the community uses intimate knowledge of past and present individuals *qua* individuals to support popular legends and norms for the general social good. In the language of Freilich's model (Chapter 1), they use smart means to achieve the proper goal of social control. Only an approach to the study of deviance attribution that is qualitative, in this case merging history, the arts, humor, informal law, ethos, and an intimate knowledge of community members, can detect the many subtleties of discourse in the handling of deviance.

Faeroese excessive drinking, arrogance, sexual infidelity, belief in black magic, and other local forms of deviance may not threaten the physical or moral order of the community as directly as homosexuality, transvestism, assault, and murder might for members of more complex societies, but members of each society make popular grievances about deviant behaviors and thereby activate norms and laws. It may also be easier for Faeroese to agreeably attribute some local form of impropriety to villagers than for Americans, for example, to attribute some form of hard deviance to nearly everyone in their communities. But differences in form should not distract us from the commonplace process of folk talking and storytelling embedded in grievances and deviance attribution.

In more stratified arenas than Koppbøur some persons or groups have power over the communication channels, and they have the ability to make their stories more audible and convincing than others' stories about them. In more complex, densely populated contexts, everyday storytellers separate the myths from the person and often use the myths as the criteria for judgment and actions toward them. In Koppbøur villagers certainly judge each other, but unlike other, less egalitarian communities, there is not much difference in actions toward those judged. Villagers are amiable toward them, and still fish, hay, and play with them.

In moving from the simple, egalitarian or peasant community to the more complex society, the commonplace deviant loses his or her virtue as everyman's *legal* material for grievances and allegories. Instead he or she becomes an independent person representing only the illegal. Concomitantly the deviance is taken out of everyone and put into only some.

Even in contexts where some are deviants, the interpretation of behavior as deviant or not is open to daily individual and group discretion. Hawkins (1981) demonstrates how members of an American parole board, in making a release decision, variably interpret the acts of a potential parolee as "evil" or not. Gaffin (1986) shows how White Russian *shtetl* Jews neutralized the deviance of prostitutes if they were working to pay for their formal education. It is possible for people to create stories that refrain from attributing deviance even to those who are supposed to be deviant, just as it is possible for Faeroese to make legends out of everyone's deviance.

We Americans often believe that there are "good folks" (intelligent, law-abiding, sane) who have so little in common with bad or "evil" ones (retarded, criminal, mad) that we cannot imagine ourselves crossing into stigmatized categories. Many believe it is other folks, especially professional labelers such as police and doctors, who are responsible for handing out labels, whether they are deserved or not. Such officials are merely formal representatives of our own cultural styles of storytelling and story interpretation. Perhaps each of us, in our own professional and everyday legend making, can learn to believe in stories and people.

NOTES

1. Nader and Todd (1978: 15) also state that an "aggrieved party may escalate his or her grievance directly to the dispute level without ever confronting the offender." A person may not know that someone thinks he or she committed a deviant act or is a deviant.

2. In a discussion of Apache caricatures of the white man, Basso (1979: 44) discusses "epitomization": "Western Apache jokers pursue invention and interpretation through caricature and hyperbole, portraying their characters so as to make them appear ludicrous and ridiculous. These affects are achieved in accordance with a single overarching strategy—I shall call it epitomization—that is informed and guided by two major principles: contrast and distortion."

3. See West (1972) and Wylie (1986) for histories of the islands.

4. The names of the island, village, and people are pseudonyms.

5. Several anthropologists have discussed the role of nicknames in socialization and social control. See particularly Pitt-Rivers (1971), Lévi-Strauss (1966) and Rosaldo (1984).

6. See the legend of Snopprikkur in Jakobsen, Hammershaimb, and Schrøter (1977).

7. For more elaborate discussion of the role of the *rukka* in Faeroese culture and social control, see my doctoral dissertation (1987), "Everyday People as Living Legends: The Art of Social Control in a Faeroese Village." See also Joensen's (1975: 200-7) historical account (in Danish) of the *rukka* and its functions aboard Faeroese fishing sloops.

8. Basso (1984) discusses Apache stories, with associated place names where they took place, as "moral narratives" that aim to educate. Faeroese stories are also moral narratives except, unlike the Apache accounts, most Faeroese stories speak of living villagers every day.

9. Villagers often asked me not to repeat their supernatural experiences to others. Generally, folks do not want to be known for believing in trolls, *huldufolk*, ghosts, and so forth.

10. Other theorists of deviance discuss how in egalitarian or small-scale communities a deviant person does not lose significant standing in the community because other, nondeviant aspects of the person are also known. In these contexts there is usually less persecution and separation of the deviant from the community (see Edgerton 1973).

CODA

The ethnographic essays utilize, or can be related to, one or more of our three models of deviance: Smart and Proper Strategies (SAPS), Hard and Soft Deviance, and Staged Deviance. We conclude with a brief overview of the connections between the models and the cultural data.

STRATEGIES

Hijras use "smart" means to achieve some of the very proper goals—such as marriage and the fulfillment of dharma—that sexually normal members of other communities pursue. In Taiwan, liumang see themselves as embodying traditional values, and often work in "smart" ways to achieve the proper goals of maintaining social order and helping others to settle disputes. Gaffin shows how people from Koppbøur use the "smart" means of tale-telling, and the proper form of taettir, to achieve the proper goals of leveling and social control. The khaddaam of Yemen use language and oratory in a "smart" way to help more proper people put others in their place. In Kenya, Kilbride considers child abuse at two different time horizons: In the traditional period, infanticide was tolerated as a "smart" method for dealing with special circumstances, whereas women who commit such an act now are seen as invoking both improper means and goals. Rose applies the SAPS model to the varied options that the Swazi use for dealing with witchcraft. She examines how formerly proper means for the community have become private, "smart," and deviant ones under the European legal system.

SEVERITY

Shaw shows that while Chinese gangsters see their deviance as "soft," public officials view these same patterns of conduct as "hard." The latter characterization has also been applied by Kilbride to child abuse and neglect in Kenya, and by Rose to Swazi witches; on the other hand, Gaffin's Faeroese gossipers, Caton's khaddaam, and Nanda's hijra all fall within the "soft" range. As Raybeck suggests, designations of "hard" and "soft" have to do not only with the severity of the deviance, but with how embedded the deviants are in social roles and networks. Softly deviant Chinese gangsters and Faeroese villagers are deeply enmeshed in the day-to-day lives of their communities, just as hijras and khaddaam play key roles in the cultural activities of others.

STAGING

The deviance of khaddaam and hijra is openly and ritually staged, just as Taiwanese gangsters and Koppbøur gossips conduct some of their affairs in a very public manner in order to make their sanctions more effective. In contrast to these patterns, other forms of deviance that have been described remain covert. Kenyan child abuse and Swazi witchcraft are hidden from view, although accusations, mob justice, and prosecutions in these cases may be carefully staged so as to highlight their moral lessons for the public at large.

The ethnographies also demonstrate a key point made in the Introduction; that is, that the models can explain much of the deviance data for a given culture, but leave other parts uncovered. Put a different way, those who use our models will still find some of their data naked, unclothed by theory. It is not surprising, therefore, to find that the ethnographic essays use other concepts to cover additional aspects of deviance. In particular, they take up the sanctions inherent in common discourse, the more formalized sanction of labeling, the deviant careers people follow, and the impact of social change. Gaffin, for example, alerts us to deviance and its sanctions as part of everyday life: People's negative reputations enter into common dialogue and reinforce concepts of proper conduct. The khaddaam also use language as a levelling device. Indian hijras, Yemeni khaddaam, and Taiwanese gangsters have all developed deviant "careers," and fulfill them as members of organized groups. In contrast to these cases, Kenyan child abusers and Swazi witches neither pursue careers or form themselves into communities. Yet the deviant statuses of the latter five groups—hijras, khaddaam, gangsters, abusers, and witches—have been labeled in their respective, complex societies, bearing out Raybeck's arguments about labeling and social scale.

Two essays bring out the dimension of social and cultural change. Kilbride's analysis of Kenyan child abuse indicates how deviant behavior can be related to modernization—in this case specific alterations in gender roles, family dynamics, and social support systems. And Rose describes the way in which European legal notions, imposed on the customary practices of the Swazi, have changed both the means and the goals that people apply in cases of witchcraft: The victims are now as likely to be regarded as deviant as the accused once were.

In this book we have attempted to integrate theory with cross cultural data. Our goal has been to promote a more comprehensive and comprehensible view of deviance, and we will consider ourselves successful to the extent that our work stimulates students of deviance to reconsider their favorite models. We suggest they ask themselves two questions: Does my preferred model fully explain deviance in America? And how much explanatory power does that model have for deviance in Africa, India, China, Taiwan, Trinidad, and other areas? We hope we have encouraged readers to rethink their conceptions of deviance and to re-view its role(s) in their own society. More generally, as a geology book may induce a traveler to see familiar terrain in a new light, we would hope this book will stimulate readers to develop a fresh perspective on themselves and on their relations with others.

BIBLIOGRAPHY

Aaronson, D. E., C. T. Dienes, and M.C. Musheno
  1984 *Public Policy and Police Discretion*. New York: Clark Boardman.
Acciaioli, Gregory L.
  1981 "Knowing What You're Doing: A Review of Pierre Bourdieu's *Outline of a Theory of Practice*." *Canberra Anthropology* 4(1):23–51.
Allen, B. and D. Bosta
  1981 *Games Criminals Play: How You Can Profit from Knowing Them*. Susanville, Calif.: Rae John.
American Association of Suicidology
  1982 "Resolution on Nuclear Disarmament." Adopted at the Annual Meeting, New York, N.Y., April 17, 1982.
American Law Institute
  1966 *A Model Code of Pre-arraignment Procedure*. Philadelphia: American Law Institute.
American Psychiatric Association
  1968 *Diagnostic and Statistical Manual of Mental Disorders*. 2d ed. Washington, D.C.: American Psychiatric Association.
Aremu, L. L.
  1971 "Cultural Conflicts in the Criminal Law of Southern Nigeria—with Special Reference to Homicide." Ph.D. thesis, London School of Economics and Political Science.
Bailey, F. G.
  1968 "Parapolitical Systems." In *Local Level Politics*. M. J. Swartz, ed. Chicago: Aldine.
Baker, Hugh D. R.
  1979 *Chinese Family and Kinship*. New York: Columbia University Press.
Bakhtin, M. M.
  1981 *The Dialogic Imagination: Four Essays by M. M. Bakhtin*. Michael Holquist, ed. Caryl Emerson and Michael Holquist, trans. Austin: University of Texas Press.

Ball, Donald W.
  1970 "The Problematics of Respectability." In *Deviance and Respectability: The Social Construction of Moral Meanings*. J. Douglas, ed. New York: Basic Books.
Barth, Fredrik
  1981 *Process and Form in Social Life: Selected Essays of Fredrik Barth*. Vol.1. Boston: Routledge and Kegan Paul.
Basham, A. L.
  1959 *The Wonder that Was India*. New York: Grove.
Basso, Keith
  1979 *Portraits of the White Man: Linguistic Play and Cultural Symbols Among the Western Apache*. Cambridge: Cambridge University Press.
  1984 "Stalking with Stories: Names, Places and Moral Narratives Among the Western Apache." In *Text, Play and Story: The Construction and Reconstruction of Self and Society*. Edward Bruner, ed. 1983 Proceedings of the American Ethnological Society, Washington, D.C.: The American Ethnological Society.
Beattie, John
  1963 "Sorcery in Bunyoro." In *Witchcraft and Sorcery in East Africa*. J. Middleton and E. H. Winter, eds. London: Routledge and Kegan Paul, 27–55.
Becker, Howard S.
  1963 *Outsiders: Studies in the Sociology of Deviance*. New York: The Free Press.
Beidelman, T. O.
  1963 "Witchcraft in Ukaguru." In *Witchcraft and Sorcery in East Africa*. J. Middleton and E. H. Winter, eds. London: Routledge and Kegan Paul, 57–98.
Bell, Rudolph
  1985 *Holy Anorexia*. Chicago: University of Chicago Press.
Bellah, Robert N., R. Madsen, W. M. Sullivan, A. Swidler, and S. M. Tipton
  1985 *Habits of the Heart*. New York: Harper & Row.
Benedict, Ruth
  1934 *Patterns of Culture*. New York: Houghton Mifflin.
Bergessen, Albert James
  1977 "Political Witch Hunts: The Sacred and Subversive in Cross-National Perspective." *American Sociological Review* 42, No. 2: 220–33.
Berliner, J. S.
  1952 "The Informal Organization of a Soviet Firm." *The Quarterly Journal of Economics* 66:342–65.
Berndt, Ronald
  1962 *Excess and Restraint: Social Control Among the New Guinea Mountain People*. Chicago: University of Chicago Press.
Bilmes, Jack
  1976 "Rules and Rhetoric: Negotiating the Social Structure in a Thai Village." *Journal of Anthropological Research* 32 (Spring):44–47.
Birenbaum, Arnold and Henry Lesieur
  1982 "Social Values and Expectations." In *The Sociology of Deviance* M. Michael Rosenberg, Robert A. Stebbins, and Allan Turowetz, eds. New York: St. Martin's, 97–122.

Birenbaum, A. and E. Sagarin
  1976 *Norms and Human Behavior.* New York: Praeger.
Bittner, E.
  1983 "Legality and Workmanship: Introduction to Control in the Police Organiza-
         tion." *Control in the Police Organization.* M. Punch, ed. Cambridge, Mass:
         MIT Press.
Blau, Peter M.
  1955 *The Dynamics of Bureaucracy.* Chicago: University of Chicago Press.
Blau, Peter M. and R. K. Merton (eds.)
  1981 *Continuities in Structural Inquiry.* London: Sage.
Bloch, Herbert A. and A. Niederhoffer
  1958 *The Gang: A Study in Adolescent Behavior.* New York: Philosophical
         Library.
Bloch, Sidney and Peter Reddaway
  1977 *Psychiatric Terror: How Soviet Psychiatry Is Used to Suppress Dissent.* New
         York: Basic Books.
Bloomhill, G.
  1962 *Witchcraft in Africa.* Cape Town: Howard Timmins.
Blumer, Herbert
  1969 *Symbolic Interactionism: Perspective and Method.* Englewood Cliffs, N.J.:
         Prentice-Hall.
Bobb, Dilip, and C. J. Patel
  1982 "Fear is the Key." *India Today.* September 15, pp. 84–85.
Bohannon, Paul (ed.)
  1960 *African Homicide and Suicide.* Princeton, N.J.: Princeton University Press.
Bok, Sissela
  1983 *Secrets: On the Ethics of Concealment and Revelation.* New York: Pantheon.
Boram, Clifford
  1973 "Kutchin Quarrelling." *Ethnology* 12(4):437–48.
Bourdieu, P.
  1979 *Outline of a Theory of Practice.* Cambridge.: Cambridge University Press.
Bourdieu, P. and J. C. Passeron
  1977 (1970) *Reproduction in Education, Society and Culture* London: Sage
Brandt, Richard B.
  1954 *Hopi Ethics: A Theoretical Analysis.* Chicago: University of Chicago Press.
Bregenzer, John
  1982 *Tryin' To Make It: Adapting to The Bahamas.* Washington, D.C.: University
         Press of America.
Broch, Harald Beyer
  1983 "The Bluefish River Incident." In *The Politics of Indianness: Case Studies of
         Native Ethnopolitics in Canada.* Adrian Tanner, ed. St. John's, Newfound-
         land: Institute of Social and Economic Research, Social and Economic Papers
         No. 12. Memorial University of Newfoundland.
Brown, M. K.
  1981 *Working the Street.* New York: Russell Sage Foundation.
Bullough, V. L.
  1976 *Sexual Variance in Society and History.* Chicago: University of Chicago
         Press.

Burawoy, Michael
  1982   "Introduction: The Resurgence of Marxism in American Sociology." In
         Marxist Inquiries: Studies in Labor, Class and States. Michael Burawoy and
         Theda Skocpol, eds. Chicago: University of Chicago Press.
Burawoy, Michael and Theda Skocpol
  1982   *Marxist Inquiries: Studies of Labor, Class and States.* Chicago: University of
         Chicago Press.
Burrell, D. B.
  1968   "Obeying Rules and Following Instructions." In *Philosophy and Cybernet-*
         ics. Frederick J. Crosson and Kenneth M. Sayre, eds. New York: Simon and
         Schuster.
Buxton, J.
  1963   "Mandari Witchcraft." In *Witchcraft and Sorcery in East Africa.* J. Middle-
         ton and E. H. Winter, eds. London: Routledge and Kegan Paul, 99–121.
Bwibo, N. O.
  1982   "Battered Child Syndrome." In *Child Labor and Health.* P. Onyango and S.
         Kayongo-Male, eds. Nairobi: Acme Press.
Carrithers, Michael, Steven Collins, and Steven Lukes, eds.
  1985   *The Category of the Person.* Cambridge: Cambridge University Press.
Carstairs, G. M.
  1967   *The Twice-Born: A Study of a Community of High Caste Hindus.* Blooming-
         ton: University of Indiana Press.
Caton, S. C.
  1985   "The Poetic Construction of Self." *Anthropological Quarterly* 58(4):141–51.
Cavell, Stanley
  1982   *The Claim of Reason.* Oxford: Oxford University Press.
Chagnon, Napoleon A.
  1977   *Yanomamo: The Fierce People.* New York: Holt, Rinehart and Winston.
Chance, Norman A.
  1966   *The Eskimo of Northern Alaska.* New York: Holt, Rinehart and Winston.
Chen Kuang-hui
  1967   "Bu liang shao nian pang hui zu zhi de tou shi." (A Look at Gang
         Organizations of Delinquent Youth.) *Xin Tian Di 5 (11):12–15.*
Chiang Siang-Tseh
  1954   *The Nien Rebellion.* Seattle: University of Washington Press.
Clifford, W.
  1978   "Culture and Crime—In Global Perspective." *International Journal of Crim-*
         inology and Penology 6:61–80.
Clinard, Marshall, ed.
  1964   *Anomie and Deviant Behavior: A Discussion and Critique.* New York: The
         Free Press.
  1974   *Sociology of Deviant Behavior.* New York: Holt, Rinehart and Winston.
Cloward, R. A. and L. E. Ohlin
  1961   *Delinquency and Opportunity: A Theory of Delinquent Gangs.* New York:
         The Free Press.
Cohen, Albert K.
  1965   "The Sociology of the Deviant Act: Anomie Theory and Beyond." *American
         Sociological Review* 30:5–40.
  1966   *Deviance and Control.* Englewood Cliffs, N.J.: Prentice Hall.

Cohen, Anthony P.
1978 "The Same—But Different: The Allocation of Identity in Whalsay, Shetland." *Sociological Review* 36 (3): 449–69.
1985 *The Symbolic Construction of Community.* London: Tavistock.
Cohen, Lawrence and Richard Machalek.
1988 "A General Theory of Expropriative Crime: An Evolutionary Ecological Approach." *American Journal of Sociology* 94(3): 465–501.
Cole, S.
1957 "The Growth of Scientific Knowledge: Theories of Deviance as a Case Study." In *The Ideal of Social Structure.* L. A. Coser, ed. New York: Harcourt, Brace Jovanovich, 175–220.
Collier, Jane Fishburne
1973 *Law and Social Change in Zinacantan.* Stanford, Calif.: Stanford University Press.
Collins, Randall
1981 "The Normalcy of Crime." In *Sociological Insight: An Introduction to Non-Obvious Sociology. Essays by Randall Collins.* Oxford: Oxford University Press.
1982 *Sociological Insight: An Introduction to Non-Obvious Sociology.* New York: Oxford University Press.
1985 *Three Sociological Traditions.* New York: Oxford University Press.
Colson, Elizabeth
1974 *Tradition and Contract: The Problem of Order.* Chicago: Aldine.
Connor, Walter D.
1972 "The Manufacture of Deviance: The Case of the Soviet Purge, 1936–1938." *American Sociological Review* 37: 403–13.
Coser, Lewis A.
1980 *The Pleasures of Sociology.* New York: New American Library (Mentor Books).
Coser, Lewis A., B. Rhea, P. A. Steffan, and S. L. Nock
1983 *Introduction to Sociology.* New York: Harcourt, Brace Jovanovich.
Crawford, J. R.
1967 *Witchcraft and Sorcery in Rhodesia.* Oxford University Press for International African Institute.
1969/1970 "The History and Nature of the Judicial System of Botswana, Lesotho and Swaziland." *The South African Law Journal* 87:76–86.
Cressey, Donald R. and Elg Elgesem
1968 The Police and the Administration of Justice. *Scandinavian Studies in Criminology* 2:53–72.
Current Digest of the Soviet Press
1980 The "Expediter" and Why He's Necessary. 34(1):1–3.
Dahrendorf, Rolf
1968 "Homo Sociologicus." In *Essays in the Theory of Society.* Stanford, Calif.: Stanford University Press.
Das, T.
1945 *The Purums.* Calcutta: University of Calcutta Press.
Davis, Fei-ling
1971 *Primitive Revolutionaries of China.* Honolulu: University Press of Hawaii.

Davis, Fred
  1979 *Yearning for Yesterday: A Sociology of Nostalgia*. New York: The Free
        Press.
Davis, Nanette J.
  1980 *Sociological Constructions of Deviance: Perspectives and Issues in the Field*.
        Dubuque, Iowa: W. C. Brown.
Dentan, Robert K.
  1968 *The Semai: A Nonviolent People of Malaya*. New York: Holt, Rinehart and
        Winston.
Deutsch, W. O., et al.
  1982 "My Neighbours are My Enemies: A Survey of Witchcraft Belief in Swazi-
        land." Unpublished paper for Committee for Education and Training, Coun-
        cil of Swaziland Churches.
Dewey, John
  1939 *Freedom and Culture*. New York: Capricorn Books.
Dexter, L.
  1981 "Marketers, Not Donors." *Society* 18(6):58–61.
Diamond, S.
  1972 Review of: Man and Culture: A Philosophical Anthropology. A. W. Levy,
        ed. *American Anthropologist* 74:10.
Diggs, B. J.
  1964 "Rules and Utilitarianism." *American Philosophical Quarterly* 1:32–44.
Dittmer, Lowell
  1983 "The Study of Chinese Political Culture." In *Methodological Issues in
        Chinese Studies*. Wilson, Amy Auerbacher, Sidney L. Greenblatt, and Rich-
        ard W. Wilson, eds. New York: Praeger.
Dougherty, R.
  1964 "The Case for the Cop." *Harper's Magazine*, April 1964, 129–33.
Douglas, Jack D.
  1970a "Deviance and Order in a Pluralistic Society." In *Theoretical Sociology:
        Perspectives and Developments*. John C. McKinney and Edward A. Tiryak-
        ian, eds. New York: Appleton-Century-Crofts, 367–402.
  1970b "Deviance and Respectability: The Social Construction of Moral Mean-
        ings." *Deviance and Respectability: the Social Construction of Moral Mean-
        ings*. J. Douglas, ed. New York: Basic Books.
  1970c *The Social Meaning of Suicide*. Princeton, N.J.: Princeton University
        Press.
  1971 *American Social Order: Social Rules in a Pluralistic Society*. New York: The
        Free Press.
Douglas, Jack and Frances Chaput Waksler
  1982 *The Sociology of Deviance: An Introduction*. Boston: Little, Brown.
Douglas, Mary
  1963 "Techniques of Sorcery Control in Central Africa." In *Witchcraft and
        Sorcery in East Africa*. J. Middleton and E. H. Winter, eds. London:
        Routledge and Kegan Paul, 123–41.
  1966 *Purity and Danger*. London: Routledge and Kegan Paul.
Drabek, T.
  1968 *Disaster in Aisle 13*. Columbus, Ohio: Disaster Research Center, The Ohio
        State University.

Dumont L.
1977   *Homo aequalis*. Paris: Gallimard.
Durkheim, Emile
1938   [1895] *The Rules of the Sociological Method*. New York: The Free Press [reprinted 1964].
1951   [1897] *Suicide*. New York: The Free Press.
1953   "Value Judgments and Judgments of Reality." D. F. Pocock, trans. In *Sociology and Philosophy*. Glencoe, Ill: The Free Press.
1964   [1893] *The Division of Labor in Society*. George Simpson, trans. New York: Collier Books.
Dworkin, Ronald
1967   "The Model of Rules." *University of Chicago Law Review* 35:14–46.
Eberhard, Wolfram
1965   *Conquerors and Rulers: Social Forces in Medieval China*. Leiden, Netherlands: Brill.
Edel, May M.
1960   "Some Reflections on Chiga Ethics" In *Men and Cultures*. A. F. C. Wallace, ed. Philadelphia: University of Pennsylvania Press.
Edgerton Robert B.
1973   "Deviant Behavior and Cultural Theory." *Addison-Wesley Module in Anthropology* No. 37. Reading, Massachusetts.
1976   *Deviance: A Cross-Cultural Perspective*. Menlo Park, Calif: Cummings.
1980   "The Study of Deviance—Marginal Man or Everyman." In *The Making of Psychological Anthropology*. G. Spindler, ed. Los Angeles: University of California Press.
1986   *Rules, Exceptions and Social Order*. Berkeley: University of California Press.
Erchak, Gerald
1984   "Cultural Anthropology and Spouse Abuse." *Current Anthropology* 25(3):331–32.
Erikson, Erik H.
1963   *Childhood and Society*. 2d ed. New York: W. W. Norton.
Erikson, Kai T.
1964   "Notes on the Sociology of Deviance." In *The Other Side: Perspectives on Deviance*. Howard S. Becker, ed. New York: The Free Press.
1966   *Wayward Puritans: A Study in the Sociology of Deviance*. New York: Wiley.
Etienne, M. and Eleanor Leacock
1980   *Women and Colonization: Anthropological Perspectives*. New York: Praeger Publishing.
Evans-Pritchard, E. E.
1937   *Witchcraft, Oracles, and Magic Among the Azande*. Oxford: Oxford University Press.
Fiedler, Leslie
1978   *Freaks: Myths and Images of the Secret Self*. New York: Simon and Schuster.
Finckenauer, J.
1976   "Some Factors in Police Discretion and Decision Making." *Journal of Criminal Justice* 4 (1976):29–46.

Fireside, Harvey
  1979   *Soviet Psychoprisons*. New York: W. W. Norton.
Firth, Raymond
  1939   *Primitive Polynesian Economics*. London: Routledge.
  1961   [1951] *Elements of Social Organization*. Boston:Beacon Press.
  1964   *Essays on Social Organization and Values*. New York: Humanities Press.
Foster, George M.
  1967   *Tzintzuntzan: Mexican Peasants in a Changing World*. Boston: Little,
         Brown.
Foucault, Michel
  1973   *Madness and Civilization: A History of Insanity in the Age of Reason*.
         Howard French, trans. New York: Random House.
Fraser, G. and P. Kilbride
  1981   "Child Abuse and Neglect—Rare but Perhaps Increasing Phenomenon
         Among the Samia of Kenya." *International Journal of Child Abuse and
         Neglect* 4:227–32.
Freilich, Morris
  1970   "Toward a Formalization of Fieldwork." In *Marginal Natives: Anthropolo-
         gists at Work*. New York: Harper & Row.
  1975   "Myth, Method and Madness." *Current Anthropology* 16:207–26.
  1976   "Manufacturing Culture: Man, the Scientist." In *The Meaning of Culture*.
         M. Freilich, ed. Lexington, Mass: Xerox College Publishers.
  1978   "The Meaning of Sociocultural." In *The Concept and Dynamic of Culture*.
         Bernado Bernadi, ed. The Hague: Mouton.
  1980   "Smart-Sex and Proper-Sex: A Paradigm Found." *Central Issues in Anthro-
         pology* 2:37–51.
  1981   "Smart Means for Proper Goals: A Victimless Con-Game in Trinidad."
         Paper presented at the Annual Meetings of the Northeastern Anthropological
         Association, Saratoga, N.Y.
  1983a "Beauty in the Beast." Introduction to *The Pleasures of Anthropology*. M.
         Freilich, ed. New York: New American Library (Mentor Books).
  1983b "Ethnographic Facts and Deviance Theory." Paper presented at the 82d
         Annual Meeting of the American Anthropological Association, Chicago, Ill.
         November 16–20, 1983.
  1985   "Deviance, Decision-Making and SAPS." Paper prepared for the third
         annual meeting of the panel of "The Anthropological Study of Deviance."
         American Anthropological Association, Washington, D.C., December 4–8.
  1989a *The Relevance of Culture*. Morris Freilich, ed. South Hadley, Mass.: Bergin
         and Garvey.
  1989b " 'Sip' Not 'Toe': Strategies for Theory Development." Paper presented at
         the Annual Meeting of the Northeastern Anthropological Association, Mon-
         treal.
Freilich, Morris and F. A. Schubert
  1989   "Smart Rules, Proper Rules and Police Discretion." In *The Relevance of
         Culture*. Morris Freilich, ed. South Hadley, Mass.: Bergin and Garvey.
Fried, Martha Nemes and Morton H. Fried
  1980   *Transitions: Four Rituals in Eight Cultures*. New York: W. W. Norton.

Fried, Morton H.
  1951 "Chinese Society: Class as Subculture." *Transactions.* The New York Academy of Sciences. Series II, 14.8: 331–36.
Fung, Yu-lan
  1948 *A Short History of Chinese Philosophy.* Derk Bodde, ed. New York: The Free Press.
Gaffin, Dennis
  1986 "Indecency, Ostracism and Yiddishkayt: Being Jewish in Tsarist Russia." *International Journal of Oral History.* 7(1): 19–42.
  1987 "Everyday People as Living Legends: The Art of Social Control in a Faeroese Village." Ph.D. dissertation, State University of New York at Buffalo.
Gallin, Bernard and Rita Gallin
  1977 "Sociopolitical Power and Sworn Brother Groups in Chinese Society: A Taiwanese Case." In *The Anthropology of Power: Ethnographic Studies from Asia, Oceania, and The New World.* Raymond D. Fogelson and Richard N. Adams, eds. New York: Academic Press.
Garbarino, J.
  1977 "The Human Ecology of Child Maltreatment." *Journal of Marriage and the Family* 39(4):721–35.
Gardiner, J. A.
  1969 *Traffic and the Police: Variations in Law-Enforcement Policy.* Cambridge, Mass.: Harvard University Press.
Garfinkel, H.
  1967 *Studies in Ethnomethodology.* Englewood Cliffs, N.J.: Prentice-Hall.
Gatewood, John B.
  1984 "Cooperation, Competition and Synergy: Information Sharing Groups Among Southeast Alaskan Salmon Seiners." *American Ethnologist* 11(2):350–70.
Geer, Blanch, et. al.
  1967 "Learning the Ropes." In *Among the People: Studies of the Urban Poor.* Irwin Deutscher and Elizabeth Thompson, eds. New York: Basic Books.
Geertz, C.
  1973 *The Interpretation of Cultures.* New York: Basic Books.
Gelda, Beth
  1978 "After-hours at the Sandstone Bar." In *Strangers No More: Anthropological Studies of Cat Island, The Bahamas.* Joel Savishinsky, ed. Ithaca, N.Y.: Ithaca College.
Gelfand, M.
  1967 *The African Witch: With Particular Reference to Witchcraft Beliefs and Practice Among the Shona of Rhodesia.* London: E. & S. Livingstone.
Gelles, J. and C. Cornell
  1985 *Intimate Violence in Families.* Beverly Hills, Calif.: Sage.
Gibbs, J. P.
  1966 "Conceptions of Deviant Behavior: the Old and the New." *Pacific Sociological Review* 9:9–14.
  1981 *Norms, Deviance and Social Control: Conceptual Matters.* New York: Elsevier.

Glassner, Barry
  1982 "Labeling Theory." *The Sociology of Deviance*. M. Michael Rosenberg, R. A. Stebbins and A. Turowetz, eds. New York: St. Martins.

Gluckman, M.
  1944 "The Logic of African Science and Witchcraft: An Appreciation of Evans-Pritchard's *Witchcraft, Oracles and Magic among the Azande of the Sudan.*" *Human Problems in British Central Africa* 1:61–71.
  1963 "Gossip and Scandal." *Current Anthropology* 4:307–16.
  1965 *Politics, Law, and Ritual in Tribal Society*. Oxford: Basil Blackwell.

Goffman, Erving
  1959 *The Presentation of Self in Everyday Life*. Garden City, N.Y.: Doubleday and Co.
  1961 *Asylums: Essays on the Social Situation of Mental Patients and Other Inmates*. Garden City, N.Y.: Doubleday Anchor.
  1963a *Behavior in Public Places*. New York: The Free Press.
  1963b *Stigma: Notes on the Management of Spoiled Identity*. Englewood Cliffs, N.J.: Prentice-Hall.
  1967 *Interaction Ritual: Essays in Face-to-Face Behavior*. Chicago: Aldine.
  1974 *Frame Analysis*. New York: Harper Colophon Books.
  1980 "On Cooling Out the Mark." In *The Pleasures of Sociology*. Lewis A. Coser, ed. New York: New American Library.
  1981 "Response Cries," In *Forms of Talk*. Philadelphia: University of Pennsylvania Press: 78–123.

Good, Anthony
  1981 "Prescription, Preference and Practice: Marriage Practice Among the Kondaiyankottai Maravar of South India." *Man* (NS) 16:108–29.

Goodenough, Ward H.
  1981 *Culture, Language and Society*. Menlo Park, Calif.: Benjamin/Cummings Publishing.

Gouldner, Alvin W.
  1959 "Organizational Analysis." In *Sociology Today*. R. K. Merton et al., eds. New York: Basic Books.
  1980 *The Two Marxisms*. New York: Seabury.

Green, R.
  1984 "Law by the Numbers." *Forbes Magazine* January 30, p. 66.

Greenberg, David
  1978 "The Label of Tourist." In *Strangers No More: Anthropological Studies of Cat Island, The Bahamas*. Joel Savishinsky, ed. Ithaca, N.Y.: Ithaca College.

Gregor, Thomas
  1977 *Mehinaku: The Drama of Daily Life in a Brazilian Indian Village*. Chicago: University of Chicago Press.

Gregory, J.
  1984 "The Myth of the Male Ethnographer and the Woman's World." *American Anthropologist* 86 (2):316–27.

Hall, E. T.
  1969 *The Silent Language*. Greenwich, Conn: Fawcett.

Hallowell, A. I.
1941 "The Social Function of Anxiety in a Primitive Society." *American Sociological Review* 7: 869–81.
Halperin, Morton H., J. J. Berman, R. L. Borosage, and C. Marwick
1976 *The Lawless State: The Crimes of the U.S. Intelligence Agencies.* New York: Penguin Books.
Harkness, S. and P. Kilbride, eds.
1983 "The Socialization of Affect." *Ethos* 11 (4).
Hawkins, Keith
1981 "The Interpretation of Evil in Criminal Settings" In *Law and Deviance*. H. Laurence Ross, ed. Beverly Hills: Calif.: Sage.
Hawkins, Richard and Gary Tiedman
1975 *The Creation of Deviance: Interpersonal and Organizational Determinants.* Columbus, Ohio: Merrill.
Hayes, Betsy
1974 "Night Life in Tarpum Bay: Roosevelt's Jolly Roger Bar." In *Anthropological Perspectives on Eleuthera*. Garry Thomas, ed. Island Environmental Studies, The Bahamas, Reports 1973–74. Corning, N.Y.: College Center of The Finger Lakes.
Hobsbawm, Eric and Terence Ranger, eds.
1983 *The Invention of Tradition.* Cambridge: Cambridge University Press.
Hocart, A. M.
1970 *The Life-Giving Myth and Other Essays.* Rodney Needham, ed. London: Methuen.
Hollos, Marida
1976 "Conflict and Social Change in a Norwegian Mountain Community." *Anthropological Quarterly* 49(4):239–57.
Holmberg, Allan R.
1969 *Nomads of the Long Bow: The Siriono of Eastern Bolivia.* Garden City, N.Y.: The Natural History Press.
Honigmann, John J.
1981 "Expressive Aspects of Subarctic Indian Culture." In *Subarctic,* June Helm (ed.). Vol. 6 of *Handbook of North American Indians*. Washington, D.C.: Smithsonian Institution.
Howard, A.
1963 "Land, Activity Systems and Decision-Making Models in Rotuma." *Ethnology* 2:407–440.
Hsiao, Kung-chuan
1960 *Rural China. Imperial China in the Nineteenth Century.* Seattle: University of Washington Press.
Huang, Philip C. C.
1985 *The Peasant Economy and Social Change in North China.* Stanford, Calif.: Stanford University Press.
Hunn, E.
1982 "The Utilitarian Factor in Folk Biological Classification." *American Anthropologist* 84(4):830–47.
Hymes, D.
1970 "Discovering Oral Performance and Measured Verse in American Indian Narrative." *New Literary History* 20:431–57.

1974   *Foundations in Sociolinguistics.* Philadelphia: University of Pennsylvania Press.

Jacob, H.
   1978   *Justice in America: Courts, Lawyers and the Judicial Process.* Boston: Little, Brown.

Jakobsen, Jákup, W. U. Hammershaimb, and J. H. Schrøter.
   1977   *Suðuroyarsagnir.* Torshavn, Faeroe Islands: Einars Prent.

Joensen, Joan Pauli
   1975   *Faerøske Sluppfiskere: Etnologisk undersøgelse af en erhvervsgruppes liv.* Lund: Gleerup.

Jordan, David K.
   1985   "Sworn Brothers: A Study in Chinese Ritual Kinship." In *The Chinese Family and Its Ritual Behavior.* Jih-chang Hsieh and Chuang Ying-chang, ed. Taipei: Institute of Ethnology, Academia Sinica.

Kakar, Sudhir
   1981   *The Inner World: A Psychoanalytic Study of Childhood and Society in India.* Delhi: Oxford University Press.

Kamisar, Y.
   1965   "When the Cops Were Not Handcuffed." *The New York Times,* November 7, p. 34.

Kant, I.
   1966   *The Fundamental Principles of the Metaphysics of Ethics.* Trans. and with an introduction by O. Manthey-Zorn. New York: Appleton-Century-Crofts.

Katzenstein, James
   1978   "Alcohol Consumption on Cat Island." In *Strangers No More: Anthropological Studies of Cat Island, The Bahamas.* Joel Savishinsky, ed. Ithaca, N.Y.: Ithaca College.

Keniston, Kenneth
   1970   "Youth: A 'New' Stage of Life." *American Scholar.* Autumn.

Kent, J.
   1979   "Helping Abused Children and Their Parents" *Families Today.* DHEW Publication No. (ADM) 79–915, pp. 607–33.

Kilbride, P.
   1979   "Barmaiding as a Deviant Occupation Among the Baganda of Uganda." *Ethos* Vol. 7(3):232–55.
   1980   "Sensorimotor Behavior of Baganda and Samia Infants: A Controlled Comparison." *Journal of Cross-Cultural Psychology* Vol.11 (2):131–52.
   1985   "Cultural Persistence and Socio-economic Change Among the Abaluyia: Some Modern Problems in Patterns of Child Care." Seminar Paper No. 170, Institute of African Studies, University of Nairobi.

Kilbride, P. and J. Kilbride
   1990   *Changing Family Life in East Africa: Women and Children at Risk.* University Park, Pa.: Penn State Press.

Kitsuse, J. I.
   1962   "Societal Reaction to Deviant Behavior." *Social Problems* 9:247–256.
   1980   "Coming Out All Over: Deviants and the Politics of Social Problems." *Social Problems* 28(1):1–13.

Kluckhohn, Clyde
   1967   *Navaho Witchcraft.* Boston: Beacon Press.

Koestler, Arthur
  1941 *Darkness at Noon.* New York: Macmillan Co.
Korbin, Jill
  1977 "Anthropological Contributions to the Study of Child Abuse. *Child Abuse and Neglect* 1:7–24.
  1980 "The Cultural Context of Child Abuse and Neglect." In *The Battered Child.* 3d ed. C. Henry Kempe, ed. Chicago: University of Chicago Press.
  1981 Jill Korbin (Editor) *Child Abuse and Neglect: Cross-Cultural Perspectives.* Berkeley: University of California Press.
Korzybski, Alfred
  1933 *Science and Sanity.* Lancaster, Penn.: Science Press.
Krige, J. D.
  1947 "The Social Function of Witchcraft." *Theoria* 1: 8–21.
Kroeber, A. L.
  1952 *The Nature of Culture.* Chicago: University of Chicago Press.
  1957 *Style and Civilization.* Ithaca, N.Y.: Cornell University Press.
Kuper, H.
  1947 *An African Aristocracy Rank Among the Swazi.* London: Oxford University Press, for the International African Institute.
Kupferer, Harriet J.
  1979 "A Case of Sanctioned Drinking: The Rupert's House Cree." *Anthropological Quarterly* 52(4):198; 203.
Lachman. John
  1960 "The Model in Theory Construction." *Psychological Review* 67:113–29.
LaFlamme, Alan
  1985 *Green Turtle Cay: An Island in The Bahamas.* Prospect Heights, Ill.: Waveland Press.
LaFontaine, J.
  1963 "Witchcraft in Bugisu." In *Witchcraft and Sorcery in East Africa.* J. Middleton and E. H. Winter, eds. London: Routledge and Kegan Paul, 187–220.
Lakoff, George
  1987 *Women, Fire and Dangerous Things: What Categories Reveal About the Mind.* Chicago: University of Illinois Press.
Lakoff, George and Mark Johnson
  1980 *Metaphors We Live By.* Chicago: University of Chicago Press.
Lakoff, George and Mark Turner
  1989 *More Than Cool Reason: A Field Guide to Poetic Metaphor.* Chicago: University of Chicago Press.
Langness, L. L.
  1981 "Child Abuse and Cultural Values: The Case of New Guinea." In *Child Abuse and Neglect.* J. Korbin, ed. Berkeley: University of California Press.
Lattimore, Owen
  1962 *Studies in Frontier History.* London: Oxford University Press.
Largo Eight
  1982 *Eagle-Tribune*, Lawrence, Mass. February 4, p. 8.
Leach, E.
  1954 *Political Systems in Highland Burma.* London: Bell.
  1961 *Pul Elia: A Village in Ceylon.* Cambridge: Cambridge University Press.

Lee, Richard B.
1979 *The !Kung San: Men, Women, and Work in a Foraging Society*. New York: Cambridge University Press.

Lemert, Edwin
1967 "Stuttering among the North Pacific Coastal Indians" and "Stuttering and Social Structure in Two Pacific Island Societies." In *Human Deviance, Social Problems, and Social Control*. Englewood Cliffs, N.J.: Prentice-Hall.
1981 "Issues in the Study of Deviance." *Sociological Quarterly* 22:285–305.
1982 "Issues in the Study of Deviance." In *The Sociology of Deviance*. M. Michael Rosenberg, Robert A. Stebbins, and Allan Turowetz, eds. New York: St. Martin's.

LeVine, R. A.
1963 "Witchcraft and Sorcery in a Gusii Community." In *Witchcraft and Sorcery in East Africa*. J. Middleton and E. H. Winter, eds. London: Routledge and Kegan Paul.

LeVine, S. and R. LeVine
1981 "Child Abuse and Neglect in Sub-Saharan Africa." In *Child Abuse and Neglect*. J. Korbin, ed. Berkeley: University of California Press.

Lévi-Strauss, Claude
1966 *The Savage Mind*. Chicago: University of Chicago Press.

Liazos, A.
1972 "The Poverty of the Sociology of Deviance: Nuts, Sluts and Perverts." *Social Problems* 20:103–120.

Liebow, E.
1967 *Tally's Corner*. Boston: Little, Brown.

Lin, Tsung-yi
1958 "Tai-pau and Liu-mang: Two Types of Delinquent Youths in Chinese Society." *British Journal of Delinquency*. 8 (4):244–56.

Liu, James J. Y.
1967 *The Chinese Knight-Errant*. London: Routledge and Kegan Paul.

Lofland, J.
1978 "Conversion to the Doomsday Cult." In *Deviance: The Interactionist Perspective*. E. Rubington and M. Weinberg, eds. New York: Macmillan.

Luckenbill, David F.
1986 "Deviant Career Mobility: the Case of Male Prostitutes." *Social Problems* 33(4):283–96.

Luckenbill, David F. and Joel Best
1981 "Careers in Deviance and Respectability: the Analogy's Limitations?" *Social Problems* 29(2):197–206.

Lundman, R. J.
1974 "Routine Police Arrest Practices: A Commonwealth Perspective." *Social Problems* 22:128–41.

MacAndrew, Craig and Robert B. Edgerton
1969 *Drunken Comportment: A Social Explanation*. Chicago: Aldine.

MacCannell, Dean
1976 *The Tourist: A New Theory of The Leisure Class*. New York: Schocken Books.

Madsen, Richard P.
1981 "The Maoist Ethic and the Moral Basis of Political Activism in Rural China." In *Moral Behavior in Chinese Society*. Wilson, Richard W., Sidney L. Greenblatt, and Amy A. Wilson, eds. New York: Praeger.
1984 *Morality and Power in a Chinese Village*. Berkeley: University of California Press.

Mair, A. W.
1951 "Greek and Roman Suicide" In *Encyclopedia of Religion and Ethics*, 2:26–33. James Hastings, ed. New York: Scribner's.

Mair, L.
1969 *Witchcraft*. London: Weidenfeld and Nicolson, World University Library.

Mak Lau Fong
1981 *The Sociology of Secret Societies*. Oxford: Oxford University Press.

Malinowski, Bronislaw
1966 [1926] *Crime and Custom in Savage Society*. London: Routledge and Kegan Paul.
1970 "Magic, Science, and Religion." In *Witchcraft and Sorcery: Selected Readings*. M. Marwick, ed. Harmondsworth, England: Penguin Books.

Marcuse, H.
1964 *One Dimensional Man*. Boston: Beacon Press.

Marshall, Lorna
1976 *The !Kung of Nyae Nyae*. Cambridge, Mass.: Harvard University Press.

Marshall, Mac
1979 *Beliefs, Behaviors and Alcoholic Beverages*. Ann Arbor: University of Michigan Press.

Marwick, B. A.
1940 *The Swazi: An Ethnographic Account of the Swaziland Protectorate*. Cambridge: Cambridge University Press.

Marwick, M.
1950 "Another Modern Anti-Witchcraft Movement in East Central Africa." *Africa* 20:100–12.
1964 "Witchcraft as a Social Strain-Gauge." *Australian Journal of Science* 26:263–68.
1965 *Sorcery in Its Social Setting: A Study of the Northern Rhodesian Cewa*. Manchester: Manchester University Press.
1967 "The Sociology of Sorcery in a Central African Tribe." In *Magic, Witchcraft and Curing*. John Middleton ed. Garden City, N.Y.: The Natural History Press.
1970 *Witchcraft and Sorcery*. Harmondsworth, England: Penguin Books.

Marx, Gary T.
1981 "Ironies in Social Control: Authorities as Contributors to Deviance through Escalation, Nonenforcement and Covert Facilitation." *Social Problems* 28(3):288–318.

Matza, David
1964 *Delinquency and Drift*. New York: Wiley.
1969 *Becoming Deviant*. Englewood Cliffs, N. J.: Prentice Hall.

Matza, David and Gresham M. Sykes
1961 "Juvenile Delinquency and Subterranean Values." *American Sociological Review*. 26(5):712–19.

Mayer, P.
   1954   "Witches." Inaugural Lecture, Rhodes University, Grahamstown, South Africa.
Mbiti, J. S.
   1969   *African Religions and Philosophy*. London: Heinemann.
McHugh, Peter
   1970   "A Common-Sense Conception of Deviance." In *Deviance and Respectability: The Social Construction of Moral Meanings*. J. Douglas, ed. New York: Basic Books.
Mead, George Herbert
   1934   *Mind, Self, & Society*. Chicago: University of Chicago Press.
   1964   *On Social Psychology: Selected Papers*. Chicago: University of Chicago Press.
Meadows, Paul
   1957   "Models, Systems and Science." *American Sociological Review* 22:3-9.
Medvedev, Zhores A.
   1971   *The Rise and Fall of T. D. Lysenko*. I. Michael Lerner, trans. Garden City, N.Y.: Doubleday.
Medvedev, Zhores A. and Roy A. Medvedev
   1971   *A Question of Madness*. Ellen de Kadt, trans. New York: Knopf.
Meeker, M.
   1976   "Meaning and Society in the Near East: Examples from the Black Sea Turks and the Levantine Arabs. *Journal of Middle East Studies* 7:243-70;383-422.
Merton, Robert
   1957   *Social Theory and Social Structure*. New York: The Free Press.
Meskill, Johanna M.
   1979   *The Lins of Wu-feng. A Chinese Pioneer Family*. Princeton, N.J.: Princeton University Press.
Middleton, J.
   1969   "Oracles and Divination Among the Lugbara." In *Man in Africa*. M. Douglas and P. M. Kaberry, eds. New York: Tavistock.
Middleton, J. and E. H. Winter, eds.
   1963   *Witchcraft and Sorcery in East Africa*. London: Routledge and Kegan Paul.
Mills, C. Wright
   1971   *The Marxists*. Harmondsworth, England: Penguin.
Moore, Sally Falk
   1987a   "Explaining the Present: Theoretical Dilemmas in Processual Ethnography." *American Ethnologist*. 14(4);727-36.
   1987b   "Legal Systems of the World: An Introductory Guide to Classifications, Typological Interpretations and Bibliographical Resources." In *Law and the Social Sciences*. Leon Lipson and Stanton Wheeler, eds. New York: Russell Sage Foundation.
Nadel, S. F.
   1951   *The Foundations of Social Anthropology*. New York: The Free Press.
   1952   "Witchcraft in Four African Societies: An Essay in Comparison." *American Anthropologist* 54:18-29.
   1953   Social Control and Self Regulation. *Social Forces* 31:265-73.

Nader, Laura and H. F. Todd Jr., editors.
   1978   "Introduction: The Disputing Process." In *The Disputing Process: Law in Ten Societies*. New York: Columbia University Press.
Nagel, T.
   1959   "Hobbes on Obligation." *Philosophical Review* 68:68–83.
Nanda, Serena
   1984   "The Hijras of India: a Preliminary Report." *Medicine and Law* 3:59–75.
   1985   "The Hijras of India: Cultural and Individual Dimensions of an Institutionalized Third Gender Role." *Journal of Homosexuality* 11(3–4):35–55.
   1990   *Neither Man Nor Woman: The Hijras of India*. Belmont, Calif.: Wadsworth.
   1991   *Cultural Anthropology*. 4th ed. Belmont, Calif.: Wadsworth.
Newton, Esther
   1972   *Mother Camp: Female Impersonation in America*. Englewood Cliffs, N.J.: Prentice-Hall.
Nhlapo, R. T.
   1982   "Legal Duality and Multiple Judicial Organization in Swaziland: An Analysis and a Proposal." In *The Individual Under African Law*. Peter N. Takirambudde, ed. Kwaluseni: University of Swaziland.
Onyango, P. and D. Kayongo-Male
   1982   *Child Labor and Health*. Nairobi: Acme Press.
Opie, Peter and Iona Opie
   1959   *The Lore and Language of Schoolchildren*. New York: Oxford University Press.
Opler, M.
   1947   "Rules and Practice in Jicarilla Apache Affinal Relatives." *American Anthropologist* 49:453–62.
Orwell, George
   1946   *Animal Farm*. New York: Harcourt Brace.
   1950   *1984*. New York: New American Library.
Page, C.
   1946–47   "Bureaucracy's Other Face." *Social Forces* 25:89–94.
Parrinder, G.
   1976   [1962] *African Traditional Religion*. Westport, Conn.: Greenwood Press.
Parson, T.
   1951   "Deviant Behavior and the Mechanism of Social Control" in *The Social System: Essays by Talcott Parsons*. New York: Glencoe Free Press.
Pelto, P.
   1973   *The Snowmobile Revolution*. Menlo Park, Calif.: Cummings.
Peng, Ming-min
   1971   "Political Offenses in Taiwan: Laws and Problems" *China Quarterly* 47:473–93.
Perry, Elizabeth J.
   1980   *Rebels and Revolutionaries in North China*. Stanford, Calif.: Stanford University Press.
Pevin, F. F.
   1981   "Deviant Behavior and the Remaking of the World." *Social Problems* 28:489–508.

Pfohl, Steven
  1981 "Labeling Criminals." In *Law and Deviance*. Laurence Ross, ed. Beverly Hills, Calif.: Sage.
  1985 *Images of Deviance and Social Control: A Sociological History*. New York: McGraw-Hill.
Pimpley, P. N. and S. K. Sharma
  1985 "Hijras: A Study of an Atypical Role." *The Avadh Journal of Social Sciences* (India) 2:42–50.
Pitt-Rivers, Julian
  1971 *The People of the Sierra*. Chicago: University of Chicago Press.
Poggie, J. and R. Lynch, eds.
  1974 *Rethinking Modernization: Anthropological Approaches*. Westport, Conn.: Greenwood Press.
Pollner, Melvin
  1974 "Sociological and Common-Sense Models of the Labeling Process." In *Ethnomethodology*. Roy Turner, ed. Harmondsworth, England: Penguin Books.
Popper, Karl
  1968 *The Logic of Scientific Discovery*. London: Hutchinson.
Prus, Robert
  1983 "Deviance as Community Activity: Putting 'Labelling Theory' in Perspective." Paper presented at the Canadian Ethnology Society Meetings. Hamilton, Ontario, May 7–19, 1983.
  (N.D.) "Anthropological and Sociological Approaches to Deviance: An Ethnographic Prospect." Paper presented at "Deviance in a Cross-Cultural Context." Waterloo, Ontario, June 2–5, 1984.
Pye, Lucian W.
  1968 *The Spirit of Chinese Politics*. Cambridge, Mass.: M.I.T. Press.
Ranade, S. N.
  1983 "A Study of Eunuchs in Delhi." Ministry of Social Welfare, Government of India. New Delhi (unpublished).
Rawls, J.
  1955 "Two Concepts of Rules." *Philosophical Review* 64:3–32.
  1973 *A Theory of Justice*. Cambridge, Mass.: Harvard University Press.
Rawski, Evelyn S.
  1985 "Economic and Social Foundations of Late Imperial Culture." In *Popular Culture in Late Imperial China*. David A. Johnson, A. Nathan, and E. Rawski, eds. Berkeley: University of California Press.
Raybeck, Douglas
  1981 "The Ideal and the Real: The Status of Women in Kelantan Malay Society." *Women and Politics*, 1(4):7–21.
  1983 "Anthropology and Labeling Theory: Are Deviants Created or Recognized?" Paper presented at the 82nd Annual Meeting of the American Anthropological Association, Chicago, Illinois, November 16–20, 1983.
  1986 "The Elastic Rule: Conformity and Deviance in Kelantan Village Life." In *Cultural Identity in Peninsular Malaysia*. S. Carstens, ed. Athens, Ohio: University of Ohio Press.
  1988 "Anthropology and Labeling Theory: A Constructive Critique." *Ethos* 16(4):371–97.

Redfield, Robert
1953   *The Primitive World and Its Transformation.* Ithaca, N. Y.: Cornell University Press.
1960   *The Little Community and Peasant Society and Culture.* Chicago: University of Chicago Press.
Reisman, W. M.
1979   *Folded Lies: Bribery, Crusades and Reforms.* New York: The Free Press.
Reynolds, B.
1963   *Magic, Divination, and Witchcraft Among the Barotse of Northern Rhodesia.* Berkeley, Calif.: University of California Press.
Richards, A.
1935   "A Modern Movement of Witchfinders." *Africa* 8(4):448–61.
Robarchek, Clayton A.
1977   "Frustration, Aggression and the Nonviolent Semai." *American Ethnologist* 4(4):762–79.
1979   "Conflict, Emotion and Abreaction: Resolution of Conflict Among the Semai Senoi." *Ethos* 7(2):104–23.
Robbins, M. C. and R. Pollnac
1969   "Drinking Patterns and Acculturation in Rural Buganda." *American Anthropologist* 71:276–85.
Roberts, J. M. and T. Gregor
1971   "Privacy: A Cultural View." In *Privacy.* J. R. Pennock and J. W. Chapman, eds. New York: Atherton.
Rogers, J. and M. D. Buffalo
1974   "Fighting Back: Nine Modes of Adaptation to a Deviant Label." *Social Problems* 22:101–18.
Rohner, R.
1975   *They Love Me, They Love Me Not.* New Haven, Conn.: HRAF Press.
Roland, Alan
1982   "Toward a Psychoanalytical Psychology of Hierarchical Relationships in Hindu India." *Ethos* 10(3):232–53.
Rosaldo, Renato
1984   "Ilongot Naming: The Play of Associations." In *Naming Systems.* Elisabeth Tooker, ed. 1980 Proceedings of the American Ethnological Society. Washington, D.C.: The American Ethnological Society.
Roscoe, J.
1911   *The Baganda.* New York: Macmillan Co.
Rosenberg, M. Michael, Robert Stebbins, and Allen Turowetz, eds.
1982   *The Sociology of Deviance.* New York: St. Martin's.
Rosenhan, D. L.
1973   "On Being Sane in Insane Places." *Science* 179:250–58.
Rubenstein, Donald H.
1983   "Epidemic Suicide Among Micronesian Adolescents." *Social Science and Medicine* 17(10):657–65.
Rubenstein, J.
1972   *City Police.* New York: Farrar, Straus and Giroux.
Rubington, Earl
1982   "Deviant Subcultures." In M. Michael Rosenberg, R. A. Stebbins and A. Turowetz eds. *The Sociology of Deviance.* New York: St. Martin's.

Rubington, E. and M. Weinberg, eds.
  1968 *Deviance: The Interactionist Perspective.* New York: Macmillan.
Sagarin, Edward and Robert Kelly
  1982 "Collective and Formal Promotion of Deviance." In *The Sociology of Deviance.* M. Michael Rosenberg, R. A. Stebbins, and A. Turowetz, eds. New York: St. Martin's.
Sahlins, Marshall
  1976 *Culture and Practical Reason.* Chicago: University of Chicago Press.
Sanders, L.
  1978 *The Second Deadly Sin.* New York: G. P. Putnam.
Santayana, G.
  1955 *The Sense of Beauty.* New York: Dover.
Sapir, E.
  1915 "Abnormal Types of Speech in Nootka," In *Selected Writings in Language, Culture, and Personality: Essays of Edward Sapir.* David G. Mandelbaum, ed. 1985, Berkeley: University of California Press.
Sartre, Jean-Paul
  1965 *Anti-Semite and Jew.* George J. Becker, trans. New York: Schocken Books.
Savishinsky, Joel S.
  1974 *The Trail of The Hare: Life and Stress in An Arctic Community.* New York: Gordon and Breach.
  1977 "A Thematic Analysis of Drinking Behavior in a Hare Indian Community." *Papers in Anthropology* 18:43–60.
  1982 "Vicarious Emotions and Cultural Restraint." *Journal of Psychoanalytic Anthropology* 5:115–135.
  1983 "Pet Ideas: The Domestication of Animals, Human Behavior, and Human Emotions." In *New Perspectives on Our Lives with Companion Animals.* Aaron Katcher and Alan Beck, eds. Philadelphia: University of Pennsylvania Press.
  1990 "The Hare and Their Dogs: Human-Animal Bonds in An Arctic Community." *The World and I* 5(3):642–53.
Savishinsky, Joel S., ed.
  1978 *Strangers No More: Anthropological Studies of Cat Island, The Bahamas.* Ithaca, N.Y.: Ithaca College.
Scheff, T. J.
  1974 "The Labeling Theory of Mental Illness." *American Sociological Review* 39(June):444–52.
Schur, E. M.
  1965 *Crimes Without Victims.* Englewood Cliffs, N.J.: Prentice-Hall.
  1971 *Labeling Deviant Behavior: Its Sociological Implications.* New York: Harper & Row.
  1980 *The Politics of Deviance: Stigma Contests and the Uses of Power.* Englewood Cliffs, N.J.: Prentice-Hall.
  1983 *Labeling Women Deviant.* Philadelphia: Temple University Press.
Scott, Robert
  1970 "The Construction of Conceptions of Stigma by Professional Experts." In *Deviance and Respectability: The Social Construction of Moral Meanings.* J. Douglas, ed. New York: Basic Books.

1976 "Deviance, Sanctions and Social Integration in Small Scale Societies." *Social Forces* 54(3):604–20.

Searle, J.
1964 "How to Derive 'Ought' from 'Is.' " *Philosophical Review* 73:43–58.

Segal, J.
1979 "Child Abuse: A Review of Research." In *Families Today* (2) DHEW Publication No. (ADM) 79–815, pp. 577–607.

Selby, Henry
1974 *Zapotec Deviance*. Austin: University of Texas Press.

Shaw, Thomas A.
1988 *Emerging Persons: Youth Subculture, Social Identity, and Social Mobility in an Urban Chinese Setting*. Ph.D. dissertation, Department of Anthropology, Columbia University.

Shils, Edward
1981 *Tradition*. Chicago: University of Chicago Press.

Sirianni, Carmen
1981 "Production and Power in a Classless Society: A Critical Analysis of the Utopian Dimensions of Marxist Theory." *Socialist Review* 59:33–82.

Shostak, Marjorie
1983 *Nisa: The Life and Words of a !Kung Woman*. New York: Vintage Books.

Shweder, Richard A. and Robert A. LeVine, eds.
1984 *Culture Theory*. Cambridge: Cambridge University Press.

Simon, D. R. and D. S. Eitzen
1982 *Elite Deviance*. Boston: Allyn and Bacon.

Singer, Merrill and Maria Borrero
1984 "Indigenous Treatment for Alcoholism: The Case of Puerto Rican Spiritism." *Medical Anthropology* 8(4):246–73.

Sinha, A. P.
1967 "Procreation Among the Eunuchs." *Eastern Anthropologist* 20:168–76.

Skolnick, J.
1966 *Justice Without Trial*. New York: Wiley.

Slotkin, J. S.
1950 *Social Anthropology*. New York: Macmillan.

Smith, Hedrick
1983 "Would a Space-Age Defense Ease Tensions or Create Them?" *The New York Times*, March 27, Section 4:1.

Solomon, Richard
1971 *Mao's Revolution and the Chinese Political Culture*. Berkeley: University of California Press.

Sontag, Susan
1978 *Illness As Metaphor*. New York: Farrar, Straus and Giroux.

Spacks, Patricia Meyer
1983 "In Praise of Gossip." In *The Pleasures of Anthropology*. M. Freilich, ed. New York: New American Library.

Spradley, James
1979 *You Owe Yourself a Drunk*. Boston: Little, Brown.

Starr, June
1978 *Dispute and Settlement in Rural Turkey*. Leiden, Netherlands: Brill.

Stebbins, Robert A.
   1988   *Deviance: Tolerable Differences*. New York: McGraw-Hill Ryerson.
Steiner, George
   1983   "Killing Time." *The New Yorker* (December 12):168–88.
Steward, Julian H.
   1973   *The Theory of Culture Change*. Urbana: University of Illinois Press.
Stoddard, E. R.
   1968   " 'The Informal Code' of Police Deviancy: A Group Approach to 'Blue Coat
          Crime.' " *Journal of Criminal Law Criminology and Police Science* 59:2.
Stone, Lawrence
   1982   "Madness." *The New York Review of Books* 29:28–36.
Stone, M.
   1979   "Why Cheating Grows." *U.S. News and World Report* 87:100.
Storz, Moni Lai
   1978   "Effects of Official Labeling on Husbands' Perceptions of Their Wives: A
          Study of Mental Illness." *Australian and New Zealand Journal of Sociology*
          14(1):46–50.
Strathern, Marilyn
   1982   "The Village as an Idea: Constructs of Village-ness in Elmdon, Essex." In
          Belonging: Identity and Social Organisation in British Rural Cultures. An-
          thony P. Cohen, ed. Institute of Social and Economic Research. Memorial
          University of Newfoundland.
Strauss, M. and R. Gelles
   1979   "Physical Violence in Families." *Families Today* (2) DHEW Publication No.
          (ADM) 79–815, pp. 553–77.
Szasz, Kathleen
   1969   *Petishism: Pets and Their People in the Western World*. New York: Holt,
          Rinehart and Winston.
Szent-Gyorgyi, Albert
   1972   "Dionysians and Apollonians." *Science* 176:966.
Takagi, P.
   1974   "A Garrison State in a 'Democratic' Society." *Crime and Social Justice*:
          Spring and Summer, vol. 30.
Taylor, A. J. P.
   1962   *The Course of German History*. New York: Capricorn Books.
Taylor, Ian
   1982   "Moral Enterprise, Moral Panic, and Law-and-Order Campaigns." In *The
          Sociology of Deviance*. M. Michael Rosenberg, R. A. Stebbins and A.
          Turowetz, eds. New York: St. Martin's.
Thio, A.
   1978   *Deviant Behavior*. Boston: Houghton Mifflin.
Thomas, Elizabeth Marshall
   1959   *The Harmless People*. New York: Vintage Books.
Thomas, Garry, ed.
   1974   *Anthropological Perspectives on Eleuthera*. Island Environmental Studies,
          The Bahamas, Reports 1973–74. Corning, N.Y.: College Center of The
          Finger Lakes.

1976   *Slices of Time on Rum Cay: Undergraduate Efforts in Ethnography.* Island Environmental Studies, The Bahamas, Reports 1975–76. Corning, N.Y.: College Center of The Finger Lakes.

Thomas, Jim
1982   "New Directions in Deviance Research." In *The Sociology of Deviance.* M. Michael Rosenberg, R. A. Stebbins and A. Turowetz, eds. New York: St. Martin's.

Tittle, Charles R.
1975   "Deterrents or Labeling." *Social Forces* 53(3):399–410.
1977   "Introduction." *Social Forces* 56(2):315–19.
1980   "Labeling and Crime: An Empirical Evaluation." In *The Labeling of Deviance.* Walter E. Gove, ed. Beverly Hills, Calif.: Sage.

Tönnies, Ferdinand
1967   [1887] *Community and Society.* Charles P. Loomis, trans. New York: Harper Torchbooks.

Turk, A.
1969   *Criminality and Legal Order.* Chicago: Rand McNally.

Turnbull, Colin
1961   *The Forest People: A Study of the Pygmies of the Congo.* New York: Simon and Schuster.
1976   *Wayward Servants: The Two Worlds of the African Pygmy.* Westport, Conn.: Greenwood Press, Publishers.

Turner, R. H.
1970   *Family Interaction.* New York: John Wiley and Sons.

Turner, Victor
1957   *Schism and Continuity in an African Society: A Study of Ndembu Life.* Manchester: Manchester University Press.
1964   "Witchcraft and Sorcery: Taxonomy Versus Dynamics." *Africa* 34:314–24.
1969   *The Ritual Process: Structure and Anti-Structure.* Chicago: Aldine.

Van Maanen, J.
1978   "The Asshole." In *A View from the Street.* P. K. Manning and J. Van Maanen, eds. Santa Monica, Calif.: Goodyear.

Vansina, J.
1969   "The Bushong Poison Ordeal." In *Man in Africa.* M. Douglas and P. M. Kaberry, eds. New York: Tavistock.

Wagatsuma, J.
1981   "Child Abandonment and Infanticide: A Japanese Case" In *Child Abuse and Neglect,* J. Korbin, ed. Berkeley: University of California Press.

Wagner, G.
1949   *The Bantu of North Kavirondo* Vol. 1. London: Oxford University Press.
1956   *The Bantu of North Kavirondo* Vol. 2. London: Oxford University Press.

Wallace, Anthony F. C.
1970   *Culture and Personality.* New York: Random House.

Wanjala, C.
1985   "Twilight years are the Years of Council and Wisdom" In *History and Culture in Western Kenya.* S. Wandibba, ed. Nairobi: G. S. Were Press.

Weber, M.
1947   *The Theory of Social and Economic Organization.* New York: Oxford University Press.

West, John F.
  1972 *Faroe: The Emergence of a Nation.* London: C. Hurst.
West, W. F.
  1983 "Institutionalizing Rationality in Regulatory Administration." *Public Administration Review,* July/August, 326–34.
Westly, W. A.
  1970 *Violence and the Police.* Cambridge, Mass.: M.I.T. Press.
Whittaker, Edmund
  1958 *From Euclid to Eddington: A Study of Conceptions of the External World.* New York: Dover.
Wieder, D. Lawrence and Charles W. Wright
  1982 "Norms, Conformity and Deviance." In *The Sociology of Deviance.* M. Michael Rosenberg, R. A. Stebbins and A. Turowetz, eds. New York: St. Martin's.
Wilshire, Bruce
  1982 "The Dramaturgical Model of Behavior: Its Strengths and Weaknesses." *Symbolic Interaction* 5(2):287–97.
Wilson, D.
  1981 "Fudge Mixed with Politics Leaves a Bad Taste." In *The Meaning of Culture.* M. Freilich, ed. Cambridge, Mass.: Schenkman.
Wilson, J. Q.
  1968 *Varieties of Police Behavior.* New York: Atheneum.
Wilson, M. H.
  1951 "Witch-Beliefs and Social Structure." *American Journal of Sociology* 56:307–13.
Wilson, Richard W.
  1970 *Learning to be Chinese. The Political Socialization of Children in Taiwan.* Cambridge, Mass.: M.I.T. Press.
Winckler, Edwin A.
  1981 "Roles Linking State and Society." In *The Anthropology of Taiwanese Society.* Emily A. Ahern and H. Gates, eds., Berkeley, Calif.: University of California Press.
Wolf, Eric R.
  1969 *Peasant Wars of the Twentieth Century.* New York: Harper & Row.
Woon, Yuen-foong
  1984 *Social Organization in South China, 1911–1949.* Center for Chinese Studies. Ann Arbor: University of Michigan.
Wrong, D.
  1961 "The Oversocialized Conception of Man in Modern Sociology." *American Sociological Review* 26:183–93.
Wylie, Jonathan
  1986 *The Faroe Islands: Interpretations of History.* Lexington: University of Kentucky Press.
Yang, Lien-sheng
  1957 "The Concept of 'Pao' as a Basis for Social Relations in China." In *Chinese Thought and Institutions.* John H. Fairbank, ed. Chicago: University of Chicago Press.

Yeats, William Butler
   1926   "Among School Children." In *The Major Poets: English and American.*
          Charles M. Coffin, ed. New York: Harcourt, Brace and World (1954).
Yngvesson, Barbara
   1976   "Responses to Grievance Behavior: Extended Cases in a Fishing Commu-
          nity." *American Ethnologist* 3:353–82.
Ziman, John
   1981   "What are the Options: Social Determinants of Research Plans." *Minerva*
          19:1–42.

INDEX

ABOUT THE EDITORS AND CONTRIBUTORS

MORRIS FREILICH, who brings to this study 30 years of research and 20 years of the teaching of anthropology on deviance related topics, is Professor of Sociology and Anthropology at Northeastern University, and is the author of *The Relevance of Culture* (1989).

DOUGLAS RAYBECK is currently Professor of Anthropology at Hamilton College. He has contributed to a wide range of journals including *Ethos*, *Medical Anthropology Quarterly*, and *The Journal of Cross-Cultural Psychology*.

JOEL SAVISHINSKY, Professor of Anthropology at Ithaca College, has conducted numerous case studies of human adaptation to extreme environments throughout the world, and is the author of *The Trail of the Hare*, as well as articles in anthropology, ecology, and psychology journals.

STEVEN C. CATON is an Associate Professor of Anthropology at the University of California at Santa Cruz. He is the author of *"Peaks of Yemen I summon": Poetry as Cultural Practice in a North Yemeni Tribe*.

DENNIS GAFFIN is an Assistant Professor of Anthropology at the State University of New York College at Buffalo. His writing and work have centered around various aspects of social control in the United States, the *shtetl*, and peasant Europe.

PHILIP L. KILBRIDE is a Professor of Anthropology at Bryn Mawr College. He is the author (with Janet Kilbride) of *Changing Family Life in East Africa: Women and Children at Risk*. Other recent publications include *Encounters with American Ethnic Cultures* (edited with Jane C. Goodale and Elizabeth Ameisen).

SERENA NANDA is Professor of Anthropology at John Jay College of Criminal Justice (CUNY). She is the author of *Neither Man nor Woman: The Hijras of India* and co-author of *American Cultural Pluralism and Law*, a study of law and cultural diversity in the United States.

LAUREL ROSE received a Ph.D. in Anthropology from the University of California at Berkeley. Her research includes fieldwork in Swaziland, supported by grants from the Wenner-Gren Foundation and the Fulbright I.I.E. program. She is currently conducting research in Africa.

THOMAS A. SHAW is an Assistant Professor in the department of Human Development and Psychology at the Harvard Graduate School of Education. His studies include youth culture, adolescent identity and the life cycle, and has written about youth in Chinese society.